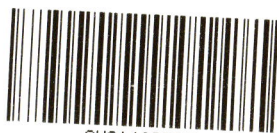

DARK LADY OF THE SILENTS

DARK LADY
OF THE
SILENTS

MY LIFE IN EARLY
HOLLYWOOD
BY MIRIAM COOPER

WITH BONNIE HERNDON

THE BOBBS-MERRILL COMPANY, INC.

Indianapolis   *New York*

ISBN 0-672-51725-6
Library of Congress catalog card number 73-3907
Designed by Winston Potter
Manufactured in the United States of America

First printing

ACKNOWLEDGMENTS

With special thanks to Booton Herndon, whose advice, encouragement and expertise made this book possible; also thanks to Walter Korte, professor of film theory and esthetics at the University of Virginia; David Parker, Paul Spehr and the Motion Picture Section of the Library of Congress; Eileen Bowser of the Museum of Modern Art; and Walter Coppedge, professor of film history at Virginia Commonwealth University.

MIRIAM COOPER & BONNIE HERNDON

DARK LADY OF THE SILENTS

« 1 »

Most little old ladies I know who are pushing eighty sit in front of TV sets in nursing homes. Not me. At the age of seventy-eight I started having a ball. Somebody sent a limousine 125 miles for me to be on TV. I made my first trip by airplane to talk to university classes. All of a sudden my little house was full of young people chattering away. All because somebody discovered what I had known all along—I'm Miriam Cooper.

For a long time if I'd made a statement like that you'd have said, "Who the hell is Miriam Cooper?" I was completely forgotten and, to tell the truth, I didn't give a damn. Then all of a sudden people began getting interested in early movies. They're on TV every night. People even go to school and study them. And it came as a pleasant shock to me that all those people knew that I played leading roles in the two greatest pictures ever made, *The Birth of a Nation* and *Intolerance.*

Dozen of books have been written in the last few years about the silent films. People are always showing them to me. A funny thing is that the authors are usually young people who weren't even born at the time they're writing about. How can they do that? I know they look up things in books and magazines, but what makes them think what they read is the truth?

When I was in pictures, back in the teens and twenties, the studio publicity people wrote more untrue stuff about me than you could imagine. According to some of those stories, I designed sets for D. W. Griffith, the greatest director of all time. Well, I never even thought about designing a set, and if I had Mr. Griffith wouldn't have paid any attention to me. I've read that I kept pigeons on the roof of a Fifth Avenue hotel. Can you imagine a Fifth Avenue hotel letting anybody keep pigeons? Then there was the story about my "skill with the boxing gloves." Boxing gloves! Jesus!

I've read articles, all supposedly written by me, on how I became a movie star, and even some telling *you* how to become a movie star. I never even saw those stories until I picked up the magazines that printed them.

Maybe I'm old-fashioned, but the only way I can see for anybody to write about anything is to be a part of it. Well, I was certainly a part of the picture business in the days when it grew from nothing into something. People who are interested in early films associate me with Mr. Griffith. But I was in films before I went to work for Griffith and after I left him. I was in so many I don't even remember a lot of them. And as the wife of another great director, Raoul Walsh, I was involved in a lot more.

At first when reporters, movie buffs and even college professors began calling me, wanting to know about my life as a silent film star, I didn't understand why. Who cares about what happened way back then?

A nice young man named Walter Korte told me. "There's a great new interest in the cinema," Walter said. Cinema! We called it pictures. People talk about films today the way we used to talk about the stage.

Walter turned out to be a professor at the University

of Virginia with a Ph.D. in Film Theory and Esthetics. I had no idea that university students studied films at all, much less theory and esthetics. When I was that age we studied literature and drama and music and art. Pictures were something you were ashamed to go to, much less be in. I remember the time when, if an actor from the legitimate stage made a quick buck appearing in a movie, he'd do it under another name so nobody would find out.

They now say that movies are the art form of our time. If they are, it's because of Mr. Griffith. Before he came along movies were little more than flickering figures on a screen. They lasted ten minutes, cost ten cents—or a nickel—and were shown in vacant stores. Only poor people and immigrants went to the movies. They did not have to understand the language to enjoy the show, because of course all movies were silent then. That's who pictures were made for, and they looked it.

Mr. Griffith changed all that with *The Birth of a Nation*. He also changed my life in the process. When I went to work for him I was just another girl. Mae Marsh, who worked with Mr. Griffith for several years, used to call him Mr. Heinz—he was always adding a new girl to the cast, and Mae said he had fifty-seven varieties. Most of the girls were like me: poor, with a pretty face and a family to support. Few of us knew anything about acting; Mr. Griffith simply told us what to do and we did it in front of the camera. Mary Pickford, Blanche Sweet and Lillian and Dorothy Gish had been on the stage for most of their lives, but Mae Marsh, Constance Talmadge and I got in the movies on looks alone. And that was the looks of our faces, not our bodies. Griffith wouldn't have hired Raquel Welch as a five-dollar extra. He liked his young ladies to be thin, ethereal types. I don't think there was a big bosom in the bunch. We were all flat as pancakes.

All the girls were young, too. If you were an old hag

of twenty-five you got character parts. I wanted to stay a sweet romantic lead so I started lying about my age before I was twenty. I'd subtract years by day and slap cold cream all over me at night.

One time years later I subtracted a little too much, and Archie Selwyn, an old friend who'd formed Goldwyn Productions with Sam Goldfish, said, "For Christ's sake, Miriam, what did they do, roll you out on the set in a bassinet?"

I was embarrassed to go back to doctors because I'd forgotten how old I'd told them I was the last time. Finally I even forgot myself. I wrote to Baltimore, where I was born, and asked for a copy of my birth certificate. Hell, it was even worse than I thought: 1891.

At least I can look back on my years in pictures with some objectivity. Those were the years in which the industry came together. The coming of age of the movies is as great a story as any ever put on film, and I was part of it. It happened all around me, on the sets, in my house. Because I've been away so long, I can look back on that vital period, see the good and the bad, and tell it the way it was.

During *The Birth of a Nation* I was making thirty-five dollars a week. During *Intolerance* I got a raise to sixty-five dollars. Even though I'd retired temporarily, my next job paid $1,000. Mae Marsh and some of the others went up to as much as $3,000 a week. From one-room apartments with Murphy beds we went to houses in Beverly Hills with six servants and chauffeur-driven cars a block long. We were like kids let loose in a candy store. We spent money like water. One year we were nobodies, poor, untrained and uneducated. Overnight we were treated like royalty. People followed us everywhere and wrote about everything we did. And if we didn't do anything they'd make something up.

That's why I am writing what I remember of my days making movies. I'm not making anything up. I was *there*.

« 2 »

When I was a girl my mother did not let me go to the movies. No nice girl's mother did. I saw only one movie before I started being in them. The only reason I went to that one was because the janitor's daughter had found a quarter. That was enough to pay for both of us with plenty left over for Crackerjacks. We sat on the edge of our rickety chairs reading the subtitles out loud to each other.

I haven't the faintest memory of what the movie was about. It must have been pretty bad. We were more impressed with the woman playing the musical accompaniment on a tinny piano in the corner than we were with the action on the screen. She'd be playing a slow waltz, looking around at the audience. Suddenly she'd remember the movie, look back at the screen, and rush into chase music. She was more of a show than the movie.

The movie theater was really just a vacant store. That's what most of them were back in those days before World War I. Somebody would rent a store cheap and paint the windows black, both to make it dark and to keep people from looking in. For a nickel you could sit on folding chairs and watch figures in stark black and white move jerkily and silently on a dirty bed sheet hung on the wall. The only thing fancy about those places was the name: nickelodeon. The men who jumped on the movie bandwagon thought it was just a fad, like hula hoops. They didn't think it would last, and they wanted to make money while it did.

The next time I got near a movie I wound up being in it. I was going to art school at Cooper Union. Another student named Rita Wood suggested that we walk over to the Biograph Studio after school and see what they were doing there.

Don't get the idea that this was an exciting tour of a glamorous motion picture studio. Biograph was just a big brownstone house at 11 East 14th Street. A millionaire had lived there once, but the wealthy people had long since left the neighborhood, and all the lovely old mansions were now rooming houses, restaurants, shops and this one movie studio.

We walked up the worn front stairs to the first floor and into a large foyer. Nobody stopped us. We saw men and women lounging against the walls and talking to each other. There were stairs on the left, and a big archway into a huge room on the right. It looked as though the walls had been knocked out to make one big high-ceilinged room out of what had been the front parlor and the back parlor.

We looked into the room and saw what appeared to be a ballroom scene. The lights in the room were so bright they hurt my eyes. There was a big camera mounted on a platform; a man sat next to it in a camp chair with D. W. GRIFFITH in big black letters on the back. He was wearing a huge, floppy straw hat. He turned his head and I saw his profile—it was all nose. I remember asking Mae Marsh years later why he always wore his hat indoors. She said, "It hides his bald spot and his big ugly nose."

Rita Wood and I stared at the scene fascinated. Just then we heard Mr. Griffith tell a young man standing beside him, "We need more pages and scullery maids. Can you find some extras?"

The young man looked around and saw us. "Are you girls extras?" he asked.

We didn't know what he was talking about. Extra what? "No," we said, expecting to be thrown out, "we're just watching."

"Would you like to be in the movie instead of just watching?"

We looked at each other. Nice girls didn't work in the movies; they didn't even go to movies. My mother still didn't know I'd ever seen one.

"It pays five dollars a day," he said. Suddenly the movies became more respectable. Mama, my sister and two brothers and I were living on handouts from relatives and whatever we could pawn. I said yes, and Rita nodded.

"Go down to the basement and get some clothes," the man said. We went down the steep flight of stairs to where the costumes were kept, giggling and holding onto each other. There was an old woman sitting at a sewing machine in the corner. She looked at us but didn't say anything.

"Is this where we get costumes?" I asked her.

"Scullery maids or page boys?" she growled at us.

Scullery maids sounded terrible, but page boys sounded romantic. "Page boys," we both said.

The woman got up and walked back to the wardrobe baskets. Just then a girl came out of the ladies room across the hall wearing black tights, a striped ruffle around her middle and a hat with a feather on her bleached blond hair. She walked past us, her bottom wiggling under the ruffle. We'd never seen anybody walk like that before—and in tights. You could see her *legs!* I knew I wouldn't dare put those things on. Neither would Rita; her parents were Christian Scientists.

I turned back to the woman, who was rooting around in the wardrobe baskets, and said, "Miss, I think you better make that scullery maids."

She never changed expression, just kept looking

cranky, and handed us two bundles of patched and ragged clothes.

"Dressing room's down the hall," she said.

We walked down the hall and opened the door to a long, narrow room. Girls were smearing on makeup and undressing and dressing right there in front of each other.

Rita and I huddled together, shy and scared, and looked around the room. A red and white checked oilcloth covered board ran the length of the room, under a long mirror. The shelf was scattered with cans of cold cream, sticks of greasepaint and balls of cheese cloth. Kleenex hadn't been invented. At the far end of the room was a worn-out chaise longue and an overstuffed chair. On the other long wall clothes hung from wooden pegs.

"What a mess," Rita said. She untied her package and held up a patched gingham dress. It was wrinkled and miles too big. "I wouldn't wear this germy thing for a million dollars!" she said. "You can stay here if you want, but I'm going home."

I couldn't say anything. The gingham dress may have made Rita want to go home; to me it brought back the bitterest memory of my life. When I was just a child Papa left us and Mama became seriously ill. I was taken to a Catholic orphanage in New Jersey until she recovered.

At the orphanage one of the nuns told me to put on an ugly, patched gingham dress and scrub the floor. I didn't mind scrubbing the floor, but even then I had this thing about being neat and clean. I refused to put on that dress. The nun beat me with a cat-o'-nine-tails and forced me into it.

I wasn't in the orphanage long, and it became a hazy memory pushed out of my mind. Now, as I held another ugly gingham dress in my hands, it all came back. I was afraid I was going to throw up.

Right there I made the decision that changed my life. I wanted to run out of there as fast as I could, but I wanted that five dollars, too. I had to have it, bad enough to fight back my memories and my nausea.

"If you go I'll never speak to you again," I told Rita, but by that time she was already at the door. And I really didn't speak to her for years.

So there I was alone with a bunch of painted women. I had never undressed in front of anyone before; the Sisters at the convent I had gone to didn't approve of that. But once I had decided to stay, the rest was easy. When I make up my mind to do something, I don't let anything or anybody stop me.

I took off my dress, hung it on a peg, and pulled on the ugly big shapeless gingham costume. Then I sat down in front of the makeup shelf and started moving things around. The girl sitting next to me on the wooden bench watched me in the mirror. "Is this your first day?"

The Sisters had taught me not to lie. "Yes," I said, "and I don't know what to do with all this stuff. I've never used makeup before."

"You look it," she said bluntly. I was to discover in the next few years that this girl was always blunt. "But don't worry," she said. "I'll help you." Then she showed me what to do. "Clean your face with this cold cream and be sure to rub the pink stuff in good. Then put a lot of this powder over it. When you're ready, I'll bead your eyes."

I was embarrassed and grateful and I mumbled thanks. "Don't mention it, my deah; it's nothing a'tall," she said in a broad British accent. Then she began singing in her native Brooklynese. Crazy actress. While I smeared on the greasepaint and the powder, she asked my name and told me hers was Teddy Sampson. Teddy put some black color on my eyelids. Then she heated some black grease in a tiny frying pan over a can of sterno. With a small gray pencil in one hand, the hot grease in the other, she came at me. I pulled back.

"Hold still, for Christ's sake," she said. "I'm not going

to put your eyes out." She beaded my lashes and then stood back admiring her work.

I looked in the mirror. Yellow powder over pink greasepaint, heavy black eye shadow, long stiff lashes tipped with black beads. I looked like Halloween.

When I got upstairs one of the actresses watching the scene stared at me. "Who made you up?" she asked me.

"Teddy Sampson helped me," I told her.

"That Teddy," the girl said. "Mack," she said to a heavy-set young man standing next to her, "look what Teddy did to this kid."

He turned to look at me. "What a lousy trick," he said, shaking his head. "C'mon, I'll fix you up."

My new friend took my hand and pulled me toward the men's dressing room. I sat on a bench while he wiped some of the paint off and fixed my eyes. What he was doing to me was a complete mystery at the time. He seemed to be a nice man, and I sat there and held my face still for him to work on. I learned later that there were two reasons for makeup. One was to hide wrinkles from the glare of the lights. The other was because red photographed black, and people with tanned or reddish skins had to cover them with greasepaint.

But I didn't need much makeup. I was hardly old enough for wrinkles, and my skin was very white; I looked anemic, but I photographed well. Anyone looking at the makeup Teddy had pasted on me would assume that I was covering wrinkles *and* dark skin. Either Teddy didn't know what she was doing—or she did.

When Mack thought I looked all right, I thanked him and left the men's dressing room. I ran right into the young man who had hired me. "What are you doing in there?" he said. "Don't you know girls aren't allowed in the men's dressing room? Don't go in there again, ever."

I didn't see why he was so upset. I went on up to the set.

A banquet scene was in progress when I got there. The movie was a seventeenth-century melodrama. Later on I learned it was called *A Blot on the 'Scutcheon,* with Dorothy Bernard playing the lead. Mr. Griffith was telling everybody on the set what to do. He had a strong, resonant voice, and when he spoke everybody listened.

In between times we could talk and move around. This was in the silent days, remember. Teddy stood next to me. We didn't mention my makeup. When I saw the man who'd made me up leaning against the wall talking to a young woman, I asked Teddy who they were.

"That's Mabel Normand and Mack Sennett," she said. "She's a comedienne and he directs comedies. Everybody thinks they're going to get married." They never did get married, but they did make very successful comedies together when Mack Sennett started his Keystone Kops.

Not many people have been made up the first day by Mack Sennett in the men's dressing room. He later became one of the great names in pictures, but even if he had been famous at that time I wouldn't have known it. Biograph didn't identify who was in its films. When Mary Pickford was with Biograph she was known only as "The Biograph Girl," or "The Girl with the Curls."

Other studios were beginning to give the names of the players but not Mr. Griffith. He didn't believe any actor was so good that he couldn't be replaced. If anyone wanted to leave Biograph for another studio and more money and publicity, that was all right with him. He'd look around the studio and pick someone else for the part.

The banquet scene took two or three hours. I just stood around. My feet hurt and my face felt funny under the makeup. When the banquet was finally over, Mr. Griffith said, "Bring on the scullery maids."

There were four or five of us, all in our shapeless dresses and beaded eyelashes. We walked on the set with our buckets and mops and started cleaning up. Mr. Griffith told us how to push our mops around, as if we didn't know. Then he said, "All right, all right."

While we were rehearsing I must have moved away from the others a little. "Wait a minute," he said, and pointed to me. "You—little dark-haired girl—get back in camera range." I didn't know what that meant, but I hustled back close to the others. "Fine, fine," he said. Then he shouted, "Lights! Camera!"

With all the other girls pushing mops too, I didn't feel self-conscious. It couldn't have been more than two minutes before Mr. Griffith yelled, "Cut!" and walked away. The loud grinding of the camera stopped and the lights went out. The stage was dark and silent. Two minutes' work and I'd made five dollars. It had taken longer to put the goo on my face. This was the kind of work I liked.

I had started for the dressing room when the same young man stopped me. By this time I knew his name was Christy Cabanne. "Don't take off your makeup," he said. "Mr. Griffith wants to see you."

I wondered why, but I went back. Mr. Griffith was talking to his cameraman. He turned and looked at me. Then he looked back at his cameraman.

"Billy," he said, "I want a test of this young lady."

I had no idea what Billy was going to test, but I never thought of questioning this man. He had a strong, decisive manner; you did what he told you to do.

G. W. "Billy" Bitzer, who I learned later was Griffith's favorite cameraman, told me where to stand and then turned on the lights. They looked like two huge pencils with the points touching. When they came on I couldn't see anybody or anything, but I could hear Mr. Griffith giving me directions. "Tilt your head up, now turn your head to the right, now to the left. Look front, now straight at me. Now smile." I did what he said, but I wished he'd hurry up so I could get my money and go home.

Mr. Griffith thanked me, but, more important, someone else gave me five dollars. It took a long time to get all the makeup off my face, and it was dark when I left the studio. I knew Mama would be worried. I ran to the subway. But as I passed Luchow's, the famous German restaurant, I glanced in and saw many of the movie people in there, eating and drinking. I slowed down. They looked happy and, to me, rich. I couldn't help thinking about the poor artist's models who posed for us at school for fifty cents an hour. I clutched my five dollars a little tighter.

All the way home I worried about what I would tell Mama. Even when I stopped off after school at Wana-maker's Department Store for their free cookies and tea, I was never this late.

When I walked in, my brother Gordon said, "It's about time. Where have you been? Mama was going to go to the police."

I babbled something about how I'd been working so hard at art school I didn't think about what time it was. I certainly couldn't tell Mama I'd been in a movie. I had often heard her say she couldn't understand parents allowing their children to go to those dreadful moving-picture places. Mama would never have understood, not even for five dollars.

« 3 »

Mama was straight out of a soap opera. She was a Stewart, one of the fine old families of Baltimore. She met my father, Julian Cooper, when she was going to Visitation Convent and he was attending Loyola University. They'd meet on Sundays; she'd be coming out of church, he'd be coming from a poker game.

Papa was handsome, well mannered and rich, but Mama's parents, who were devout Catholics, didn't approve of him. Her parents were wiser than Mama was, for after they had eloped and Mama had had five babies in five years, one of whom died, Papa took off for Europe. I guess he was unable to cope with so many children so fast. I loved Papa and wished he had stayed. But then, if he had, I doubt if I would have been desperate enough to even think of going into pictures.

After Papa left, his mother supported us. We lived in a comfortable apartment in Washington Heights, which was then a charming little village an hour-and-a-half's ride away from New York City by streetcar. Across Broadway was an old Dutch cemetery. It was forbidden territory, so we loved to play there. We'd climb the gray stone wall surrounding it and play hide and seek among the headstones.

It was peaceful and quiet, and the flowers were beautiful. It was like another world.

Mama sent the other children to parochial school, but I was a dreamy kind of child and she thought I needed stricter discipline, so she sent me to a convent school, St. Walburga's Academy.

This was a gray stone building overlooking the Hudson River. From my desk near the window I could see the huge ocean liners silhouetted against the Palisades on their way to China or Rome. I would be standing on the deck, watching the skyline fade in the distance as the big ship started across the ocean. Sometimes I'd be in China, riding in a rickshaw; other times I'd be in Rome, having tea with the Pope.

And then I'd be right back in St. Walburga's, with Sister Rosalita calling my name. "Miriam Cooper, what was I talking about?"

"I don't know," I'd answer. How could I know what she was talking about? I was half the world away.

"Of course you don't. You've been daydreaming again," Sister Rosalita said. "Get on your knees and face the wall. Pray to God to forgive you."

That's how I spent most of my school years, on my knees, facing the wall, saying Hail Marys.

I was still a child when Grandmother Cooper died. Her entire estate went to Papa. I'm sure she thought he would take care of his wife and children, but he was not the gentleman she thought he was. He stayed in Europe and never sent us a cent.

With Grandmother's financial help gone, we were very poor. We moved from our comfortable apartment in Washington Heights to a flat on 116th Street in what was called "Little Italy." I hated it. I hated the hand-me-down clothes and the smells of the tenement, over-cooked food and the toilet in the hall. The women sat on the stoops, flopped out their breasts and nursed their children in front of everybody. Little boys took out their things and peed in the street. I'd never heard or smelled or seen anything like that in Washington Heights. It's hard to make the adjustment from well-to-do to dirt poor at any age; to a proper, neat little girl like me it was too much to bear.

So I didn't bear it; I just slipped away from it. I don't remember when I first learned how to do it. Maybe I never learned, I just did. I've since heard that this strange ability to be somebody else, somewhere else, is called astral projection. All I really did was just some high-powered daydreaming, but anyway, I developed this faculty early in life.

Even back in Washington Heights, when life would have seemed to be much more pleasant, there were times when I needed to escape. In a family without a father and with a bewildered, helpless mother whose reaction to any problem was to get a sick headache and lie down, the other kids, more often than not, raised hell. My brothers would fight and scream at each other, and Lenore could always get away with murder.

Like the fights we had over rice pudding. We all loved rice pudding. On the nights we had rice pudding we ate everything on our plates. That way we knew we'd get dessert. All except Lenore, the baby of the family. She'd eat practically nothing, waiting for that rice pudding. Mama never scolded her for it. Instead she'd give Lenore—we called her Nonie—a heaping plate of rice pudding and the rest of us little dabs.

"The poor child has to have something to eat," Mama would say. Nelson and Gordon would kick Lenore under the table and she'd scream and holler, but she'd get the rice pudding.

Nelson and Gordon were really tough. Nelson had freckles and red hair with a cowlick that stuck up in back like Skeezix. He was always doing something he shouldn't and Mama was always chasing him with a hairbrush. He was even fresh to the parish priest. Every year Monsignor McMahon read the final marks in front of the whole school. When he came to Nelson's he would stare at the report card and frown. "Nelson Cooper, Conduct D," he read. And Nelson had to walk to the front of the auditorium and get his report. Once the priest said to him, "Do you know, young man, where you're going to end? You're going to wind up in hell."

"That's great," Nelson said. "I'll meet you there, too." That was the end of Nelson's schooling. He was expelled from school and took a job delivering groceries. But he later went to night school and then to Columbia University, and eventually became an architect.

Gordon was just as bad. He loved to say things to shock Mama. Even though she was mad at Papa, Mama didn't mind bragging about his ancestors. One time she was telling about Grandfather Cooper who discovered Navassa Island, a pear-shaped rock in the Caribbean. It was rich in guano and he had made a fortune from its sale as fertilizer. Gordon said, "A million dollars for bird shit." Mama had a fit when he talked that way.

I always tried to please Mama, but she didn't seem to accept me, for a reason I couldn't comprehend at that age. Lenore was her favorite. She even slept with her. I was the only one who slept alone. The boys were together, as were Mama and Lenore, but I slept on the couch in the living room way down the hall, far away from everybody else. One night I had a terrible nightmare and I woke up screaming. Nelson, Gordon and Mama all came running in to see what the matter was.

"There's a man at the window," I cried.

"Where?" said Gordon.

"Right there, climbing up the curtain," I said. But he wasn't there anymore, now that I was awake.

"She's nuts," Gordon said. "We're not coming in any-more, no matter how loud you scream."

They didn't, either, although the nightmares got even worse, and I dreaded night and that lonely room. Why couldn't Lenore and I sleep together, and Mama take the couch? She was a grown woman; she shouldn't have been scared. Of course, now I'm a grown woman, too, and I'm still afraid of the dark. I'm eighty-two years old and I keep the light on all night—and wear a dark eye shade to keep it out of my eyes. (I also wear an adhesive patch on my forehead at night. I don't want to get wrinkles.)

I had to have something to get me away from the bickering, the fears, and also the misery of the tenement and poverty. I probably discovered my version of astral projection in the peace and beauty of the old Dutch grave-yard, which was across the old bridge over upper Broadway. I used to climb the gray stone wall with the iron pickets on top and jump down inside. Lying down on a grassy grave just a few feet above the coffin of someone long gone from this world, I, too, would go away.

I could be a princess in an exotic land or a nun serving God and mankind on a remote tropical island. I could be anywhere I wanted to be. At night, alone and scared in my room far down the hall from my mother and sister and brothers, I'd be somebody else in order to keep the night-mares away, some happy person in a happy place at a happy time.

Sometimes my imagination got me in trouble. I had heard Sister Rosalita say how brave Mama was, bringing up four children all by herself. Well, one day when the parents of one of my classmates took me to the circus with them, I made her even braver. The lion tamer was a woman. I thought she was wonderful. I wanted Mama to be the best thing that ever lived, so I told my friend and her parents that Mama had been a lion tamer.

When the story got back to Mama she said, "How could you? I'll never understand you, not if I live to be a hundred." Then she went to bed with one of her sick headaches.

Mama may not have understood me, but my imagination kept me going through childhood, and later it became an important factor in my career. I don't think I was ever a great actress. But when Mr. Griffith told me, "You're a Southern girl watching your brother go off to war," I didn't have to act, I *was* that girl.

There was something else that helped me get to the top in pictures, something I discovered after a temper tantrum at school.

When we moved away from Washington Heights Mama couldn't afford to keep sending me to St. Walburga's. But the Mother Superior and the Sisters were kind, and arranged for me to continue without paying tuition. They even paid my carfare, a nickel each day.

All the girls knew my obsession with being neat. We wore uniforms to school and I pressed my pleated skirt until it was so shiny you could see yourself in it. We wore white dickeys over a blue serge middy. I had only two dickeys, but I was always washing and ironing them. I starched them so much that they rubbed my neck raw. I was in agony, but I wore those dickeys anyway.

One day at school I went to the bathroom and when I came back I found a big blob of ink on my desk. Somebody had spilled it to tease me. When I saw this big ink blob spreading all over my neat, clean desk, I got mad and threw my ruler across the room.

Mother Mary Christopher looked at me for a long moment. Then she said, "Come here, Miriam." I stood in front of her. "How could you hurt Our Lord so cruelly when He suffered and died on the cross for love of you?"

This was the first time I ever thought that, with all the

millions of people in the world, Our Lord knew I existed, that He cared about what I did. I suddenly felt very special. I was determined not to hurt Our Lord again.

That night when my brothers started fighting I left the room and didn't get in it. I did all the household chores before I was told to. One of my brothers said, "What's the matter with Miriam—is she sick?"

I wasn't sick; I was devoutly dutiful in the knowledge that Our Lord was watching me. It gave me security.

Although with Our Lord watching me all the time I had to get the chores done, that didn't mean I couldn't have help. Lenore was supposed to help me do the dishes, but she often griped about the job or dropped the towel and sneaked out.

One night I had an inspiration. I told her a famous poem had been written about her, and I recited my version of "The Raven," waving my soapy arms all around. Lenore watched me, enthralled, waiting for another dish to dry. I repeated the performance every night, holding my audience.

On summer nights the audience included everybody in the apartment house. "Lenore, Lenore," I'd shout. "Nevermore, nevermore!" My voice carried up and down the air shaft and through the open windows of everybody else's kitchen. "Pipe down, Miriam," they'd yell. "Shut up, up there." But I didn't care what they said as long as I kept Lenore drying dishes.

Later, when I was working in pictures, I didn't care who was on the set or what they said. I just went about trying to hold my audience.

I may have learned how to hold an audience in a tenement kitchen, but it was also in that kitchen that I had one of the most wounding experiences of my life. I don't remember what I was doing there; as far as I know I was just standing around. Mama came in and saw me. The good Lord only knows what she had been thinking of, but it must have had something to do with Papa and his leaving her in this grubby tenement. She had a bitter, angry expression on her face. All of a sudden she snapped at me.

"Get out of my sight," she said. "I hate the sight of you. You look just like that Julian Cooper." Seventy years later those words still hurt me. I used to cry then, and I still cry now when I remember it.

I had never realized that I looked like Papa. He was mostly a blur in my mind, but I did have one vivid childhood memory of him. He was walking jauntily toward me on the street, slapping his thigh with a rolled-up newspaper. He was tall and slender, wearing a red carnation in his buttonhole, with a carefully trimmed moustache and goatee. He had black hair, dark eyes and a fair complexion. He was a very good-looking man.

And that was his entire legacy, his good looks, and he left them to me. I must have been a constant reminder of him to Mama. Maybe that was why she put me down the long hall, why she favored Lenore. It wasn't my fault. I didn't ask to be born looking like Papa.

But it was my Julian Cooper face that supported Mama, my brothers and sister for as long as I was in pictures and many years after. That was my primary attribute. I can talk about my face objectively now, for I've seen it often enough in rushes, on the screen, in stills, in newspapers and magazines. It was a pretty face—black hair, dark eyes and white skin. My eyes were my dominant feature. Recently I sat through a showing of *The Birth of a Nation* with two young professors of film history, Walter Coppedge of Virginia Commonwealth University and Walter Korte. Walter Korte said my eyes were sensual. Walter Coppedge said they were liquescent. I had to ask him how to spell it. Anyway, even though they were talking about the girl on the screen, I loved it. So much for objectivity.

It was my Julian Cooper face, plus the combination of a lively imagination, the ability to transport myself into different places and be somebody else, and the feeling that I was somebody special whom Our Lord cared about that helped me become an actress. Whenever directors asked me to do daring things, whenever they yelled at me, I wasn't afraid. Even when the high moguls of the movie industry tried to push me around, I wasn't afraid to fight back. Nobody was bigger than Our Lord, and He was my Friend.

« 4 »

The first money I ever made came about solely because of my face. At St. Walburga's I spent more time drawing and doing caricatures of my classmates than I did on my studies. Monsignor McMahon, pastor of our parish, suggested to Mama that I use the talents God had given me. He arranged for me to go to art school at Cooper Union. He even paid for my paints, brushes and canvases, and gave me twenty-five cents a day for carfare and lunch money.

When I got home from school one day, shortly after I was old enough to put up my hair, Mama had a visitor, an old lady in a beat-up black hat. She told Mama that Harrison Fisher and Charles Dana Gibson, the famous illustrators, were looking for models and that they paid fifty cents an hour. She offered to go with me to their studios in Greenwich Village. Mama was a little doubtful, but the old lady with the black hat and I talked her into it. Funny, but all that I remember about the woman who first made it possible for me to make money with my Julian Cooper face was her hat.

The first painting Gibson ever did in oils was of me. He painted me in a mantilla with my décolletage, what there was of it, covered by a big artificial rose. When I left the studio that day, I took the rose. It's the only time I can remember that I forgot God was watching me, keeping me from temptation. I kept the stolen rose and later, when I had no money for makeup and wanted to impress a beau, I pulled off a petal, wet it, and painted my cheeks with it.

It was about this time that Rita Wood and I went to the Biograph Studio. The five dollars I earned that day went to my head. I couldn't give it to Mama—how could I explain it?—so I spent it all on candy and sodas for the girls at school. After it was gone I wanted more, and now I knew where to get it.

Biograph never sent for me, so I tried the other two big studios in New York, Edison and Vitagraph, with no luck. That left Kalem, a small studio in the attic of a building on 23rd Street. Kalem's name came from the initials of the three men who organized it, George Kleine, Samuel Long and Frank Marion. They started with a cash capital of $400. Kalem made the first western movie—in the badlands of Coytesville, New Jersey. Today there's a great deal of interest in Kalem films, for they are among the forerunners of the modern cinema. There's one in the Library of Congress, with me in it!

I stuck my head in the door of the Kalem attic and asked if they needed an extra. They did. I stood around with makeup on and was paid for it. I kept going back. Some days they would use me, some days they wouldn't. When I didn't work I would go to art school; on working days I would pretend to go. My roles in those long-forgotten two-bit one-reelers grew larger. And then, one autumn day, my big chance came, and it scared me to death.

Movie studios were just beginning to move out of New York for the winter. The IMP Company had sent Mary Pickford to Cuba, and other studios were taking advantage of the sunshine and warm weather in California. They still came back to New York like robins in the spring, for it would be another few years before the permanent move to southern California. Kalem had several stock companies and was sending one to Florida. Mr. Marion asked me to go with this company as the ingenue. He would pay me thirty-five dollars a week and expenses, take it or leave it; they were going next week.

I told him I'd let him know. All that money sounded wonderful, but Florida was a long way away from Mama. Even if I got up the nerve to go, she'd never let me. Working in pictures in those days was a half-step up from being in burlesque. I didn't know what to do. I dreaded going home.

But when I got home that night nobody would have been interested if I had said I was going to China. There was other big news. A big box had arrived from Baltimore! We all opened it together. It was from Aunt Margaret's estate. She had died recently, and not only had she been rich, but Mama had been named for her.

First we pulled out several party dresses, then long wide petticoats with embroidered ruffles, then muslin corset covers. One of the dresses was of black silk trimmed with jet beads. It looked as though it had been made by Omar the tentmaker.

"Boy," Gordon said, "she must have been the fat lady in the circus."

Mama said Aunt Margaret had swelled up a bit with dropsy. Then she held up a pair of the biggest shoes I'd ever seen. They were the high-button type with pointed toes and scallops around the top. They were wide enough for all four of us kids to get into together. "Golly," Gordon said. "Cowboy boots!"

Mama held the shoes in her hands, looking at them thoughtfully. "Well," she said, "Miriam does need shoes."

That did it. I could just see myself walking into Cooper

Union or Kalem in those enormous hideous shoes. I told Mama I wasn't going to wear those shoes, I wasn't going back to school, I was going to Jacksonville, Florida, to make movies. Mama said calmly that she wanted me to stay in school and become an artist. "Why, someday you'll be famous," she said. "In a hundred years you might be as famous as Michelangelo."

"I don't give a hoot about a hundred years from now," I said. "We need some money right now. I'm going to Florida."

"How can you do this to me?" Mama said, and she went to bed with a sick headache. For hours, while I packed, I could hear her moaning in her bedroom. Mama really enjoyed her headaches. She should have been the actress, not me.

The boys wouldn't speak to me. The only one who approved was Lenore, the youngest. "I think it will be fun to have an actress in the family," she said.

Before I left I gave Mama ten dollars and told her I would send her fifteen dollars a week out of my salary. That would be like coming into an inheritance. But all Mama said was, "I want you to promise me one thing, that you will never write to the family in Baltimore. It will be bad enough when they find out themselves."

So with those words of encouragement, I got on the boat to Florida.

« 5 »

In Jacksonville we lived in a big old house called Fairfield
owned by two old ladies. One took care of the housekeeping,
the other sewed all our clothes. From my bedroom window
I could look out on lush green growth and see the big
steamers going up and down the St. John's River. It was
beautiful and I loved it, but at the same time I was so homesick that I cried myself to sleep many a night.

Anna Q. Nilsson and Guy Coombs were our leads.
Helen Lindreth and Henry Hallam played the character
parts and Hal Clements was the heavy. I was the ingenue.
The director was Kennan Buel, and Storm Boyd was assistant director. That was the total company. If we needed
extras, we hired local people. The big star of Kalem was
Alice Joyce, who worked in New York.

Perhaps because it was the fiftieth anniversary of the
Civil War, we did a lot of war pictures. I was in so many
Civil War one-reelers for Kalem that they all run together
in my mind. We'd do one a week. Often the story called for
me to be disguised as a boy. I remember one in which I had
a cap over my long hair. At the dramatic moment my cap
fell off and, big surprise, I was a girl doing the dangerous
job of a boy. In another I was the Drummer Girl of Vicks-

burg. I learned to play a drum for this picture—de-dum, de-dum, de dum dum dum. And I played it over and over and over. I drove everybody crazy with my de dum dum dum. And then nobody heard it in the picture.

When I wasn't working in a scene there were many other things to do. I kept busy so I wouldn't be homesick. I learned to ride horseback. The company rented lots of horses for the war scenes, and the local people taught me. Soon I began playing roles on horseback.

I had always loved animals, but I'd never been able to have one. Hal Clements gave me a dog and on St. Valentine's Day one of the men gave me a kitten. How I got the pet alligator I don't remember. He was just a little one, only eight inches long. Hal nailed a box together for him to live in, put a pan of water in it, some river sand, and a piece of screen on top. Then he painted it white. In the evenings we would all sit around watching the dog and the cat chase the alligator. But he was too smart for them. He'd get behind them and bite their tails, and boy, could he bite! Helen Lindreth made a little brown book for me with pictures of Nifty, the black cat, pasted in it. Then she wrote a few lines about each picture and gave it to me. I still have it.

And that was what glamorous movie stars did in 1912.

When the light started to fade in the afternoon and shooting was over, I'd go swimming in the river. I had learned to swim in the Hudson River at what was then called Manhattan Beach, only a few blocks from where we lived. Can you imagine a clean sandy beach on the Hudson today? Swimming runs in my family. My father had been one of the first people to attempt to swim the English Channel and my brother had once swum across the Hudson River. It was narrow up at Washington Heights where he did it, but he was only eleven at the time. A couple of generations later, my niece, Donna de Varona, won a gold medal in the 1964 Olympics to become a world champion.

Keenan Buel, the director, seeing me swimming in the river, decided to write some scenes around me. This was common practice in those days. If anybody did anything well, a director would find a way to use it. Buel wrote swimming scenes into several movies. One was entitled *The Tide of Battle*. That's the one in the Library of Congress.

My big scene started with me on the horse riding into the river. I hadn't become the world's greatest horsewoman at that time, and as the horse entered the water I held onto the pommel with one hand and tried to look calm. The horse wasn't very happy either, especially when the bottom dropped off sharply into the channel and he had to swim.

I slid off his back into the cold, black water and grabbed his tail. I had to kick like mad to keep my body on top of the water, out of range of the horse's hooves. I was wearing a shirt, pants and shoes—as usual I was disguised as a boy—and it wasn't easy. I had to remember to keep my face toward the camera. The director and the cameraman were in a boat moving downstream ahead of the horse and me. They were trying to hold the boat steady, crank the camera, and shout at me at the same time. At least I didn't have to smile.

In another one-reeler I rowed a boat out to set fire to the bridge and cut off the Yankees. Recently I read in *The Moving Picture World of 1912* some of the synopses of Kalem films. They called me plucky, brave, intrepid and courageous. I ran trains, shot cannons, burned bridges, spied, all for the Confederates. I don't see how the Yankees won the war.

One of the blurbs sent out to exhibitors said:

Miriam Cooper looks out upon the world with large dreamy eyes that belie her ability to swim, dive, shoot and ride with a fearlessness that has put many a thrill into Kalem pictures. Also she is expert in the use of boxing gloves and spends her spare time in the pretty spots of Jacksonville with her sketching outfit. And Miss Cooper is only 18 years old. She was born in Baltimore and gained much of her theatrical experience in school plays. But to see her in the role of a southern heroine, as in the spectacular production, *The Battle of Pottsburg Bridge,* in which her role is a most daring one, one could pronounce her a graduate of the legitimate stage.

Imagine how I reacted when I ran across that in my scrapbook recently. I have absolutely no idea what that thing about boxing gloves referred to; I don't remember it at all. Over the years I've developed some respect for the printed word—and now I run across that kind of stuff written about me.

At that time, doing daring things was just part of the business. We all risked our necks. Mabel Normand had gone even further that I had in *The Squaw's Love.* She fought with another girl on top of a cliff, dove into the water, swam underwater and wrecked the canoes of the Indians who were following her. She really did it, all of it, and nobody thought anything of it. She got paid, didn't she?

In *The Little American* a few years later, a film about the sinking of the *Lusitania,* Mary Pickford had to flounder around in the ocean wearing an evening dress. She couldn't swim very well and she nearly froze in the cold water. And who can ever forget Lillian Gish in *Way Down East,* floating toward the waterfall on an ice floe in the middle of a blizzard? That was the bravest thing any actress ever did.

We didn't use stunt men for the simple reason that we were supposed to be our own stunt men; it was part of the job. The businessmen making money off us thought actors were expendable. I found that out the hard way. My parts had been getting bigger all along. In many of the pictures Anna Q. Nilsson had started out as the lead but Buel kept enlarging my part until it was as big as hers and harder work besides. She was getting sixty-five dollars a week; I was getting thirty-five, and I was the one who got all wet. It got my goat.

After a particularly grueling role, running the train or some other damn thing, I went to see Mr. Marion and Mr. Long. "I'm playing leads," I told them, "and I think I ought to get more money."

They didn't say anything, so I thought I was getting the raise. The next Saturday when I ran down to collect my pay and looked in the envelope, there was my regular salary, thirty-five dollars. There was also a pink slip saying "Your services are no longer required."

I went home, back to art school, back to fifty cents an hour.

For weeks I tried to get a job and couldn't. One day I met Anna Q. Nilsson, who was back in New York, and Alice Joyce for lunch. I told them I was having trouble getting a job. Finally I said, "I'm going down to see Griffith."

"What!" Anna said. "*You're* going to see *Griffith*? What makes you think he'll see you? You're nobody."

"Well," I said, "he is the best in the business, isn't he?"

All my life I've gone to the best. Even when I thought I ought to be more graceful, I didn't go to just any old dancing teacher; I got Martha Graham to give me private lessons. When I wanted a divorce, I didn't go to just a divorce lawyer, but to the best corporation attorney in California. If I'd done what other people wanted me to do I'd probably have been a cook instead of a movie star. First Mama told me not to go in pictures, then Anna and Alice told me not to see Griffith. When I did what I wanted to do, I was always right and I got what I wanted. It's been that way all my life.

I got on a subway to go see Griffith.

« 6 »

Outside the studio on 29 Union Square there was a long line of people. It looked as though half of New York wanted to work for Mr. Griffith. I joined the line, and when I got inside the studio, I made myself comfortable on the hard benches reserved for the hopefuls who sat around waiting for somebody to notice them and give them a job.

I hung around all that day and came back every day for the next week. I knew that if I wanted to work for the best director in the business, he would have to see me. Every day I hoped he'd notice me, but he never did. I was there, but I might as well have been part of the wallpaper. Nobody paid any attention to me. Terribly discouraged, I went back to Cooper Union. If I couldn't be in pictures maybe I'd do what Mama said and get to be as famous an artist as Michelangelo after all.

I was coming out of the school one day when I ran into the young man I'd seen at Mr. Griffith's studio, Christy Cabanne. He had been an expendable young actor, too, but he'd moved up to be one of Mr. Griffith's assistant directors.

"Where've you been?" he asked. "I've been looking for you. You're not in the phone book."

"I don't have a telephone," I said. In our neighborhood

nobody had a telephone; we all used the corner drugstore.

"Well, Mr. Griffith wants to see you. Come to the studio at nine o'clock in the morning."

I couldn't believe it. I didn't think he knew I existed. Christy told me Mr. Griffith had been running through old tests when he came to that one I had made for him the day I worked as an extra. When he saw my test he told Christy, "Get that girl."

Christy had been trying to find me, though I couldn't understand why they hadn't looked out on the bench at their own studio. I'd been sitting there for weeks.

The next day I walked right by the bench and reported to Christy Cabanne. He took me in to see Mr. Griffith immediately. Mr. Griffith greeted me courteously, but from then on it was all strictly business. He asked me to take off my hat. Then he asked me to take down my hair, which I did, and my long dark hair, pinned so carefully that morning, came tumbling down below my shoulders. He looked at me full face and in profile again, just as he had done the first time I had seen him. Then he said, "Thank you, that's all."

When I went back outside, my hair all disheveled, my hat in my hand, I heard a man say, "Wow, that must have been some interview!" I can still remember my face getting hot.

Four more times that day Mr. Griffith called me back into his office. I began to think he was nutty. But I guess he was making up his mind about me. Each time he would ask me more questions about myself. I told him I was from Baltimore, that I lived with my mother, brothers and sister, and that my father was long gone.

Most of the girls in the Griffith company had the same kind of background. None of us had fathers; they had all disappeared before we ever saw Mr. Griffith. I learned later that this was the kind of girl Mr. Griffith liked—young, beautiful and supporting her mother. He didn't care particularly about talent since he felt he could mold anyone into the type of performer he wanted.

The last time he called me in he said, "We're going to rehearse a short scene. Bobby Harron is your sweetheart. He's a Confederate soldier going off to war. He's come to say goodby."

Robert Harron was one of the few people who had been at Biograph before Mr. Griffith. He was a poor boy who had gotten a job at the Biograph Studio through his parish priest, and had worked as general office boy before becoming one of the actors. He had soulful brown eyes and was always smiling. Everybody liked him. He had a way of slapping his thighs, clapping his hands and laughing as he walked past you. Bobby came over to me and said, "Don't be nervous. What's there to be afraid of?"

We went through the scene several times in the bare rehearsal room. Mr. Griffith sat on one of the kitchen chairs telling us what to do. I was like a stick. I was so in awe of Mr. Griffith I could hardly move. "Now remember," he said, "you are not Miss Cooper. You are a girl living during the War Between the States." I forgot myself and let my imagination take over, and I became just the girl he wanted me to be. When he was satisfied he walked out of the room and went to his office. A few minutes later he sent for me.

"We'll be leaving for California soon," he said. He didn't ask me if I wanted to go. He never asked anybody anything. He told you. "I'm going to be making a picture out there. It will be a story about the Civil War." Even then, some months before he started work on *The Birth of a Nation,* it was the only picture he had on his mind. "I have you in mind for the Southern girl."

There must have been something about me that Mr. Griffith felt expressed his symbol of Southern womanhood. There was never any conversation about my being in other pictures; to Mr. Griffith I was the Southern girl in the Civil War picture. It was only later that I realized what significance this was to have in a picture that changed the motion picture industry.

"Your salary will be thirty-five dollars a week," Mr. Griffith said. "Mr. Cabanne will give you all the details. That's all for now. Thank you."

He'd never given me a chance to answer. He never mentioned a contract. He just assumed I'd say yes and be on the train to California when the time came.

I did and I was.

I left New York to go 3,000 miles away from my family with no contract and only ten dollars in my pocket. What actor would do that today? But that was how strong my faith was in this man. I never doubted his word.

« 7 »

I had placed my faith in a man of honor and dignity. D. W. Griffith was also a very private man who rarely, if ever, told anyone his future plans or anything about his personal life. At the time I didn't even know that he was married. His wife was Linda Arvidson, an actress who worked with Biograph until she left it and him in 1911.

Mr. Griffith was a perfect gentleman. All those men were back then—Thomas Edison, the inventor of both the electric light and the kinetoscope that started moving pictures, Mr. Marion and Mr. Long of Kalem, and Albert E. Smith and J. Stuart Blackton of Vitagraph. They all wore white collars and cuffs and talked like gentlemen. You never saw them in shirtsleeves; they always wore suits. None of them were the fresh kind who would throw you down on a couch when you walked in, as the high moguls did years later.

Mr. Griffith looked like a gentleman and dressed like any successful businessman, conservatively and immaculately. He also looked like a general, with his erect carriage, piercing blue eyes and hawk nose. The only theatrical touches to his dress were his high-button suede shoes and his broad-brimmed hat which he wore indoors and out; when he did take his hat off you could see his bald spot under the thin, light brown hair he combed over it.

All his movements were quick, and he never wasted time. Even when he was walking, he kept talking. But he never gossiped. He was very patient and never spoke harshly to anyone, although he could be very sarcastic.

One time I said good morning to him and he didn't answer me. He probably had something on his mind and didn't hear me. At first I was only hurt, but by the time I reached the dressing room I had worked myself into a fury. Mae Marsh looked at me in amazement.

"Griffith'll have a long gray beard before I speak to him again," I said.

"What happened?" Mae said.

"He didn't answer me when I said good morning to him, that's what."

"Maybe he had something else on his mind," Mae said, trying to calm me down.

"He looked right through me. He's nothing but a common, ill-bred old man."

Mae didn't say anything more but she must have told him what I said. In fact I *know* she did. She was one of Mr. Griffith's girls at the time and she was afraid Griffith liked me. She didn't want any more competition.

The next day at rehearsal he said: "Where's the queen? Let's see what the Queen of Sheba can do."

He looked straight at me as he said it, and I knew he meant me. I stood up, stiff as a board, and walked on the set. The whole cast snickered. I was terribly embarrassed and thought he was cruel to draw attention to me this way. I was the only inexperienced girl there; they had all worked with him before. I needed his help, not his sarcasm. He made me feel about two inches high.

When we were leaving for home he told me to wait.

"I understand you think I'm a common, ill-bred old man," he said, repeating my exact words. "Is this true?"

I burst into tears and didn't answer. I was furious with Mae for telling him what I'd said, and I was scared to death he was going to fire me.

"Is this true?" he repeated.

"Yes," I sobbed.

"Why do you think that?"

"Because you didn't speak to me when I said good morning."

"I don't recall seeing you."

"And you called me the Queen of Sheba before everybody."

He put his hand under my chin. When I looked up he was smiling. "All right," he said. "In the future I'll try to be a gentleman." Then he took my hand. "Now are we friends again?"

We may have been friends but he continued to call me Queen for months.

I learned something very important from this incident. Jealousy can make even your dearest friend hurt you if she happens to be an actress and thinks you're going to get something she wants. I learned never to say anything to anybody that I did not wish repeated.

When Mr. Griffith wasn't calling me Queen, he called me Miss Cooper. The only people he called by their first names were Bobby Harron and Billy Bitzer, and he had known them since his first days in pictures. The men were all called by their last names—Walsh, Walthall, Pallette— but he always referred to the girls as Miss Marsh, Miss Cooper and Miss Gish.

He acted like the Victorian father none of us had. He was very strict with us. We were not allowed to drink or go to wild parties. One night we all went to dinner with Roy and Harry Aitken, financial directors of Mutual Film Corporation. Roy was sitting next to me and asked me if I'd like a beer. Mr. Griffith overheard him and told him sternly that I couldn't have it. I thought he was awfully fresh talking to one of his backers that way.

As long as I knew him he never swore or took a drink. He treated everybody very fairly, but he did like to keep everybody off balance. He didn't give you any opportunity to get a swelled head. In one picture you would be a lead, in the next little more than an extra. Lillian Gish played the lead in *The Birth of a Nation* and then appeared very briefly in his next big spectacle, *Intolerance*. Constance Talmadge was the lead in one sequence in *Intolerance:* in another, an extra.

He seemed to treat me differently. In each picture I made for him I had a bigger part. Actually I never cared how big my part was. I was only interested in pictures for the money I could make, and my salary was the same no matter what the role.

Even then D. W. Griffith was considered one of the great directors. I was just beginning, with experience only as little more than a stunt girl. But I realize now that the great director and I had one thing in common—money; that is, we both got into pictures simply because we needed money.

Mr. Griffith had started out as a playwright, and from what I learned about him later, he had earnestly devoted his early years in the theater to this one ambition. He had one play produced, but it ran only two weeks. That one play, a poem and a short story were all he ever had published. In order to keep eating while he wrote these unsuccessful plays he tried acting. He toured with a New York company, but he was no big success on the legitimate stage.

Purely in hopes of getting a few dollars to support himself and his wife, he took a story to Edwin Stratton Porter, head of the Edison Company. That was sinking pretty low, but he sank even lower when Porter turned the story down, then offered him a role in a one-reeler. Griffith took it, and played the lead in *Rescued from the Eagle's Nest*. It's still around today, all ten minutes of it, and it's so bad it's funny. I never heard Mr. Griffith comment on his heroic role fighting with a stuffed eagle, and I doubt if anybody else did either.

He worked for Edison for a while as an actor, but he still wanted to write. He went to the American Mutoscope and Biograph Studios to try to get them to buy his scripts. They did, for fifteen dollars each, and he began working for them, under the name Lawrence Griffith, as both actor and playwright.

Then he had an offer from a summer stock company for forty dollars a week. He would be in the theater, but what would he do come fall? Steady employment won out, and he agreed to stay with Biograph as a director, with the understanding that if he failed they'd keep him on as an actor.

My decision to go into the movies affected my whole life. Mr. Griffith's decision affected his life, the entire industry, and the lives of scores of other people. Money was his major reason, but not too long after he must have begun to feel that movies could be more than a peep show. In 1910, at contract time, he had signed his real name, David Wark Griffith.

In those days the director was the most important man in pictures. He chose the story, hired the actors and determined how much they would be paid. The actor had no rights, no contract—only the director's word. And Mr. Griffith always kept his word. When you worked for him, you were one of Griffith's players. He changed companies many times, and when he left one for another, everyone considered it an honor to be asked to go with him: nobody ever wanted to be left behind.

With his cameraman, Billy Bitzer, he brought many technical innovations to films. Whatever Griffith wanted, Bitzer could do. If Billy hadn't been such a fine cameraman, some of the shots Griffith wanted wouldn't have been possible.

The big Pathé camera and the tripod Billy used were so heavy and bulky he needed a camera boy to help him move them. Shortly before I came along, the company bought him a motor-driven camera. He continued to crank it himself, however, because he could control the action better that way. If a man took a long time getting on a horse, for instance, Billy could crank a little slower. When it was run on the screen it would look as though the rider got on quickly and easily.

We always talked about the camera as a person. We never referred to Billy but to the camera itself. "Stop picking your nose," we'd say. "The camera's grinding."

Griffith's ideas and Billy's expertise made an unbeatable combination. However, they didn't use photography to be arty, but to tell a story. Mr. Griffith's films were about ordinary people and the things that happened to them. I guess that's why his pictures appealed to the masses of ordinary people who went to see them. He hired young, inexperienced players who lived the same kind of lives as the characters in the movies he made. They were poor, young, in love, overcoming the obstacles in a cold, hard world. They were believable.

"You have to suffer," Mr. Griffith told us, "to know something about life."

Years later, when movies became respectable, society girls from uptown would try out for parts. They were always terrible. Then I thought it was because they didn't need the money and weren't willing to work as hard as we were. But now I think it was because they didn't know what it was like to be poor and in trouble. They couldn't *be* the part. Mr. Griffith was always polite to them after the tryouts, but he never asked them to come back.

His players included many movie immortals—Mary Pickford, Lillian Gish, Mae Marsh, Mack Sennett and Lionel Barrymore. Movie buffs will remember some of the lesser lights—Constance Talmadge, Blanche Sweet, Henry B. Walthall, maybe even Miriam Cooper. You'll notice that most of the names are female. Mr. Griffith was most effective working with women. He could get his young ladies to give performances they didn't know they could give. Many never did very well once they left his company.

Maybe it's because we would have done anything to please him. I mean in the way of acting—there were no casting couches in Mr. Griffith's office. He may have had some lady friends, but he treated all of us with great respect.

In his first five years in pictures Mr. Griffith produced over 400 films. By then he was the master of the camera and could use it as part of the story to portray emotion and achieve many dramatic effects.

When Harry and Roy Aitken offered him the position of head of production of their companies, he took it. He could direct films himself, supervise the other directors and make two more films a year independently.

It was during this period, when Mr. Griffith was making films for the Aitkens, that I hung around the studio at 29 Union Square with the rest of the hopefuls. I was one of the few who made it. I left for California and a whole new life.

« 8 »

It was a dreary, cold January day when I left New York for my first trip across the continent. I hated to leave my family and friends, but not the dirty slush and snow. I was looking forward to California's sunshine.

Mama said she had a headache and sent Gordon and Nelson to Pennsylvania Station to see me off. Although she looked down on picture people and didn't want to have anything to do with them herself, she wanted them to see that I had some family. The boys were far more interested in the big locomotive and in Eagle Eye than they were in seeing me off. Eagle Eye was an American-Indian actor making the trip with us. He wore his hair in shoulder-length braids and dressed in cowboy clothes. He drew a crowd wherever he went.

Christy Cabanne was in charge of the company. Christy was now a director himself with his own assistant, a handsome young actor named Raoul Walsh. Our leads, Irene Hunt and Eugene Pallette, were already on the West Coast. I was the ingenue, and the cameraman and a character actor made up the rest of the company. Christy's wife, Vivian, his three-month-old baby and his mother-in-law made the trip with us.

Christy's mother-in-law took it upon herself to chaperone me. Every night at nine o'clock she'd come for me in the club car. "It's not safe for you to be with those men and that Indian this late," she would say, and hustle me off to my upper berth.

She was right, but she was only half right. *I* was safe; my money wasn't. Raoul and Christy taught me to play poker and cheated me outrageously. I would sit next to the window with my cards held out in front of me. "Hold your cards up, Miriam," Raoul said. When I did, the cards were reflected in the train window, and he and Christy could see everything I had. I was losing all my money. But Christy's mother-in-law caught on, bawled them out, and I arrived in California well rested, with my ten dollars intact.

Eugene Pallette, looking more like a cowboy than an actor, met the train in Los Angeles. Pallette, then young, slender and handsome, was an important leading man for years. Later, when he developed his paunch, he made the transition to talkies as a gravel-voiced character actor and comedian.

Pallette had hired a car to take us to the Gates Hotel on Figueroa Street on the edge of Los Angeles. Our leading lady, pretty blue-eyed Irene Hunt, was already there. The Gates was one of the few hotels where picture people could stay. The townspeople shared Mama's feelings about the movies. People had signs on their lawns advertising apartments for rent, saying "No dogs or picture people allowed." Most Californians at that time were either retired Midwesterners with very middle-class ideas, or second-generation Californians who were just far enough away from their Gold Rush ancestors to be bluenoses.

In 1914 Los Angeles was a big unattractive hick town. Hollywood, a few miles away, was a sweet little country village, sedate and quiet. It was a residential community, no stores, just quiet streets with big old comfortable houses sitting back from the street behind well-kept spacious lawns.

Hollywood Boulevard connected the two towns. It was a picturesque street lined with palm trees and masses of multicolored geraniums. Sitting on a small knoll, well back from the street, was the Hollywood Hotel. It was a yellow frame building about two blocks long where people lazed away the hot afternoons in rocking chairs on the porch. Many picture people lived there and it was the scene of much merriment and parties in later years.

Streetcars ran on the main streets in and out of Los Angeles. Where there were no streetcars you could usually find a jitney, a large open touring car that cruised the city looking for passengers. To get one you stood on a corner with your arm extended and yelled "jitney" whenever one passed by. You'd squeeze in with four or five other people, and for a dime the driver would take you almost anyplace you wanted to go.

Beverly Hills, today one of the most expensive and exclusive areas surrounding Los Angeles, was way out in the country. Some of the rich Texans who came to California to escape the torrid Texas summers had large Victorian houses there, but nothing ostentatious. I don't remember anyone having a swimming pool.

Another posh area today, San Fernando Valley, was nothing but a desert then. Some of the more prosperous actors and directors had begun to invest in land there, Christy told me, but everybody thought they were taking a gamble.

Smog was nonexistent, and California was a land of warmth and sunshine except during January and February, the rainy season. Then rain would come down in such torrents that you had to use a rowboat to get across streets at the bottom of the hills.

Nothing was glamorous—not the people, the town or

the studio. Reliance Majestic, Mr. Griffith's new studio, occupied a large corner lot on Sunset Boulevard between Hollywood and Los Angeles. It was a rural area, with only a few turn-of-the-century houses in the neighborhood. A dark gray two-story frame house had been converted to offices for Mr. Griffith, Frank C. "Daddy" Woods, the business manager, and Johannes Charlemagne Epping, who handled Mr. Griffith's finances for years. Mr. Woods was a dignified gray-haired man who ran everything. Mr. Epping, who was only as big as a peanut, gave us our pay. The building also contained developing, cutting and rehearsal rooms. Outside was a bench where the extras sat from morning to night, day after day, waiting for a job. Nearby were the projection room, the dressing rooms and the lunchroom. A sandwich sold for ten cents and milk and pie for five cents each.

Behind the buildings on the front lot were two outdoor stages built six inches off the ground, like dance floors. There were no indoor stages then. To control the sun, muslin diffusers were pulled back and forth over the stage on pulleys, depending on what kind of lighting Mr. Griffith wanted. There were also pieces of hard stiff cardboard painted silver that could be moved around so the sun would hit the actor where the director wanted the light, behind you, on your cheeks, anyplace.

We arrived in California before Mr. Griffith did, but we didn't wait for him to start working. Christy Cabanne began filming one- and two-reelers immediately to keep us busy and make some money. In one of them I had my first scene-stealing experience.

A scene called for Irene Hunt and me to talk to each other, profiles to the camera. During rehearsals everything went off all right, but once the camera started grinding I somehow wound up with the camera taking a lovely picture of Irene's face and the back of my head. During the third take, as Irene inched her way upstage, Cabanne shouted, "Cut!" He walked over to Irene. "Would you mind, Miss Hunt, if we saw just a little bit of Miss Cooper's face?" he said very sarcastically. "Just a teensie bit?"

Irene blushed and stopped upstaging me, but she wouldn't speak to me all the rest of the time we were shooting.

We had finished that picture when Mr. Griffith arrived with almost a hundred people—actors, actresses, directors, assistants and cameramen, and their relatives. The place started humming. Carpenters and electricians were everywhere, banging and sawing and putting up wires. Several directors were working on one of the big stages at the same time. There were people dressed as cowboys, Mexicans, Indians, and in period costumes all mixed up together. Directors shouted orders, and actors and actresses laughed and talked together, with the sound of hammering always in the background.

It was very confusing and noisy but nobody minded. Mr. Griffith was here and we all felt confident and secure. It's funny how we never worried about anything in those days. It was only after the high moguls came in, and we had lawyers and contracts, that we worried.

Mr. Griffith lived at the Alexandria Hotel, the best and most expensive place in town. The people with families found apartments and bungalows, while the rest of us lived in one-room apartments with a Murphy bed, a small kitchenette and a bath.

The Murphy bed was hidden behind a mirrored wall. To go to bed you pulled the bed out of the wall; in the morning you pushed it back in. It was very convenient and space saving, except that the clothes closet was behind the bed. You couldn't get your clothes out without pulling the bed out of the wall.

My room was in the Stowell, where I paid thirty-five

cents for dinner and seven dollars a week for rent. The Stowell was what I needed financially, because I was sending Mama fifteen dollars a week, but if she had known what it was like she'd have had a sick headache. It was a traveling salesman's hotel, and many a night whoever occupied the room next to mine jiggled my doorknob to see if he could come in. I kept the door locked. I was lonely, but I wasn't that lonely.

Most of the other girls lived with their mothers. The girls were the breadwinners and the rest of the family followed them wherever they went. Once the big money began rolling in, it was amazing how many relatives wanted to follow you around.

In those days mothers played the role of business manager, chaperone and agent. All the leads—Lillian and Dorothy Gish, Mae Marsh, Constance Talmadge—lived with their mothers. None of them had fathers. Lillian and Dorothy's father was a ne'er-do-well who had walked out on their mother while the girls were very young. Mae Marsh's father had died in the San Francisco earthquake, leaving her mother with six children to bring up. The Talmadge girls—Norma, Natalie and Constance—hadn't seen their father since they were teenagers. They had gone to work at the Vitagraph Studios across the street.

From the time Lillian and Dorothy Gish were child actors, their mother had advised them on what jobs to take and how to handle their money. She was a sweet, frail woman who stayed in the background, unlike Mary Pickford's mother, who was considered one of the toughest businesswomen around. Dorothy Gish told me Mary's mother was always there when Mary was working for Mr. Griffith. She fought for larger parts for Mary and bigger salaries. One producer said of her: "It often took longer to make one of Mary's contracts than it did to make one of Mary's pictures."

Peg Talmadge, mother of Constance, Norma and Natalie, was an uneducated woman, and she looked terrible. She was fat, with big bosoms that fell all the way to her waist. She tied her belt up underneath them. But she had a mind like a steel trap. She advised her girls to put their money in trust funds so they would never be broke. She had a terrific sense of humor and was always jolly. Everybody liked her. I was crazy about her. Anita Loos got the idea for the heroine of *Gentlemen Prefer Blondes* from stories Peg told her.

Mae's mother was something else. She was a slender red-haired woman who was very nice, but stupid. But she still looked out for Mae. Once Mae had promised to go to Mass on Easter Sunday with Raoul Walsh. She was all dressed to go when Mr. Griffith asked her to spend the day with him. Mae's mother made up Mae's mind in a hurry. Raoul was just an assistant director then, but Griffith was Mae's bread and butter.

I had no one to advise me. Mama would never fraternize with picture people, not with her famous ancestors. It would never have occurred to her to fight for bigger parts or bigger salaries for me. I was on my own. Fortunately I was never envious of other actresses when they got them. I did my job as best I could and accepted the parts Mr. Griffith gave me.

All during the spring Mr. Griffith supervised other directors who were making one- and two-reelers while at the same time he was directing four- and six-reelers. One of the longer films was *Home Sweet Home*, based on the life of the man who composed the song, John Howard Payne. It was an early classic and, according to film histories, I played Bobby Harron's fiancée.

But if I was in *Home Sweet Home* I must have been unconscious at the time. I don't remember a thing about it, and I never saw it. What probably happened was that one of Mr. Griffith's assistants asked me to work in some scenes with Bobby Harron and I did. I had no idea what the picture was.

I am not the only one who has forgotten what she was in. Recently, when Lillian Gish came to visit me in Charlottesville, I asked her if she remembered every film she'd ever been in.

"You know," she said, "only recently I was in the Museum of Modern Art looking at an old film and I saw myself on the screen. But I still didn't believe it. I'd never heard of that movie before. There I was moving around up there and I kept saying, 'No, no, that's not me.' "

Lillian assured me I was in *Home Sweet Home.* "Everybody in the company was in it," she said. "You were part of the company, weren't you, Miriam?"

I was, so that's that.

It may sound strange today, but there was a good reason for not knowing what we were doing. Making pictures in the days before World War I was informal, casual and confusing. We worked for any director who needed us. I'd be in a Christy Cabanne picture one day, and a Tod Browning the next. The pictures were short, and if it wasn't a big part, it was hard to keep track of them. I played beautiful Mexican girls, beautiful Spanish and Algerian girls and beautiful American girls. I'd be walking across the lot and somebody would call me to come be in a scene. Things like that happened all the time.

Recently I saw an old photograph of myself with a brown calf in the Museum of Modern Art files. The picture is identified as a still from *The Greaser* and I'm identified as Billie West, a young actress who did look a little bit like me. The New York Public Library for the Performing Arts has the same picture; its description says that the girl is me, and that the calf is a present from a fan. A clipping from a newspaper of that time says that I kept the calf in my backyard.

They are all crazy. The truth about that picture is that I was walking across the lot one day and somebody yelled, "Hey, Miriam, put your arm around that calf. I want to take your picture." I did and he did, and that's the whole story.

Eileen Bowser, the Museum of Modern Art's Griffith expert, said, "It's very hard to identify people in these early pictures, and the cast isn't always identified. Lillian Gish and Blanche Sweet are easier to identify because they use characteristic gestures. But sometimes I'll say, 'That looks like Mary Pickford in the background'; but I can't be sure even after having seen so many films."

To make things even more confusing, titles were sometimes changed. During the spring of 1914 I made two or three cowboy pictures. One featured Sam De Grasse and Eugene Pallette. In that picture Gene takes me over his knee and spanks me. It hurt, and that's how I happen to remember that picture so well. I know very well, from my seat of memory, that its name was *The Gunman*. But I have a page of photographs that appeared in *Reel Life* advertising the picture and in the ad it's called *The Horse Wrangler*.

If a picture didn't sell, often the producer would change the title and send it out again. Some unscrupulous exhibitors would even go so far as to retitle a successful picture and give it another play.

A lot of the confusion ended as the names of the players became known, although other companies had publicized their leads for years before Mr. Griffith finally gave in.

In the *Moving Picture World* issue of September 12, 1914, the Reliance Majestic ad said: "We advise Exhibitors to advertise the names of these stars when showing any of the above-named pictures." The company began offering enlargements of the Griffith players to be put in the lobby of the theaters. An exhibitor could get a fourteen-by-seventeen-inch for fifty cents, or a giant five-foot-high picture for $2.50. At first only enlargements of Mae Marsh, Blanche Sweet and the Gish sisters were available, but after a couple of months my name was added to the list. After *The Birth of a Nation,* there were enlargements of everybody in the cast.

The motion picture producers were beginning to be aware that a name, a "star" was something people wanted to see. But it would take the pants pressers and the glove salesmen who came into the business later to turn this awareness into big money.

We had to be at the studio six days a week, whether we were scheduled to work or not. We learned a way to get there that was cheaper than jitneys and a lot more fun. We'd stand out on the corner and stick out our thumbs. We wouldn't ride with anybody who looked scroungy, or with the old men. But when a young handsome man stopped for us we were always willing to ride with him.

I'm surprised they stopped, for we always looked like bums. I don't know what happened to that neat little girl with the starched dickey; maybe it was just a matter of not wasting time. There was no point in combing my hair because I'd just have to do it all over again when I got to the studio and found out who I was going to be that day.

Neither could we afford fancy clothes the way actresses in other companies could. Mr. Griffith never paid big salaries and we were always broke.

But we stuck together, especially the girls. Like the time we tried to protect Gertrude Bambrick, one of the dancers Mr. Griffith had brought from New York. She was pregnant and her husband, Marshall Neilan, was cheating on her. Mickey Neilan was very talented; he later directed some of Mary Pickford's best pictures. But at the time we were all mad at him. He'd tell Gertrude he had to work late, but we all knew where he was.

Poor Gertrude, who looked like she'd swallowed a

watermelon, wouldn't leave her room without Mickey. "I'm not parading around any hotel in this condition without my husband," she said.

We all took turns spending the evening with her so she wouldn't be alone. She had a book called *The Do's and Dont's for Pregnant Mothers* which, among other things, said to massage her stomach daily with olive oil. That was my job. I was more interested in motherhood than I was in pictures.

Aside from such excitement as rubbing Gertrude's stomach, life was dull and I was lonely. One night Teddy Sampson asked me to join her and some men friends for dinner at the Alexandria Hotel. I was so lonely I said I would. That evening Teddy and her friends called for me in a black, chauffeur-driven limousine.

The automobile was big and beautiful but the men were terrible. They were rough traveling salesmen from New York who drank too much, but they were better than nothing. That Saturday night we all went out to Vernon's, a popular roadhouse with a shady reputation.

At dinner everybody was too busy drinking to eat. I asked for a cup of coffee. "What's the matter with you?" Teddy asked. "Why don't you have a real drink?"

"I don't like the way it tastes," I said. They all looked at me with disgust. But I really didn't like the taste of whisky, and besides, it made me sick.

During the soup course I felt a hand caressing my thigh under the table. I jumped up, gave the man a shove that almost knocked him off his chair, and ran into the ladies room. Then I realized I couldn't get home—I didn't have enough money for a taxi.

Teddy came lurching into the ladies room. "What's the idea of being so damn upstage?" she asked.

I didn't want to get into an argument, so I ducked into one of the cubicles and pulled the chain so I couldn't hear what she said. She rattled the door until she got tired and left, but I stayed there. Sometime later she came back. "We're leaving now, if you want a ride home," she said and slammed the door.

I got into the car and they took me home. Nobody talked to me.

On Monday morning I could hear sounds of angry, loud talking coming from the dressing room long before I reached it. Teddy was ranting and raving. "I'll run my private life as I damn please, and anybody who thinks I won't is crazy." Then she mimicked Mr. Griffith. "The company doesn't approve of this, the company doesn't approve of that. Who the hell does the old bastard think he's kidding? He's the company, nobody else but."

Now don't think all Griffith girls talked that way; they didn't. Lillian Gish and Mae Marsh would never have said things like that. Neither would I. Of course the language I heard in the studio was certainly stronger than that I had heard in the convent. When I first went back to New York I said "Oh, my God" in front of my mother and she nearly fainted. But that was about as bad as we got then.

Teddy was different. She played in comedies and went with Ford Sterling, one of Mack Sennett's Keystone Kops. I don't know why, but all the comedians talked tough and swore a lot.

Mr. Griffith didn't use such language himself and didn't want his girls using it, either. When he heard about this scene in the dressing room he fired Teddy. He'd never fired anyone before. He'd never even raised his voice. He didn't have to; he could make you feel like a worm just by looking at you. We were all upset. We all liked Teddy even though she was a terrible gossip and you couldn't believe a word she said.

But Teddy didn't care. She went over to the Sennett company and got a job there.

A day or so later Mr. Griffith called me to his office. I thought he was going to fire me, too. When I entered the room he didn't look up from the papers he was working on.

"Sit down, Miss Cooper," he said, going right on with what he was doing. I sat down on the edge of a chair. He kept working and I sat there, waiting for the ax to fall. He did this all the time: called you, then kept you waiting while he did something else. It made you feel like two cents. He was the master of dramatic suspense off the screen as well as on. Finally he looked up.

"Don't you know it is against company rules for young ladies to drink or patronize roadhouses?"

I kept my head down and nodded.

"The company has decided it isn't safe for you to live alone in a hotel," he said. Then a long silence. "How would you like to live with Miss Alden?"

I just stared at him open-mouthed. Mary Alden was a character actress who had appeared on the legitimate stage. She is remembered today as the mulatto mistress of Senator Stoneman in *The Birth of a Nation.*

"I hardly know Miss Alden," I said. "I don't think she . . ."

"Miss Alden would be delighted to have you," he said. "Think it over. I'll talk to you in the morning." Then he strode out the door without waiting for me to answer.

I knew very well that I had no choice in the matter. When Mr. Griffith told you to do something there was no doubt in his mind that you were going to do it—and usually there wasn't any doubt in your own mind, either.

I moved in with Mary. Her apartment consisted of two rooms, a kitchen and a bath. I slept in the Murphy bed in the living room.

My life changed drastically with Mary. She was a fine actress and an accomplished woman. Each evening she would help me with difficult scenes. She gave me little hints about how to get an emotion across to the audience and she gave me self-confidence.

She also started me on a lifelong habit of taking lessons. Believing that it would help me to learn more about English literature, she found a high school teacher to tutor me.

When I wasn't studying or rehearsing, I could enjoy the people who came to see Mary. John Emerson was one. He had been a stage actor and playwright and now worked as an actor, writer and director for Mr. Griffith. He was crazy about Mary, though he later married Griffith's young scenario writer, Anita Loos.

Now that I was with Mary I wasn't lonely, so I didn't do things to get myself in Dutch. Nevertheless, I did think Mr. Griffith's rules were pretty puritanical.

We didn't even have boy friends. Dorothy Gish was the only one who had dates. She was going with Bobby Harron. They were in love for years, but she never married him. Lillian and Mae went out, but only with Mr. Griffith; that didn't count. Our only friends were other Griffith players. We were different from the actors at other studios. We had no money and no glamor; we just worked harder.

But we weren't saints. Smoking and drinking were forbidden, so that's what we wanted to do. We started a Hens' Club that met at a different person's house every Thursday night. We'd buy a pack of cigarettes and a couple of bottles of beer. Then, behind closed doors, we'd sneak a drink and a puff. One of us would light up, and, not even knowing how to inhale, we'd draw in. Our eyes watered and we choked a bit, but that didn't stop us. We wanted to be sports.

One night at Dorothy Gish's we must have had an extra swig of beer because we decided to do something daring indeed—go across the hall to Lillian's apartment. None of us except Dorothy had ever been in it before, since Lillian never invited the girls to visit her.

We opened her door, yelling something inane like Surprise! and then stopped in our tracks. There was Lillian,

The Kalem company in
War's Havoc. In picture
after picture we won
the war for the Confed-
erates fifty years
after the war was over.
Hal Clements, Henry
Hallam, Guy Coombs,
Anna Q. Nilsson,
Helen Lindreth and me.

Here I am bravely
setting out to dynamite
the bridge in The
Battle of Pottsburg Bridge.
It was 1912; I was 21.

I never saw this calf before, nor have I seen it since, but according to different authorities I owned it or played a scene with it.

ladies of the Florida Kalem pany in our Civil War finery—me, en Lindreth and Anna Q. Nilsson.

Kalem Company at istmastime in Jacksonville. row, second from left, heavy, Hal Clements; next im, leading man Guy Coombs; he center, our director, Keenan l. Helen Lindreth is third n right; on her left, character r Henry Hallam and assistant ctor Storm Boyd. Second from left he middle row is Anna Q. Nilsson. third from left in the bottom row.

THE BABY KALEM CO. XMAS 1911.
THE HOME OF —
MR & MRS C HEMENWAY

In order to get the tears he wanted for this scene in
The Birth of a Nation, *Mr. Griffith told me my mother was dead.*

In The Birth of a Nation *I played the role of Margaret*
Cameron, Mr. Griffith's symbol of the South.

In Intolerance, *I played a fallen woman, the mistress of gangster Walter Long. Here I'm about to shoot him in a jealous rage.*

This scene from Intolerance, *showing me agonizing after killing my lover, was one of the most intense I ever played. As Mr. Griffith wrenched the emotions out of me a still photographer took these pictures.*

Bobby Harron,
Walter Long and I
in a scene
from Intolerance.

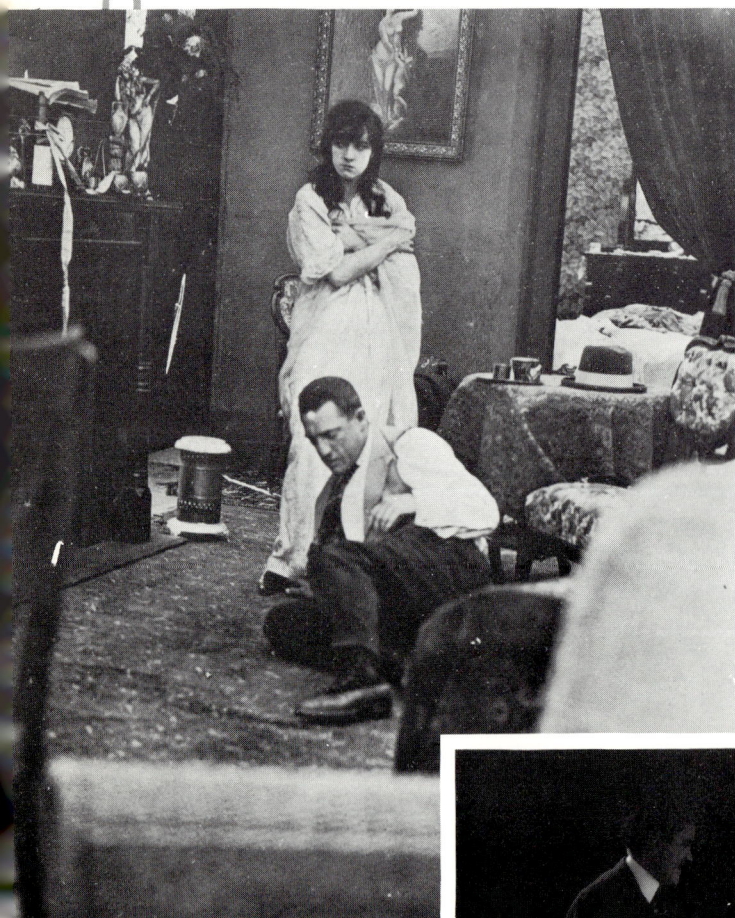

Walter Long and I
on the Intolerance
set. Like Walter,
this scene ended
on the floor—of
the cutting room.

Bobby Harron, Mae
Marsh and I on the
set of Intolerance.

lying on her bed, wearing something filmy, with her long golden hair spread out over the pillow. She was reading Shakespeare. It was the only time I ever saw her look annoyed. But she welcomed us in and was pleasantly polite during the brief time we stayed.

We couldn't help but notice the difference between her apartment and her sister's. Although the rooms were exactly the same size, no two places could have looked less alike. Dorothy's looked like a monk's cell, with only two or three pieces of Mission furniture in it. Lillian's was opulent, with velvet draperies and bed throw, gilt-framed mirrors and lace-trimmed pillows. It was hard to realize that this seductive-looking woman was the same prim self-contained girl who walked around the studio carrying a book.

Lillian and Dorothy had very different personalities. Dorothy was warm and friendly and utterly without pretense. Everybody liked her. But none of the girls was clubby with Lillian. She was stand-offish, always reading and never raising her voice. "Who the hell does she think she is?" they'd say.

In one way though, she was unlike most of the girls who criticized her. She was a lady. She may not have been friendly with the girls, but she was always polite and considerate. When Lillian came to visit me recently I saw in her those qualities I had never seen in the early days— warmth and friendliness. I don't know which one of us has changed.

She and Dorothy had joined the Biograph Studio in the summer of 1912 and had played in several one-reelers before coming to California. Dorothy, a comedienne, later gave one of her most endearing performances as the Little Disturber in *Hearts of the World*. Lillian played the lead in many Griffith films, including the one I don't remember, *Home Sweet Home*, and became one of the best-remembered actresses to have worked with Mr. Griffith.

The men on the set never paid much attention to Lillian. Everybody considered her Griffith's girl. (Though he and his wife, Linda Arvidson, had long been separated, she wouldn't give him a divorce.) And of course Mae Marsh didn't like her. Mae wanted to be Griffith's girl, but Lillian was too much competition.

After we had been in California a few months, Mr. Griffith told me to dress with Mae. Even though she had been with the company longer and was established as a lead, she was happy to share the dressing room with me.

Mae was never upstage; everybody liked her. She was always gay and merry and fun to be around. But no matter how zany she was, her wide-set gray eyes never lost their sad expression.

She never looked like a glamorous movie actress. She had freckles and more tiny wrinkles than a fifty-year-old woman. Her hair was wispy and mousy brown; but she did have one physical attribute I wished I had, a pert, retroussé nose.

I loved Mae. She was my dearest friend. When I was living alone I'd spend many nights with her and her large, warm family. She, her older sister Lovey and I would sleep three in a bed. Those were the only nights I wasn't homesick.

Mae had visited Lovey on the set when Lovey, as Marguerite Loveridge, had worked for Mr. Griffith a few years earlier. Mr. Griffith had seen Mae sitting on a bench, and her pale, wistful face appealed to him. She got her big opportunity when Mary Pickford refused to wear a grass skirt in a picture called *Man's Genesis*. Mary looked at the grass skirt and realized that if she wore it people could see her legs. All the other girls—Blanche Sweet, Mabel Normand and Dorothy Bernard—said if Mary wouldn't play the role, they wouldn't either. Mr. Griffith turned to Mae and asked her to do it. Mae didn't care if her legs showed. She played the role in the grass skirt and gave a fine performance, legs and all. Even Mary congratulated her on it. As a reward Mr. Griffith gave her the lead in *The Sands of Dee,* a part the other girls would have given their eyeteeth for.

Mae was a natural actress, and Mr. Griffith's voice guided her into giving appealing and believable performances. And she could always do something to make you laugh, like sending me a picture of herself inscribed "To Miriam, in memory of old times, 1914." I'd known her about six months.

In spite of my close friendship with Mae, she never told me about her relationship with Mr. Griffith. I found out about it in the dressing room after work. The dressing rooms were in a long weather-beaten building between the office and the lunchroom. The men's dressing rooms were on the first floor, ladies' on the second. Also on the first floor was the stars' dressing room, shared by Lillian and Dorothy Gish. Mae and I were upstairs with the other girls.

A high board fence shielded the girls from being seen from below as we ran back and forth along the balcony in our underwear to the bathroom. There were cracks in the boards. Each night Mae would look down through the cracks at Lillian's dressing room. If Lillian came out of her room all dressed up, Mae would know it was Lillian's night to go out with Mr. Griffith. If she came out looking like the rest of us, in old clothes, then Mae would change her clothes just in case.

One night you'd see Mr. Griffith having dinner at his hotel with Lillian, the next with Mae. So far as I know, Mae and Lillian were the only two girls he ever took out. I had my opportunity; in fact, I think he had a case on me. He gave me a portrait of himself with an inscription on the back: "To the brunette of brunettes.—By the river, by the river." I have no idea in the world what that river business means.

One day after shooting he offered to drive me home in his Rolls Royce. We were on location at Griffith Park. Mine being the last scene of the day, he sent the company and the hired car on ahead. "I'll see that Miss Cooper gets home," he said.

I leaned back against the cushions of the back seat, enjoying the cool evening air as the chauffeur guided the car through the hills. I was exhausted from working and happy that the day was over. I had my eyes closed so I didn't see what was happening, but I could feel an arm going across the seat behind my head. I opened my eyes just as Mr. Griffith leaned over and kissed me on the mouth. He smelled of butter; we'd had corn on the cob for lunch. I was so startled I pushed him away, and he landed on the floor. He looked so silly that I'd have laughed if I hadn't been scared. He was amazed that anyone would do this to him. I was amazed that he would make a pass at me with the chauffeur sitting in the front seat.

"Don't you want me to kiss you?" he said.

I damn well didn't, but I didn't want to be fired, either.

"Oh, no, it's not that," I said. "But I'd have to tell it in Confession."

"Do you mean your church teaches that kissing is a sin?"

"No," I said, "but the nuns taught me not to put myself in temptation's way. *That* would be a sin."

Being a temptation was something Mr. Griffith seemed to understand. He relaxed and sat back next to me, all puffed up at the thought of having put me in temptation's way. I never did understand how a man like that could be taken in by such a story.

He may have shown some naïveté, but professionally he had reached a point in his career where everything was coming together. He had technical mastery of the camera, a superb cameraman able to carry out his most innovative ideas, a company of players experienced and well qualified in the new style of movie acting; and he had experience in making longer films with large casts and scenes involving scores of people, machines and animals. He was ready for a showcase for all his talents.

« 9 »

People today know how pictures are made—today. They know that there's a script all written out in its entirety and broken down into scenes. They know the actors are familiar with the story, and with what they're going to do each day while it is being filmed.

Well, *The Birth of a Nation* wasn't like that at all. I haven't the faintest recollection of the day we began working on it, and for a long time I had no idea of what it was about. It was no big thing at the beginning.

As I said, we'd all report to the dressing rooms in the morning, not knowing whether we were going to be the rancher's daughter or the Indian maiden, or just be photographed with some dumb calf. Well, I guess one morning Mr. Griffith told us we were going to start the Civil War picture.

For me it was just another day in the life of a $35-a-week leading lady. Of course Mr. Griffith had told me in New York I was going to play a Southern girl in a movie he had in mind, but for all I knew, that morning in California, the picture could have been a one-reeler shot in two days.

As for the script, there wasn't any. In all the time I

worked with Mr. Griffith I never saw him use a script. He'd scribble out the shooting schedule for the day on any old piece of paper, and that was it.

I learned later that *The Birth of a Nation* was based on a book by Reverend Thomas Dixon called *The Clansman*. It had been dramatized for the stage and it had played around the country for years. Griffith had purchased the movie rights for *The Clansman*, but that was only the framework. Most important of all, he had his own ideas. As a child he had listened to his father's stories of the Civil War and Reconstruction days. His father, Jacob Wark Griffith, had been a colonel in the Confederate Army. It wasn't hard to tell the good guys from the bad guys.

But that was about all we could tell. As I said, we had no script. This was in the days of silent films, and there were no lines to read, memorize and deliver. If it was necessary to tell the audience what was going on, words were written and cut in later.

No script, no lines and, to add to the confusion, no sequence. Like filmmakers today, Griffith didn't shoot his films in sequence. He arranged the schedules according to his own convenience. For example, we'd shoot all the scenes on one location together, no matter in what part of the film they might appear. Those of us in one scene might not have any idea what other actors were doing on another location.

Actors today know all that and expect to work that way. But you have to remember that back in those days the stage was the important thing, and people didn't know or care how movies were made. The poor stage actors were completely confused. They were used to beginning at the beginning and going on to the end. They knew who they were. In the movies they only knew who Mr. Griffith said they were on that particular day.

So now that you know that I didn't have much idea

of what was going on when we were shooting, let me tell you the plot anyway. For although the film has been shown almost constantly since it was first made, and many cinema addicts have seen it a dozen times or more, many others have not seen it even once. We didn't know it when we were making it, but it turned out to be most controversial. It was told from the Southern viewpoint, which to Mr. Griffith was the *only* viewpoint. Today it is banned in some states, even in film history classes.

The major characters of the story are members of two families, the Stonemans from the North, the Camerons from the South. (I'm a Cameron.) Before the Civil War begins, they are friends.

Austin Stoneman, played by Ralph Lewis, is a Northern senator in favor of Negro rights. His daughter Elsie is Lillian Gish and his two sons are played by Elmer Clifton and Bobby Harron. In the opening scenes the Stoneman boys are writing a letter to their Southern friends, telling them they are coming to their plantation for a visit. While they are writing the letter Lillian Gish is playing with kittens, so you know right away she and her brothers are nice people.

In the next scene, when the Camerons receive the letter, you know we're nice people, too—we're playing with puppies.

Mr. Griffith was great on symbols, but I can't believe he really meant one that today's audiences give him credit for. I saw *The Birth of a Nation* recently with a class of sixty college students. Right after a love scene with Henry Walthall, who plays my brother Ben in the film, Lillian rushes to her room and wraps her arms around the bedpost. The students hooted and laughed.

I asked the professor, Walter Korte, what was so funny. He gulped and squirmed and said they interpreted it as a phallic symbol. I had to make matters worse by asking what he meant by *that*. Poor Walter. Poor Mr. Griffith, not to mention Lillian. They'd be shocked at the idea, just as I was. Walter agreed.

"With that wonderful Victorian sensibility," he said, "Griffith would have been horrified at the modern interpretation."

From the warm and friendly opening scenes, Mr. Griffith develops his story. War is declared and now the good friends from the North and South are enemies. The Stoneman boys are Union soldiers, the Camerons Confederates. Mr. Griffith made it easy to follow the action in the battle scenes because the Confederates were always on the left of the screen, the Union soldiers always on the right. This helped the audience to know what was going on.

The lives of the two families run together during the war. One time a Cameron is just about to bayonet a Union soldier when he recognizes it's his old friend. When Ben Cameron is wounded, Mrs. Cameron asks Elsie Stoneman to help and Elsie takes her to see President Lincoln.

The story shifts back and forth between the innocent victims of the war and the panoramic battle scenes. The first half ends with the Northern victory and Lincoln's assassination. The second half deals with the Reconstruction period. When Austin Stoneman's mulatto mistress, played by Mary Alden, is insulted, he takes her in his arms and comforts her. But when a power-mad mulatto wants to marry his daughter, Stoneman is enraged.

Meanwhile, the white Southerners are being terrorized by the newly freed Negroes. White women are no longer safe outside their homes. Ben warns his family not to leave the house. But the water supply is low, and my little sister, Flora, played by Mae Marsh, goes to get some. One of the bad Negroes follows her, and to escape him she jumps off a cliff. Ben finds her, and as she dies in his arms, he swears revenge. He sees some white children scaring black children with a white sheet and gets the idea for the Ku Klux Klan. First the Klan saves Elsie from the power-mad Northern Negro, and then when a mob is after the Cameron family the Klan rides to the rescue in spectacular triumph. The picture ends with the two sets of Cameron–Stoneman sweethearts finding happiness, and a message of hope for the future.

That's the plot, but of course I didn't know it. I also didn't know what my role as Margaret Cameron meant. I was, according to current film historians, the symbol of Southern womanhood, dark haired and beautiful, living through the war that divided our country, and helping to unite it again by marrying the Northerner, Phil Stoneman. Elsie Stoneman reinforces the theme by marrying my brother Ben, the little colonel. This was Mr. Griffith's way of uniting the country after all the war and fighting—the birth of a nation.

As we got into the picture I began getting an idea of what it was about and realized that it was no simple one-reeler, but it didn't matter much. I was living the role of one character in it. This sense of *being* Margaret Cameron didn't begin right away. At first there was the excitement of beginning a new film which, it soon became obvious, was going to be a big one.

In her book, Lillian Gish says everybody read Civil War history once rehearsals started. Well, Lillian may have read history, and Henry Walthall may have, but I don't remember anybody else doing it. I didn't, and if Mae did she surely didn't understand it. She had a third-grade education and was still writing small *i*'s in letters when referring to herself, like "i went."

Lillian, Mae and I represented the three different types of women Mr. Griffith liked to use in his films. In an article on me in *Arts in Virginia,* Walter Coppedge described the three types, starting with me. "Of dark liquescent eyes and a strangely still but magnetizing beauty, Miriam Cooper's looks were oddly provocative: she had sex and breeding, and she moved with an inviting grace. . . . Griffith probably saw her as an archetype of the dark-haired, passionate woman. . . . Griffith's 'Dark Lady,' then, struck a contrast to the two other types Griffith developed: the vivacious freckle-faced hoyden whom Mae Marsh and Constance Talmadge personified with their pert charm, high spirits and spunky character; and the ethereal innocent, best represented by the exquisite, seemingly fragile Lillian Gish . . ."

While we were working on the film we looked at many photographs of the period to help us with our hair and makeup. Mr. Griffith would bring pictures for us to see so we could copy the styles. "Can you fix your hair like this?" he'd ask us.

For the early scenes we all wore our hair in soft curls, falling on our shoulders. For the later scenes, when the North had won the war and the Southerners were poor and defeated, Mae and I changed to more severe hair styles. We did our hair ourselves; there were no Mr. Kenneths or Sidney Guilaroffs.

Nor were there any Max Factors or Westmore brothers; we did our own makeup, and it was difficult. The harsh California sunlight was hard on our faces. Billy Bitzer, the cameraman, blended a brown powder for us to wear over pink greasepaint. He showed us how to do it the first time, then we were on our own.

We didn't make our own costumes, but we were certainly excited about what we were going to wear. Our wardrobe mistress, Mrs. Harris, got a lot of old magazines from the Civil War period and we all looked over her shoulder as she consulted the pictures to make sure our clothes were authentic. Mrs. Harris had a beautiful daughter named Mildred. She had golden hair and dreamy eyes. She wanted to be an actress and followed Lillian around like a puppy dog. Later she married Charlie Chaplin and I didn't see her again for years.

All the excitement made the rehearsals pass quickly, but they were hard work. Mr. Griffith rehearsed us for hours before he shot the scene. We'd rehearse in his office or in a bare room with kitchen chairs for furniture. Outdoors, he'd place his chair under a tree. Leaning back, with his big hat hiding his bald spot, he coaxed, cajoled and wrenched believable performances out of his "children," as he called us.

He called us something else, too—damyankees. At least he called everybody else in the picture by that name. But even though I thought of myself as a Northerner—I had gotten so tired of Mama's ancestor worship that I revolted against the Southern side of my family—to Mr. Griffith I was a Southern lady. When I protested that I was a damyankee too, he wouldn't listen. I guess he was doing a little projecting himself.

We started rehearsing early in the morning, as soon as the sun came up, and went on until late in the afternoon.

"Film is very expensive," he explained, "so before the camera starts grinding, you must know your parts letter perfect."

Today's directors shoot scenes over and over again on film. Only a few years after *The Birth of a Nation* Raoul Walsh used to film one take after another until he was satisfied and I was exhausted. But Griffith shot each scene just exactly once—after a million rehearsals. When we had it right he'd give us a day off to rest up, then we'd appear before the camera fresh and eager.

At first I went through the motions, doing my job but not inspired. The opening scene, in which I'm playing with the puppy, came easily. I love dogs, and playing with the puppies was fun no matter how many times we rehearsed it.

My first really difficult scene was with Henry Walthall. It came at the end of a long day of rehearsals. Lillian Gish had just finished a love scene with Walthall and had gone back to her seat when Mr. Griffith called my name. Walthall was standing there, waiting for me.

On the screen he looked tall and imposing, but in real life he was short and slender. He was from the theater, and stage actors always thought of themselves as being superior. Picture people were friendly and easy to work with. They'd call you Toots or Kiddo or Baby Doll, whereas Henry Walthall never called me anything but Miss Cooper or Miriam.

As he looked at me, his dark eyes were sad, yet angry looking. He scared me. Suddenly my knees felt weak.

"Now, Miss Cooper," Mr. Griffith said, "in this scene you see your brother in his new uniform for the first time. You stand gazing at him in wide-eyed admiration. Point proudly to the officer's insignia on his shoulder. Then to the bronze medal on his chest. Throw your arms around him. Show us how much you love and admire this hero brother of yours."

I looked at Walthall. He was nothing but a blur. I tried to point to his decorations, but I couldn't raise my arm.

"Miss Cooper," Griffith said, "you're overcome with happiness. Smile!"

I was overcome, all right, but not with happiness. I couldn't move. I just stood there.

"All right, Miss Cooper," Mr. Griffith said patiently. "You can sit down now."

I don't remember going to my seat. Everything was blank until I felt Mary Alden's hand on my arm.

"It's nothing, dear," she whispered. "You just had a case of stage fright. It happens to all of us."

At the end of the day Griffith called to me as I was leaving.

"What happened this afternoon?" he asked.

"I don't know," I answered. "I guess I'm not cut out to be an actress."

"To be a good actress you must be natural," he said. "You don't try to *act* like the character you are portraying. You *are* that character. You are Margaret Cameron, a young Southern girl living fifty years ago."

My mind went back to that peaceful little cemetery in New York where I used to escape my childhood unhappiness by being someone else. And again I became someone else; I became Margaret Cameron. Later Mr. Griffith told me I was easy to direct. People tell me that in contrast to much of the arm-waving histrionics of that period my quiet style stands up today. But it wasn't me; it was Margaret Cameron.

I remained Margaret Cameron for the rest of the picture, though I have to admit that on one other occasion I did lapse into being Miriam Cooper again, trying, very unsuccessfully, to play a role. In one scene Henry Walthall was going off to war and I was telling him good-by. But I couldn't get worked up over it. I didn't care if Henry Walthall went to the moon.

Mr. Griffith was trying to get me to cry. "This is your brother and you love him. He's going off to war," he said. But he couldn't get one tear out of me, not for Henry Walthall.

Mr. Griffith got up, walked away, then came back again. He cleared the set and drew his chair up close to me.

"Miss Cooper, I wasn't going to tell you this until the day's shooting was over," he said sadly. "We received word this morning that your beloved mother is dead."

I started crying. Great tears rolled down my cheeks. Mr. Griffith gave the signal to Billy Bitzer to start the camera. It kept grinding until Mr. Griffith had all the tears he wanted. "Cut!" he said, and walked off the set.

I didn't find out for several minutes that no such word

had been received. My mother was alive and well. But Mr. Griffith got his tears.

When I told Kevin Brownlow, film historian and author of *The Parade's Gone By* . . . , about it he said, "How cruel! How could he have done such a thing?"

Another chronicler of the early days, Alexander Walker, wrote in *Stardom* that Mr. Griffith was ruthless. "Beneath the porcelain exteriors of Griffith's stars," he wrote, "there must have been wills of steel."

Well, whether ruthless or cruel, when Mr. Griffith wanted a certain emotion from you, he didn't care how he got it. The most important thing to him was getting the emotion he wanted on film. That's what made stars out of the girls with the porcelain exteriors.

Oddly enough, I wasn't angry with Mr. Griffith for the trick he had played on me. None of us ever was when he did something cruel for the sake of the movie. Whatever Mr. Griffith did was always all right with us.

That second experience with Walthall was my only lapse out of character. During the rest of the film, whether rehearsing or in front of the camera, I was Margaret Cameron. I really didn't realize to what extent I had become someone else until recently, when I was talking with friends after seeing *The Birth of a Nation* again. I mentioned two scenes which impressed me.

One was the death of Mae Marsh. She jumped from the cliff rather than submit to Walter Long, the bad Negro. I remember distinctly going to the location where the scene was shot that day. Watching the episode, even from behind the camera, affected me so deeply that tears came to my eyes. And when I saw it again, years later, I was just as touched.

The other scene was pure Griffith, and pure delight. One of his most popular devices was to build up tension or tragedy, then suddenly switch to something comic. I remember his saying that whenever you had drama, you also had to have comedy.

During a battle Henry Walthall is wounded and taken to a hospital. Lillian, his sweetheart, visits him there. The scene is tense and dramatic. But as Lillian leaves the hospital a young sentry gazes after her. He looks so mawkish the audience bursts into laughter. Later Mr. Griffith looked for the extra who had played the lovestruck sentry to offer him a role, but he had disappeared.

After discussing these two scenes one of my friends, a middle-aged man who had seen *The Birth of a Nation* in a Southern town as a boy, brought up another scene. He said it was much funnier than the one I mentioned; he'd remembered the audience shouting and roaring with laughter.

This is the scene in which the fleeing Camerons are trapped in a small farmhouse by a gang of murderous Negroes. They are battering down the door and trying to come in through the windows. The Klansmen are riding to the rescue, but it doesn't look as though they'll get there in time. My poor sick father is huddling in his shawl and I'm fluttering around. It looks like curtains for the Camerons. In the melee our faithful old colored mammy bops one of the intruders over the head.

Thinking about it now, I can see why people find the scene funny. First of all, it's slapstick comedy of the kind you're always seeing on television and in movies. The tension makes it funnier. And also, my friend explained, it's Griffith, the natural-born Southerner, editorializing. At that time white Southerners wanted to believe that *their* Negroes were affectionately loyal to them, and this episode, with the faithful old mammy hitting the bad black man, proved it. It went over big.

Why didn't I think the scene I was in was so funny, while being moved by two in which I did not appear?

I'd like to say it's because I knew that it was an unfair picture of the Negro during Reconstruction days. But the real reason is that I was seeing the other two episodes as a spectator; the scene I was in was real to me. It still is.

I remember how frightened I was when it was being shot. Actually no one was battering at the door; that scene was probably taken in another room on another day. The people breaking in to kill us weren't really Negroes; there were few Negroes in California at the time, and with few exceptions all were played by white people wearing dark makeup. Even our faithful black mammy was really white; she was a pleasant fat woman named Jenny Lee.

But I—or Margaret Cameron—was still scared when the scene was being shot, so scared that there was nothing funny at all in Jenny Lee's swatting the man who was coming to get me, regardless of what color either of them was.

If I wasn't in a scene, I would be on the set watching. The most exciting scenes were the battles. When they were being filmed I'd jump into one of the big open touring cars and ride out to watch them. Mr. Griffith had rented a whole county to shoot those scenes. He needed it for all the artillery and trenches, plus a camping spot for the horses and the stunt and rodeo performers who worked as extras.

Money was still a big factor, and although in *The Birth* it appears that Griffith used a cast of thousands, it was actually only a few hundred. After an extra would die in one battle scene, he'd wait for the camera to pass him, then get up and run around the scenery to die again in another scene. All the battle scenes were filmed to give the illusion of vast numbers, but the effects were achieved with a much smaller number of people.

Almost every well-known actor and director for years to come played a part, and everybody on the lot was in it. Directors became actors, and actors doubled as featured players and extras. Only Mae, Lillian and I never were extras. I don't know why that was; maybe it was because we would have been too easily recognized.

Students of film history disputed my claim that I was never an extra in *The Birth of a Nation*. I was at a showing recently when a dark-haired girl walked across the screen, and everybody said she was me. Well, she wasn't; she was my sister Lenore.

In 1914, when Mama remarried and went to Europe on her honeymoon, Lenore came out to California to stay with me. One night Mr. Griffith took us to dinner. He had been looking for a girl with brown eyes to play Lillian Gish's Negro maid. When he saw my sister's beautiful brown eyes he asked her if she'd do it. Lenore was still a schoolgirl and was delighted at the prospect of being in pictures. But I knew Mama wouldn't like it.

"Lenore can't do it," I told Mr. Griffith. "I promised Mama I wouldn't let her near the studio."

"But," Mr. Griffith said, "with all that makeup on, nobody will know who she is. Your mother will never know."

He and Lenore talked me into it, and Lenore played Lillian's maid. She was an extra four or five times more in the picture before she went back to New York.

Some years later Lenore worked in pictures as both an extra and bit player, but she didn't photograph as pretty as she was. There's a mystery about the camera. It enhances some people's looks, destroys others. The best example I know is Mae Marsh. Mae was never really pretty, yet the camera did marvelous things for her face—and caught all her warm happy personality.

Not only did everyone but Lillian, Mae and me double up, but some played several roles. Bobby Harron, who was one of the leads, took part in the battle scenes as an extra, and played a Negro in blackface. Raoul Walsh was an assistant director, but he also played the role of John Wilkes Booth, the man who assassinated Lincoln, and he was in the battle scenes, too.

To control these scenes with hundreds of men scattered over the landscape, Mr. Griffith worked out a careful plan. He stood on a forty-foot wooden tower and shouted orders through a large megaphone to his directors down in the battle. When the first man heard the order, he passed it on to the next, and so on down the line. Each director would shout orders to his little group of soldiers, then, dressed as a soldier himself, get in the scene with them.

Mr. Griffith strove for authenticity in every detail of the shooting. He consulted Civil War books and West Point military strategists. He used photographs taken by the famed Civil War photographer, Matthew Brady, as examples for Billy Bitzer and his crew to follow in taking photos of battle sequences.

But Billy didn't have anything to consult on how to shoot the artillery duel that went on into the night. Bonfires were lit and figures moved eerily around, barely distinguishable. It was the first time a scene had been photographed at night.

Billy obliged Mr. Griffith with another first, one that might easily have been Billy's last. They were filming the chase scenes, and Mr. Griffith wanted the camera right where the action was, actually *under* the action. He had Billy dig a trench, lie in it and photograph the mass of galloping horses thundering over him.

One Monday morning when I came to work the studio was quiet. There was no sound of hammering on the stages and no carpenters carrying parts of sets around. A few stagehands and electricians were playing cards behind the sets, while some of the actors were standing around talking. Nobody wore costumes or makeup.

Mae wasn't in our dressing room, although it was almost eight o'clock. I went down to the big dressing room at the end of the balcony. Mary Alden and some of the girls were sitting there, talking.

"What's going on?" I asked. "Are we having a holiday?"

"We don't know," Mary said. "Mr. Epping said not to make up till we were told."

I went downstairs and saw Rosie Smith, one of Mr. Griffith's cutters, coming out of the projection room. "Where is everybody?" I asked her.

"Everybody? Do you mean Mr. Griffith?" she said. "He's in the projection room."

"At this hour of the morning?"

"Yes, and Mr. Woods and Billy Bitzer are with him. I don't know what's going on."

Mr. Woods was the head of the story department and each day looked at the film that had been shot the day before. A meeting in the projection room wasn't unusual, but it certainly wasn't normal for all other activity to stop.

All kinds of rumors flew around the lot. The picture was a flop; Mr. Griffith couldn't sell it. Everybody had something to say, but nobody knew what was actually happening.

The other girls and I could only speculate, because nobody told us anything. We were treated like ten-year-olds, kept completely in the dark about everything that was going on. Mae and I were coming out of the lunchroom when Mr. Griffith came up to us.

"Would you young ladies like to invest in this picture?" he asked. "I guarantee you'll make a handsome profit."

I didn't have any money and I said so. Mae didn't say anything. After he had gone, she wrinkled up her nose and said, "Can you imagine that? Asking me to put my $300 in his picture when it's so lousy he can't even sell it." She rolled her eyes all around, looking very dramatic. "Why, it took me a year to save that much. The man's a thief."

We found out later that the picture had run over its budget. Under the terms of his contract with Mutual, Mr. Griffith could produce two independent pictures a year. This was one of them. He had formed an independent company with Harry Aitken, who put up $25,000. That was a lot of money for a film in those days, and it was hard to raise more. Mr. Griffith left California for New York. Meanwhile, we all sat around waiting for him to return. All activity at the studio came to a standstill. But nobody left the studio. We all had faith in Mr. Griffith.

If Mae had given him her $300 she would have made many thousands. Thomas Dixon had asked $10,000 for the rights to *The Clansman* and reluctantly accepted a twenty-five percent share in the picture as payment. It made him a wealthy man.

Though we were idle, we got our pay anyway. Mr. Epping gave us our pay envelopes every week. It was always cash; we did not receive checks. There was never a week when we didn't get paid. Lillian Gish says she did not receive her salary and only the extras were paid. If that's the case I must have been a highly paid extra, for my money never stopped.

When Mr. Griffith returned with more money we began working again. I almost wished he hadn't raised it when we began shooting the cotton-picking scenes on location in Imperial Valley, which is one of the few places in California below sea level. The heat was so intense several members of the cast passed out. Even in the ninety- and hundred-degree heat I wore my costume of pantalettes and hoop skirt. To make matters worse, we couldn't take a bath. The hotel had only two rooms with baths. One was occupied by a cotton broker and the other by Mr. Griffith. All the other men shared one common bath at the end of the hall. Remember, this was in the prehistoric days before air-conditioning. There were fans, of course, but they were of the prehistoric vintage, too, and didn't do a lot of good. I was the only woman on location, and Mr. Griffith suggested I use his bath when he wasn't there. It was the greatest luxury in a nightmarish situation.

And then it turned out my suffering was for nothing. The whole episode landed on the cutting room floor.

By this time Mr. Griffith was recognized as a genius in the cutting room. He had developed techniques which were at first considered shocking. Instead of letting a scene run from beginning to end, the way it was done in the theater, he would cut it and show what was going on somewhere else. This was heresy in those days. He even trained his own technicians, a young couple named Rosie and Jimmy Smith. They had had no experience whatever when they joined the company. He hired them because their priest asked him to, the same way he had hired Bobby Harron. They didn't know enough to question Mr. Griffith's revolutionary ideas even if they had dared to.

With *The Birth of a Nation* he reached new heights in cutting. He would cut the film in two ways. One was to cut across time, going from an actor's face to what he was thinking about. The other increased tension. As the excitement mounted, Mr. Griffith would cut the scenes shorter and shorter, going from one action to another, until the audience was at an emotional high when the climax came.

You can see the same technique today. *The French Connection*, the film that won the Oscar for the best movie of 1971, has a chase scene that is a classic example of Griffith editing. In *The Birth of a Nation*, when the Klan rides to rescue my family trapped in a cabin, the action switches back and forth between the horsemen and the interior of the cabin. The scenes grow shorter and shorter. In *The French Connection* the detective is in an automobile, chasing the dope smuggler who's in an elevated train above him. Again the scenes switch back and forth, growing shorter as the tension increases.

Mr. Griffith knew what effects he wanted and how to get them. Whenever he wanted an opinion he'd turn to one of the stagehands or carpenters and say, "Joe, what do you think of that?" Then he'd listen to Joe's answer and cut the scene in or out accordingly. In her book Lillian Gish says Mr. Griffith would ask her opinion of a scene. Lillian may have been the exception, for I never remember his asking an actor's opinion on anything. He was making his films for the common man, and that's whose opinion he wanted to have, not the opinion of one of the actors.

My scenes in Imperial Valley were not the only ones that fell to the cutting room floor during the three months he spent with Rosie and Jimmy Smith cutting the film down to twelve reels. Even then it was the longest American feature ever made. It ran for three hours.

It was also the most expensive, but nobody seems to know exactly how much it cost to make it. Lillian quotes Mr. Griffith as telling her it cost $61,000. Walter Korte teaches his film history students that it cost $110,000. I once overheard Harry Aitken say it cost him $75,000, plus $30,000 for publicity and advertising. At the time everyone said Griffith had exceeded his budget and was spending so much money on this picture that they thought he was crazy.

When the picture was finished he had a musical score written to help set the emotional tone. *The Birth of a Nation* was the first film to have its own orchestral theme; it had to be played by a live orchestra at each performance, of course. The picture was advertised as a "musical spectacle."

« 10 »

When the first great American motion picture opened at the Clune Auditorium in Los Angeles on February 8, 1915, it was still known as *The Clansman.* The audience loved it. It ran for months at the Clune, but I didn't see the finished picture until the end of April in New York.

The reason was that I was sick with a hacking cough that had begun during the rainy season. I was tired and listless and miserable. The doctor said I had tuberculosis. He prescribed rest and lots of raw eggs. Once I was strong enough, the company sent a car and a nurse to take me for long rides in the California sunshine.

I began to regain my strength and wanted to see the picture. Everybody who came to visit me told me it was sensational. But the doctor advised me to stay away from crowds, for I could easily get very sick again.

While I languished with my raw eggs and healthful rides, Mr. Griffith took the picture to New York. On the train across the country he worked on improving the picture, cutting and editing sequences to make them better.

And the title was changed. The way I heard it, between the time the movie was shown in Los Angeles and its opening in New York, Mr. Griffith had a private showing for

Thomas Dixon. They sat through the film together. "It's too big to be called *The Clansman*," Dixon said when it was over. "I think it should be called *The Birth of a Nation*."

On February 18, 1915, *The Birth of a Nation* was shown "By Courtesy of the President" to President Woodrow Wilson and members of his cabinet in the East Room of the White House. The presentation of a moving picture in the White House was another first for this picture that was first in so many ways. When the picture was over, President Wilson said, "It's like writing history in lightning, and my only regret is that it's all so terribly true."

Mr. Griffith loved those flattering words and they were reported everywhere.

The next night it was shown at the National Press Club for Chief Justice Edward D. White and members of the Supreme Court. Mr. Griffith was the guest of honor.

The announcements for both of these showings were printed on vellum paper that still looks prestigious fifty-five years later. Just that paper alone is proof that movies had become respectable. Thomas Dixon gave me a copy of each announcement, autographed "To Miriam Cooper, with the love of the author."

When *The Birth of a Nation* opened at the Liberty Theatre in New York on March 3, 1915, it looked like opening night at the opera. It was a full house, with everybody who was anybody in pictures, New York society and the literary world in the audience.

Mr. Griffith had sent Mama a ticket to the opening. In her letter telling me about it she said, "At the end of the picture, the audience actually stood up and cheered." Then she added words I cherished, "I was very proud of you."

It's a good thing Mama was proud of me, because she endured a lot as the mother of an actress. When she went to Mass one Sunday shortly after the picture came out, Monsignor McMahon, the priest who had paid for my carfare and lunches at Cooper Union, said from the altar, "I'm heartbroken that one of our children has left her studies as a talented artist to be a movie star."

Mama got up and walked out of church, crying into her handkerchief.

Fortunately not everyone felt the way Monsignor McMahon did. Letters and telegrams began pouring into the studio in California. The picture we had been sure was a flop was now causing a sensation. I was dying to see it.

On toward the end of April, I began to feel more like myself, and a wire from Mr. Griffith was a wonder drug. He said: I LEAVE CHICAGO FOR LOS ANGELES TUESDAY NIGHT WILL BE AT AUDITORIUM ANNEX TUESDAY GO BACK TO CHICAGO FOR OPENING THERE MAY FIFTH ARRANGED FOR YOU WITH MR WOODS DWG.

The last sentence meant that Mr. Griffith had given me a round trip ticket to New York. One day, before I got sick, he had seen me crying. When he asked what was wrong I told him I was homesick. I said he had told me I would be in California six months and now it was over a year, and I wanted to see my family. At the time he hadn't said anything about it. Now that I was well enough to travel, he was doing something.

I was so eager to get going that I rushed through packing, picked up a ticket from Mr. Woods, and was on the train two days later.

The ride across the country seemed everlasting to me. It was so hot crossing the desert that I put a wet sheet at the window, hoping to cool the air. That hot desert air was enough to kill you.

When I got to Chicago, there were two telegrams waiting for me, one from Mae, the other from Mr. Griffith. Back in the days when the Western Union boy came riding up on his bicycle wearing his knickers and his cap, telegrams were a common means of communication and especially nice to receive when changing trains going across the country.

Mae said: I KNEW YOU WOULD BE LONESOME ON THE TRAIN SO I DIDN'T WAIT FOR YOU TO ARRIVE IN NEW YORK . . . HAVE BEEN RIDING AND AM TOO SORE AND STIFF TO PICK UP A NINETY DOLLAR BILL IF IT WERE TO FALL AT MY FEET ACCIDENTALLY BUT NO SUCH LUCK DOROTHY GISH AND ALL THE GIRLS PEEVED FOR YOU NOT SAYING GOODBY . . . LOVE MAE MARSH.

Mr. Griffith's wire disturbed me. The instructions on it read: "Try all trains arriving from Los Angeles on Santa Fe RR from seven in the morning till twelve o'clock noon April 21 until found." The message was: AM AT THE AUDITORIUM HOTEL ANNEX HERE CALL ME UP IF YOU GET THIS D W GRIFFITH.

I didn't know what to do about Mr. Griffith, but I knew I had to call him. I was aware that he had a case on me, but I didn't want to get involved with him. My feelings for him were respect and admiration, but nothing else. And I wasn't the type to have an affair; I was never a very sexy person.

I tried his hotel a couple of times, but to my great relief didn't reach him. I spent the time waiting for the train reading a detective magazine. I left Chicago that night without having seen Mr. Griffith. He never made any overtures to me again.

When the train pulled into Grand Central Station the whole family met me—Mama, Nelson, Gordon and Lenore. I'd never been so glad to see any group of people before. We had so much to tell each other we all talked at the same time. We sat around the kitchen table until the wee hours of the morning.

The next day Norma Talmadge called to ask me to have lunch with her. Norma had worked for Vitagraph Studios and was an accomplished dramatic actress. I've heard it said that her Brooklyn accent ruined her for talkies, but I didn't think she had any accent at all.

I took the subway downtown to meet Norma. "Have you seen the picture?" she asked me before I had a chance to sit down. "The whole town is talking about it."

"Mama and I are going tonight," I told her. "I wish I could take the rest of the family, too."

"Why can't you?" Norma asked.

"Five of us at $2 a head? I can't afford it."

"You don't have to pay to see your own picture, you ninny," Norma said. "Ask the manager to let you in. He'll be delighted to have a celebrity as his guest."

"A celebrity? Me? Don't be silly," I said.

"You ask him," Norma said. "You'll see whether you're a celebrity or not."

That night we got dressed up in our Sunday best and took the subway to the Liberty Theatre. The lights of the marquee shone with the name of the picture in letters two feet high. D. W. Griffith Presents, *The Birth of a Nation*. The lobby was full of people and brilliantly lighted. There were posters of the leads all over the place. Long lines of people waited to get in. I walked past them, my head high, the family following after me, and went right up to the box office. I asked to see the manager and introduced myself.

He said he would be delighted to have me and my family as his guests. Norma was right, and I loved the feeling of power "being somebody" gave me.

While the manager and I were talking, Gordon came running toward me. "Come get Mama," he said. "She's embarrassing us to death."

Mama had planted herself next to the five-foot high picture of me in the lobby and was bowing and smiling, first to the poster, then to the crowd around her.

"Yes, indeed," she was saying. "That's my daughter. She's just seventeen. Yes, indeed."

Even Mama was lying about my age. She looked like a barker at Coney Island. It was the darndest thing you'd ever seen. My mother, the Stewart, working as a shill.

But the movie was wonderful. I remember how everybody gasped when the Union Army, with General Sherman at its head, came riding toward the camera. Nobody had ever seen anything so spectacular before. Later in the film, when the Klansmen ride over the horizon, wearing their white sheets, ready to save the besieged white Southerners from the Negro raiders, the audience cheered and clapped. I didn't mind at all when people turned to stare at me.

The Birth of a Nation showed off all of Mr. Griffith's talents. Everything he had ever done before was done better in this film.

But the picture was very controversial. In the second half the audience hissed because the Negroes were shown as brutes lusting after white women. Fights and riots broke out in major Northern cities. Things like this had never happened before. On the other side of the Mason-Dixon line you would have thought the audiences were seeing another picture. While the riots were going on in Boston and Philadelphia, in Atlanta the audience cheered and clapped and gave the movie standing ovations.

All this controversy made *The Birth of a Nation* a household phrase. Everybody was talking about it, either for or against it, and so everybody had to see it. Wherever it played, there were long lines of people waiting to get in. That one movie took pictures out of the nickelodeon era and into an era of respectability. Legitimate theaters gave two performances of it every day. The days of one-reelers going on endlessly five and six times each day for a nickel or a dime were over.

The Birth of a Nation ran continuously for years. Nobody knows exactly how much money it made during that time because distribution rights were sold outright to small companies, not on a rental or royalty basis. Eileen Bowser of the Museum of Modern Art told me, "*Variety* magazine says it's impossible to determine how much the picture has made, but it's expected it's the biggest money earner of our time."

All the time the picture was making money, Mr. Griffith was startled and bewildered by the negative reaction to his picture. One night he took Mae Marsh and me to dinner with Harry and Roy Aitken. He told them that an old family servant came to visit him with her small grandchild. The child had been named David, after Mr. Griffith. He said he was so pleased to see them that he greeted them with open arms and reached for the little boy. "Hello, David," he said.

"Not David anymore, Mr. Griffith," the grandmother said, pulling the child away. "We can never call him David again after what you did to our people."

Mr. Griffith said he couldn't believe his ears. This kind of talk from a woman he had known for years and who he felt was like one of his family. Her words had hurt him deeply. He also talked about the fist fights and the riots that occurred after *The Birth of a Nation* was released. We could see it broke Mr. Griffith's heart to see his film so misunderstood. He thought its critics were intolerant.

At dinner that night he said that he would never make another picture as insignificant as a four-reeler and that he had plans for an even bigger picture. He had already written a foreword for *The Birth of a Nation* asking for "the liberty to show the dark side of wrong," and a pamphlet called "The Rise and Fall of Free Speech in America," protesting censorship of *The Birth of a Nation* and of ideas. Throughout this pamphlet the word "intolerance" occurs over and over; it is at the top of every page. The glimmerings of his next big spectacle were taking root in his head.

« 11 »

While *The Birth of a Nation* was changing the course of film history, my private life was also undergoing a radical change. For it was during this picture that I fell in love.

I had first noticed Raoul Walsh when we were both sent to California. Even if I'd never seen him again, after those five days and nights on the train together I'd never have been able to forget him. He was a wonderful companion for a long train trip, enthusiastic and full of fun. He didn't make a pass at me and he wouldn't have gotten anywhere if he had. At that time we were both proper, moral, Catholic young people.

In California we all thought he was rich. Somehow he had managed to acquire a two-seater White Steamer. He and Mr. Griffith were the only people on the lot with automobiles. Raoul was also the only person who had a two-bedroom apartment. He shared it with Eugene Pallette.

But still I couldn't see him for dust. Mr. Griffith was strict with the girls, and Raoul wasn't important enough to get into trouble over. His title of assistant director really didn't mean much. One of his duties was to wait on me. Mr. Griffith would say, "Walsh, find Miss Cooper's powder puff for her," and Raoul would run around looking for it.

He couldn't see me, either. He liked Mae Marsh. One day he asked her to go to High Mass with him on Easter Sunday. Mae asked me to go along, too. About the time we finished *The Birth of a Nation* Mr. Griffith had become more tolerant about his young ladies' having dates, but Mae had another problem—Mr. Griffith himself. Her mother advised her not to jeopardize her relationship with Mr. Griffith by going out alone with another man, even to church on Easter Sunday.

I told Mae I'd go with them, but only because if I didn't go she couldn't either. I was the only other Catholic Mae knew well enough to ask.

On Easter morning Raoul arrived with corsages of violets for Mae and me, and a box of candy for Mary Alden. Then, at the last minute, Mr. Griffith asked Mae to go to San Fernando Valley with him. He had bought land in the valley as an investment and he liked to stand on the mountainside and look down on his property in the desert below. High Mass or no, Mae couldn't afford not to go off with Mr. Griffith. So I was left with Raoul.

We put Mae's corsage in the icebox and started out for church in his low-slung White Steamer. In our new Easter outfits, with Raoul in his cap and my hat tied on with some white chiffon, we looked very jaunty. People turned to stare at us.

The church, St. Bibiano's, was a lovely old cathedral built by the Spanish in the early 1800's; it was now in the heart of the Mexican quarter. A famous opera singer who'd gone on to La Scala in Italy came all the way home to the church every year on Easter Sunday and sang Gounod's "Ave Maria" at High Mass in memory of his mother.

The atmosphere of the old church, the beautiful singing and the ritual of the Mass made me feel very emotional. Tears rolled down my cheeks and I sniffled in my handkerchief. Raoul placed his hand on mine and whispered in my ear, "Don't be such a silly little goose." It may sound corny now, but at the time it was one of the sweetest remarks I'd ever heard.

After Mass we drove down to the beach. Raoul's White Steamer was built like a racing car, low with no top. We sat almost on the floor. The wind whipped our faces and blew the chiffon around my shoulders. I'd never seen a bluer sky or a greener ocean. The car, the day, our mood, everything was all so wonderful. Raoul kept taking his eyes off the road to look at me. I didn't mind. Our eyes would catch and hold, and we'd smile.

We had lunch at Venice in a lovely glass-enclosed restaurant at the end of the pier. The view was gorgeous. We chattered and talked for hours, and finally watched the sun set into the Pacific. As the hours went by, we didn't miss Mae at all.

After that we saw each other whenever we could. It wasn't often enough for either of us. As an assistant director, Raoul would frequently be away on location. When we were both in town we'd have dinner together. Sometimes we'd spend the evening at Mary Alden's apartment, sometimes we'd drive over to Spring Street and take in a vaudeville show. And, of course, we went to the movies. Raoul liked to see what other directors were doing.

We'd drive over to Pasadena to the previews. All the movie companies liked to get reactions to new films from an audience outside the Hollywood area before releasing the picture to the general public. The previews came on about ten or eleven at night, after the last showing of the regular feature. When it was over, the ushers would pass out slips of paper for the patrons to write comments on. People in Pasadena got to be real professionals at filling out these cards.

One evening at dinner Raoul said, "I hear Mr. Griffith is going to put on another director. The rumor is that he's going to give Bob Burns the job."

He stopped and didn't say anything for a moment.

Then he looked at me and said, "I know Griffith likes you. Will you ask him to give me a chance?"

I didn't think my talking to Mr. Griffith would do any good, but if Raoul thought it would help, I'd do it for him. "You know I will," I said.

The next day I hung around the lunchroom until I saw Mr. Griffith leaving. Then I fell in step beside him. We talked about the weather and things like that. Then I said, "I hear you're thinking of making one of the assistants a director. I don't know who you have in mind, but I think Raoul Walsh would be very good."

Mr. Griffith stopped walking and looked at me sharply. "What's your interest in Walsh?" he asked me.

"Oh," I said quickly, "I have no personal interest in him at all."

I didn't want Mr. Griffith to know I was interested in Raoul, but at the same time I wanted him to get the job. I decided an appeal to his vanity would be my best bet. "I've watched him working with Christy Cabanne," I said. "He's very hard working and he's got lots of ideas." Then I added the clincher. "The way he works reminds me of you."

Mr. Griffith didn't say anything more about it, but a few weeks later Raoul was made the sixteenth director on the lot.

Raoul and I both knew the importance of his first pictures to his career in films. Other companies were beginning to make offers to Griffith players and directors. If his pictures were well received Raoul would surely receive an opportunity to get more responsibility and more money. He didn't necessarily want to leave Mr. Griffith, but he knew that other companies were paying higher salaries. The men in the Griffith company didn't have the same fatherly image of Mr. Griffith that we girls did.

Raoul had hardly begun work when he received his first offer. It was from Jesse Lasky, who had already taken

Blanche Sweet away from Griffith. He'd also signed the opera star Geraldine Farrar, though I never could understand why he hired a singer to star in silent pictures.

Raoul was undecided. He hoped that if he made a few good pictures he'd get other and better offers. He put off Lasky with the excuse that he was up to his ears with work. I can testify to the validity of that; he was working so hard to make good pictures that we rarely saw each other.

It was at this point that I went to New York. If I was going to be lonely, with Raoul working day and night, I preferred being lonely there, at home with my family, whom I hadn't seen for a year and a half. When Mr. Griffith arranged for me to go home, I caught practically the first train available. I was eager to tell everybody about the most wonderful man in the world.

While I was in New York during the run of *The Birth*, our wires crisscrossed the country. In one Raoul told me Mr. Griffith had complimented him on his pictures and had started him on a four-reel feature with Henry Walthall. I remember the picture well. It was a film version of Henrik Ibsen's *Ghosts*. In film histories the picture is listed as five reels and the director is George Nichols. But I know Raoul worked on it. For it was during *Ghosts* that I didn't hear from him for three days. I was frantic. I telegraphed him to ask if he had forgotten me already. He wired back: TO FORGET YOU ALREADY IS SO ABSURD I MISS YOU MORE AND MORE EVERY DAY. Then he explained why he hadn't written: I HAVE WORKED DAY AND NIGHT ALL WEEK WITH ABOUT FOUR HOURS SLEEP HAVE NOT BEEN AWAY FROM THE STUDIO I HAVE THE OPPORTUNITY OF MY LIFE ON THIS PICTURE AND I AM GOING TO FIGHT ALL THE WAY.

It was nice to know that the man I loved was a hard worker. Then Mary Alden, who was in the cast, wired me urging me to hurry back to California. She said Raoul was lost without me. I left New York and hurried back to him.

He met me at the railroad station wearing a brand-new moustache and looking more handsome than ever. But after we had a few deliriously happy hours together, he went back to the studio. He was now cutting the film.

And he did it well, for *Ghosts* was a good picture. Lasky got in touch with Raoul again. Then William Fox got into the act. He promised Raoul his own crew, complete charge of directing his films, and the incredible salary of $300 a week. Raoul signed with Fox.

That was the good news. Then came the bad. The Fox Studios were in New York, while the Griffith company was in California.

It was a sad day when I went to the railroad station to see Raoul off. After crying all over him, I went back to the studio to start work on the picture Mr. Griffith had chosen to follow *The Birth—Intolerance.*

« 12 »

One day Mae and I were sitting in our dressing room waiting to be told what to do. Mr. Griffith called us into his office along with Walter Long and Bobby Harron. He said he wanted to enlarge a picture we had finished shortly before *The Birth of a Nation* was released. It was a four-reeler called *The Mother and the Law* about modern-day labor troubles.

At first we thought he just wanted to add depth to it. We had no idea that this little picture was to become the keystone for Mr. Griffith's masterpiece. The criticism of *The Birth of a Nation* had gotten under his skin and he intended to do something about it. Judging from the size of the sets going up all over the lot, whatever it was would be even bigger than *The Birth of a Nation*. The new sets could be seen for miles in every direction.

One set was the court of Belshazzar, last king of Babylon. Inside the walls were tall columns with elephants on top, standing with forefeet and trunks raised to the sky. Beneath them godlike figures and laughing lions guarded the huge staircases and steps leading down into the court.

While that set was going up, a society ballroom of the early twentieth century was being built on another lot for *The Mother and the Law*. Still other sets were re-creations of the streets of Jerusalem at the time of Christ, and Paris in the 1500's.

When the word spread that they were all for one picture we couldn't believe it. Nobody could figure out how a Babylonian court and a modern ballroom could be in the same picture.

By piecing bits of gossip together, we realized that Griffith was planning to film the story of intolerance throughout the ages. Three of the four stories making up *Intolerance* were demonstrations of religious intolerance: The fall of Babylon and Belshazzar's defeat by Cyrus the Great of Persia, the story of the Crucifixion of Christ, and the massacre of the Huguenots on St. Bartholomew's Day in France. The fourth was *The Mother and the Law*, or *The Modern Story*.

In the first version, already completed, my part had been small. I was the second lead, and only those scenes absolutely necessary to the story were included. The second version had much more depth and meaning and my part was much bigger.

The Mother and the Law was the story of the struggle for survival by innocent people who had been made jobless by a bitter and bloody strike. It was also a very poignant love story in which a sweet young wife first sees her husband sent to prison for a crime he didn't commit, then has her baby taken from her by intolerant social workers who believe she is an unfit mother.

Mae plays the part of the sweet young wife, called The Dear One. Bobby Harron plays her husband. My role is called The Friendless One. In his book on the greatest American films the critic Bosley Crowther lists me as "A Prostitute." Actually I play the role of a mill-town girl who loses her job, goes to the big city, and becomes a gangster's mistress. Though I'm a fallen woman, I'm not a prostitute.

The gangster was played by Walter Long. He was a tough, homely man—he had played the villainous Negro in *The Birth of a Nation*—but easy to work with. We did have difficulty with one scene, and Mr. Griffith stepped in to show Walter how to make love to me. He wrapped his arms around me, his big straw hat blocking out our faces so that Walter couldn't have gotten any idea of what he was doing. He looked so funny that everybody snickered. He was a great director but a lousy actor.

There was a saying around the studio that Mr. Griffith could make a stone act. I was far from being a stone and there was even one scene that I put my life's blood into.

In the movie Walter tries to seduce The Dear One in her apartment. I'm out in the hall, eavesdropping on what's going on inside. During the shooting I felt the role so deeply, agonizing over my lover's wanting somebody else, that I bit my lip and drew blood. The camera stayed on my face and you can see the blood run down my chin. I didn't even feel the pain, so intent was I on what I was doing.

This scene, I learned when I saw it with a group of students in a college movie theater almost sixty years later, is noted as a classic example of a Griffith innovation. It's called the big close-up—BCU. Back in his one-reeler days, Mr. Griffith had broken precedent with the idea that a camera had to show an entire set, like a theater stage. Over the protests of his backers and some critics he had narrowed the focus to what was important to the story, even cutting off an actor's body if it was the face that was important. In this celebrated BCU he even cut off the top of my face to show my lips and chin. The next time you see a portion of a face on the movie or TV screen, think of Mr. Griffith and me. We did it first.

I had another big scene in *The Mother and the Law*. After I kill Walter, I sit playing solitaire, thinking about my crime. Directing me in this scene, Mr. Griffith sat in his usual place next to the camera. "Your conscience is bothering you," he said. "An innocent man is being hanged for something you did."

I thought about what he was saying, and just as I had become Margaret Cameron in *The Birth of a Nation*, so I projected myself into being this unhappy small-town girl who has gone wrong. At first I thought, so what, I did it and I don't care. Then I thought about the tragedy I had caused—a man would be hanged because of what I had done. I tried to play cards, but I couldn't.

As I went through the scene I could hear Mr. Griffith's voice: "Now you can't see the cards. All you can see is that young wife's face and the gallows."

I raised my hands to my face and gave an anguished cry. Then I slumped in my chair. Mr. Griffith yelled "Cut!" and the scene was over.

All the time I was emoting a young man was photographing me with a big square camera. Someone said he was from *The New York Times*. At any rate, Mr. Griffith didn't tell him to leave. Usually the stills were made at the end of a scene when the director would yell, "All right, everybody, stills!" We'd all freeze until the cameraman told us to relax. This was the first time anyone had taken still pictures while we were working.

I'm glad there was no still photographer around for the shooting of a scene in which I wore a harem skirt made of diaphanous material. It floated around my legs and was pulled in tight at my ankles. I was supposed to walk in like a fast girl in a dance hall. I couldn't understand why Mr. Griffith was so particular about this scene. He cleared the set and moved the lights about for a long time before he was satisfied. One of the lights was right behind my legs.

Just as we were shooting, Mae came on the set,

ignoring the no admittance sign. She took one look at what was going on and said, "Ooooh, boy!"

She and Mr. Griffith and everybody else could see everything I owned from my bosom to my ankles. The light behind me took care of that. It was the most vulgar thing I've ever done on the screen. Once I knew what was going on, I was furious. And Griffith was furious at Mae for revealing his secret. The scene was cut from the film, thank God.

To emphasize the difference between the lives of the rich and the poor in *The Mother and the Law,* Mr. Griffith added a ballroom scene filled with society people dancing. As usual he wanted it to be authentic, so he tried to hire real society people as extras.

At one time I had told him that Mama's oldest brother, Colin Stewart, had built the Maryland Hotel in Pasadena. Uncle Colin had drilled for oil in Bakersfield, California, but the wells appeared to be dry. He killed himself in the hotel he had built. A week later the wells came in.

His wife, Annie, was a leader in Pasadena society. Mr. Griffith asked me to ask her to be in the picture. I did and she was horrified at the idea. If Mr. Griffith asked any other society people they must have refused, too, because he finally hired extras for the scene.

We didn't know till the picture was finished that the four stories would run together. Each would reach its climax at the end of the film, with the camera cutting back and forth from one story to the other as the action quickened.

Mr. Griffith didn't shoot all four stories at one time. He finished one before he started on the next. To hold the four stories together, Mr. Griffith shot a connecting link of a woman rocking a cradle, with a subtitle that was a line from Walt Whitman: "Out of the cradle, endlessly rocking." Lillian Gish played the role of the mother rocking the cradle. It didn't make any sense to me at all.

I spent a lot of time just hanging around the studio watching what was going on. We all watched with awe as the big Babylonian court took shape. It was one of the most lavish sets ever made in Hollywood. The court of Belshazzar covered 254 acres and stood three stories high; men looked like flies against the wall. The top of the wall was so wide you could drive chariots two abreast on it.

It wasn't made of papier mâché either, but was solidly constructed and lasted for years. When I was back in Hollywood in 1940 the sets were still standing.

To photograph a set as big as that, Mr. Griffith had a moving crane built with a platform for the camera, Billy Bitzer and himself. It was the forerunner of the modern camera boom.

At the beginning of the shot the crane was far away from the set, so that the camera could take in all of it. It moved in slowly until the camera focused on a small chariot, drawn by white doves and carrying a white rose across the table from Belshazzar to his beautiful Princess. Thus, in a few seconds the whole court in all its magnificence, with hundreds of people moving around, gives way to two little white doves.

An interesting thing about the court scene is that all the time the camera was moving in, both foreground and background were in focus. For a long period the so-called film experts attributed this to the genius of Griffith and his cameraman, Billy Bitzer, but my friends who are film historians say that it was actually because of the type of film used in the early days. In *The Great Train Robbery*, which goes all the way back to 1903, there's a scene where a man's shoulder in the foreground and the train in the background are both in focus.

With plenty of money at his disposal for *Intolerance*,

Mr. Griffith could afford to hire as many extras as he wanted. The extras and the leads didn't have to run around the scenery to appear twice in the same sequence. In the total production of *Intolerance*, he used 60,000 extras, more people than there are in Charlottesville, Virginia, the city I live in today. There were 4,000 in Belshazzar's scene alone, and 16,000 on the screen at one time when the Persian army advanced on Babylon for one of the largest mob scenes ever filmed.

Although it would have been hard to find them in that crowd, both Douglas Fairbanks, the swashbuckling hero of adventure movies of the 1920's, and Erich von Stroheim, the famous actor and director (and a foul-mouthed terrible man), were extras in *Intolerance*.

To manage the crowds, Griffith used assistant directors; he had always had lots of assistants. They became some of the most important directors of the 1920's—von Stroheim, Elmer Clifton, Tod Browning, Edward Dillon and W. S. Van Dyke.

It took almost two years and $1,750,000 in production costs to make *Intolerance*. Belshazzar's feast alone cost twice as much as *The Birth of a Nation*. Promotion expenses were $250,000. If the picture were made today, Dr. Korte told me, it would probably cost $25 million.

For months after the shooting was over, Mr. Griffith edited the picture. He had originally planned it to run eight hours—you'd see one half one night, the other half the next—but the exhibitors talked him out of it. He cut 200,000 feet of film down to less than 14,000 feet, approximately three hours.

While Mr. Griffith was busy with *Intolerance*, the time dragged. I worked under other directors in three short and forgotten films—*The Fatal Black Bean, His Return* and *The Burned Hand*—but most of the time I just drew my paycheck.

In October of 1915, after Raoul and I had been apart for months, I asked Mr. Griffith for permission to go to New York again. I said my mother was sick. I didn't dare tell him I was going to see his ex-director.

« 13 »

When I got to New York Raoul had just finished the silent-film version of the opera *Carmen,* starring Theda Bara. At that time Theda was the hottest thing in pictures. She was supposed to be a mystery woman of Middle Eastern origin. Bara was Arab spelled backwards, and Theda was an anagram for death. Actually she was a Cincinnati girl named Theodosia Goodman. Theda was simply her first name shortened down, and Bara came from a name in her family, Baranger. Whatever her name, she made "vamp" a household word.

I thought she was terrible. Her only expression was to duck her head and stare at the leading man or the camera with what appeared to be a searching look. And it *was* searching. She was so nearsighted she had to look hard to see anything a foot in front of her nose. She couldn't even see the camera. She kept walking into it and knocking it over. She was overweight, coarse and unattractive, entirely different from the slender young Griffith girls. Mr. Griffith would never have hired her. But in her stage makeup she looked exotic and sultry.

Whatever I thought of Theda Bara, she returned it doubled in spades. We got off to a great start right away.

Before the formal opening of *Carmen,* Mr. Fox had a special showing for the press. Miss Bara, who was only the star of the picture, was not invited. Instead, the director's girl friend was invited—me. I was the only woman there. Theda was furious. She had a case on Raoul and she thought I had arranged the whole thing to keep her away from him. The truth is that Raoul couldn't stand her and simply didn't want her in the projection room.

This screening was the first time Mr. Fox had seen the picture. When it ended with Carmen's lover stabbing her and Theda dying on the screen, Mr. Fox jumped up, cried out, "Hold it, hold it," and blocked out the screen by putting his hand over the projector. Somebody turned on the lights. Everybody turned to look at Mr. Fox.

"Vhat are you trying to do, Raoul?" he shouted. "Who vants to see such an ending? You vant the lovers should be happy. You don't vant the audience should valk out with a bad taste in their mouth."

"But, Mr. Fox," Raoul said, "Carmen is a famous opera. That's the way it ends. You can't change an opera."

All the reporters nodded and made sounds of agreement.

But Mr. Fox still didn't understand. "Are ve vorking for love or money?" he asked. Then, not waiting for anyone to answer, he stormed out of the room.

It was a new experience for Raoul and me. With Griffith, we were used to working in an atmosphere of authenticity. This was our abrupt introduction to the fact that the big moguls cared nothing about such things. They'd have made Jesus Christ Greek if it would make money. In the case of *Carmen,* fortunately, Raoul won the argument, and the picture ran with the ending that had been written for it fifty years earlier.

While Raoul was making his version of *Carmen* for Fox, Cecil B. DeMille was directing Geraldine Farrar in *his* version of *Carmen* for Jesse Lasky. The newspapers called it the battle of the *Carmen*s. DeMille's production was marvelous, and everybody agreed that Miss Farrar was more beautiful than Theda Bara. But this was a silent picture and Miss Farrar didn't sing a note. It was Raoul's version with Theda Bara, the sexy-looking vamp who had captured the country's imagination, that was the big money maker.

After two weeks in New York I had to go back to California. Once more Raoul and I were apart. These separations were becoming unbearable. Telegrams whizzed back and forth across the country. And then—why not get married? It was a daring thing to even think of. What would Mr. Griffith do? We decided to get married secretly.

In February of 1916 I asked Mr. Griffith for a brief leave. He agreed. But where could Raoul and I get married without word of it getting back to him? Georges Benoit, Raoul's cameraman, came up with the perfect solution. He knew a justice of the peace on the Hopi Indian Reservation near Albuquerque.

The main line of the Santa Fe goes through Albuquerque; Raoul would come in from New York, I from California. My brother Gordon made the trip with me. He was going to be my witness at the marriage ceremony, then he was going on to New York with Raoul to work as his assistant. Actually all I remember about the trip was Gordon climbing into the upper berth. I can still see his long skinny legs going up past my head.

The day we reached Albuquerque was bright and sunny. We met at the Santa Fe station, Raoul and I hugging and kissing each other as though we'd been separated for years. We hired an automobile and drove over the desert to the reservation. The Indians met us and took us to Georges' friend. We had a simple ceremony on the reservation and a wedding breakfast at the Harvey House, the

Howard Johnson's of its day, at the Santa Fe railroad station. That's where we had our honeymoon, two whole days of each other. The marriage was certainly a well-kept secret; we hardly left the room.

But two days of love did not make parting any easier. This separation was the worst of all. As I rode back to Hollywood, all alone, I realized what my life would be if I continued working—I would always be saying good-by. That wasn't what I wanted. I had married Raoul to be with him. If that meant giving up a moving picture career, so what. I wanted to be a wife, not a movie star.

But I was afraid to tell Mr. Griffith. Days went by. I didn't want to stay, but I didn't have the courage to tell him I was leaving.

Late one afternoon he called me into his office. "I want to give you this book," he said. "It's my next picture. I want you to play the lead."

I stood there looking at the book, not saying a word. It was a leather-bound edition of the *Rubaiyat of Omar Khayyam* with beautiful full-color plates illustrating it. He'd even inscribed it, "David," as if I'd ever have the nerve to call him just that.

I swallowed hard and thanked him. I couldn't tell him that I planned to retire from the movies and be a housewife. I said I would read it.

When I saw Mary Alden she asked me, "Why so sad?"

I told her about Mr. Griffith's offer and showed her the book. We looked at it together, skimming through the pages. Here's a verse from it:

> But come with old Khayyam and leave the Lot
> Of Kaikobad and Kaikhosru forgot:
> Let Rustum lay about him as he will,
> Or Hatim Tai cry Supper—heed them not.

I didn't understand a word of it. How could he make a picture out of that? How could I act out something I didn't understand? Patience has never been one of my virtues. When I want something I want it immediately. The man I loved was in New York. Without telling anyone, I packed my things and left.

In New York, three thousand miles away, I took the coward's way out. I wired Mr. Griffith that I was married and had made my last movie. I expected him to wire back and fuss at me, but he was too much a gentleman. Instead he sent congratulations, adding that everybody missed me. That was the last time I heard from him. I never saw him again.

And now I could openly be what I wanted to be, Mrs. Raoul Walsh. To make it even more official, Raoul and I were later married all over again, in the same Catholic church where we had had our first High Mass together.

« 14 »

Even before *Intolerance* was released, it and *The Birth of a Nation* combined to make a tremendous impact on the entertainment world. Everyone in the industry knew of the money rolling in from *The Birth of a Nation.* They could also see the unheard-of expenditures going into the sets and cast of *Intolerance.* Although many may have commented that Mr. Griffith must have lost his mind, they still knew that he was The Master. He had done it once; he just might do it again.

That period spanning most of 1915 and 1916, after the smashing opening of *The Birth of a Nation* and during the filming of *Intolerance,* was the birth of the cinema as we know it. It was a period of great expansion. The fast-buck entrepreneurs came pouring in.

For years pictures had been made by one class of people, exhibited by another. Now the men who had started out running grubby nickelodeons saw that they could make more money by getting in on the production and distribution of films. These characters were very different from those who had started the movie industry. Men like Edison and Porter, and Marion and Long of Kalem were gentlemen interested in making movies. The newcomers who were taking over were interested in making money. They knew nothing about making movies, nothing about actors or production. But they did know about making money.

There was Louis B. Mayer, a former junk dealer who bought the New England rights to *The Birth of a Nation* on a percentage basis. Thanks to a combination of the picture's popularity and his own outrageous cheating on paying off the percentage, he made over a million dollars on this one film in one area.

Adolph Zukor was a furrier who got into the penny arcade business and went on to own big movie theaters; he started "Famous Players in Famous Plays" and had movie audiences sitting for a whole hour watching Sarah Bernhardt emote a couple of years before *The Birth of a Nation* was released.

Jesse L. Lasky had been a cornet player and vaudeville promoter. He brought his brother-in-law Sam Goldfish, a glove salesman, in with him to start the Lasky Feature Play Company.

William Fox had invested his profits from ownership of a cloth-shrinking operation in nickelodeons and legitimate theaters. He had a chain of twenty-four movie houses in and around New York when he got into producing films, too.

They were only some of the new people coming in. Their names are familiar today because they were successful. There were dozens more who failed. To add to the confusion everybody was always moving around, fighting with each other, in and out of court, and organizing new companies. It was like musical chairs. Lasky and Zukor merged to become Famous Players–Lasky. Then Zukor became head of Paramount. Goldfish left his brother-in-law to team up with a theatrical producer named Edgar Selwyn and form Goldwyn Pictures Corporation. The name came from the first syllable of Goldfish, the last of Selwyn. Sam liked it so much that he took it as his own name.

All of these wheelers and dealers were offering actors and directors more money. Salaries were skyrocketing. The three highest paid people in the industry in 1915 were Mary Pickford, getting $4,000 a week from Zukor, Douglas Fairbanks, getting $2,000 a week from Mr. Aitken, and Charlie Chaplin, getting $1,200 a week from Essanay. The next year he switched to Mutual to become the highest paid entertainer in the world at $670,000 a year.

It may seem strange, but I don't recall feeling any jealousy. We all recognized Charlie Chaplin as a great artist. He was separate from us in that he was a comedian, although when I got to know him later I found him one of the most depressing people I ever knew. In his autobiography he talked of his enchantment in 1914 at meeting the film stars, "all of them beautiful," and named me along with Mary Pickford, Blanche Sweet, Clara Kimball Young and the Gish sisters. "To meet them face to face was Elysian," he wrote. As far as I'm concerned it was also imaginary, for I don't remember him at all during that period.

As for Mary Pickford, we respected her as a pioneer in films. She was not only the Girl with the Golden Curls, but a dependable, hard-working trouper. She had started out with Griffith, of course, and jumped from one company to another for more money. In our own little family, Mr. Griffith's children might have been happy to have some of the money she was making, but not at the cost of leaving the nest. And besides, we were making *big* pictures. She was still doing four-reelers.

If there was any resentment at all, it would have been directed at Douglas Fairbanks and the other stage stars Harry Aitken hired by the dozen after *The Birth of a*

Nation. Fairbanks had never been in front of a camera until suddenly one day he appeared on the lot. I remember his standing around behind Mr. Griffith, watching what was going on, but not being a part of it. Mr. Griffith was too involved with *Intolerance* to fool with him and turned him over first to Christy Cabanne, then John Emerson, another director working for Griffith. After a couple of films he caught on and moved on. Mr. Griffith let him go, but by that time he had earned our respect. You couldn't help but like Doug. However, he was one of the few who came from the theater who survived in films.

It was *The Birth of a Nation*, made by poorly paid actors and actresses, which paved the way for these gigantic salaries. Those of us, directors and players, who worked for Griffith were the elite. We had proven ourselves, and naturally the businessmen came to us to woo us away from the man who had made it all possible.

The list of Griffith people who went on to huge salaries and successful careers would fill a page. I was involved in the decisions made by a few of my close friends. Mae Marsh's was the most agonizing. Sam Goldfish came to both of us. Since I had other plans anyway I gave him a flat refusal. He didn't waste any more time on me. Mae wavered and Goldfish kept after her.

"What'll I do, Miriam?" she wailed. She was in tears. Poor sweet little Mae. She didn't want to leave Griffith, but she had a family to support, and Goldfish offered her a lot more money. Goldfish promised her that she would be his big star, not just another member of the Griffith company.

Mae wavered more. Then he increased the offer. "Three thousand a week!" she told me. "I didn't know there was that much money in the world!"

She was only getting about the same salary I was from Griffith, sixty-five a week, but still she couldn't bring herself to leave him. It was Mr. Griffith himself who made the decision for her. He told her, gently, in that wonderful thoughtful way of his, to go with Goldfish. He made her feel that she'd be making him happy to accept all that money.

Mae did become the first Goldwyn Girl, but her stardom didn't last long. She was never as fine an actress for other directors as she was for Mr. Griffith; he brought out that natural charm of hers as no other director could. She photographed older than she actually was and started playing character parts long before other actresses her age. And she didn't hold on to her money, either.

I never could understand why Griffith let his talented players go. He would have had to pay more to keep them, of course, but it wouldn't have had to be as much as they got elsewhere. I guess he thought he could make a star of anyone; he certainly had made fine players out of raw material before. But even though he later had Bessie Love and Carol Dempster and Pauline Starke, none ever reached the dramatic heights of Mae Marsh or Lillian Gish.

Lillian, of course, stayed with him. I suppose she got the same offers I did. I remember that Jesse Lasky and Cecil B. DeMille wanted me to work for them, and there were others I've forgotten. Just being a member of the Griffith company was enough, but in addition I was versatile. I had been a sweet, pretty girl in *The Birth of a Nation*, and played a much more dramatic role in *Intolerance*. And of course I'd played in a lot of one-reelers. But until I was married I felt that I wanted to stay with Mr. Griffith all my life. Lillian felt the same loyalty.

I think she felt more than that, too. I had thought that sooner or later she and Mr. Griffith would get married. The only reason I can think of as to why they didn't was Carol Dempster.

Carol was one of the dancers in Belshazzar's Feast

in *Intolerance*. She was very graceful and a good dancer, but she was not pretty. Her nose was a hook and her chin stuck out. Compared to Lillian she had nothing, but Griffith seemed to like her very much. I never could understand what he saw in her, why he tried to make her a lead, or why he would let his relationship with Lillian be broken up.

When I left Mr. Griffith, it was not for another company, not for more money. I left him for another man, the man I married.

Raoul and I were living in New York when *Intolerance* opened at the Liberty Theatre in New York on September 5, 1916. Once again there were standing ovations and great praise from the reviewers. But the lines waiting to get in grew shorter, and only months after it had opened, Mr. Griffith realized that *Intolerance* was not the crowd pleaser he had hoped it would be.

Anita Loos, in her book *A Girl Like I,* summed up the reaction of people at the time. She sat through *Intolerance* with Mr. Griffith when he wanted her to write the subtitles. "As I sat there," she wrote, "I thought he had lost his mind. I sat in stony silence." She knew Griffith was waiting for her to say something so finally she turned to him and said, "I am moved beyond words."

There were many reasons for this negative reaction. For one thing, *Intolerance* was huge and ponderous. It showed off Griffith's technical genius, but it was hard for the audience to follow four stories at the same time. The extensive cutting jerked the viewer back and forth.

For another thing there was a war spirit growing in America: Griffith planned *Intolerance,* with its strong message against war and for peace, before the United States was involved in World War I. By the time the picture was released, two years later, the national mood had changed.

Intolerance was a financial disaster, but still it has been acclaimed by many people as one of the ten best pictures of all time. Pauline Kael, the critic, has called it *the* greatest; she said it was a folly, but also a masterpiece. Whatever its weaknesses, it stands as a monument to the first genius of the cinema.

But that didn't help poor Mr. Griffith when he needed it. *Intolerance* kept him in debt for years, and though he finally recovered financially, he never recovered spiritually.

Unfortunately, even today audiences may have trouble appreciating the picture's greatness. Periodically *The Birth of a Nation* and *Intolerance* are shown in theaters across the nation. A few years ago a movie theater in our town showed both films. The theater manager very graciously asked me to attend and reserved a whole row of seats for my friends and me. We saw *The Birth of a Nation* first. It was a smooth, beautiful film and I was proud for my friends to see me in it.

Then we saw *Intolerance* and it was terrible. I was embarrassed to death. "What's the matter?" I asked the theater manager. "Griffith didn't go backwards. *Intolerance* was made later. He did everything better in that film. Why does it look worse?"

The manager explained that he had used a projector made for the film used in *The Birth of a Nation,* but the wrong projector was used on the showing of *Intolerance,* and that was why everything was so jerky. It was like playing a record at the wrong speed.

But, in spite of that showing at the wrong speed, *Intolerance* remains a great film. After all these years I still can't believe that the whole idea for this gigantic film came from one man's head.

« 15 »

There were two directors in my life, both of them cinema immortals. One was like a father. The other was my husband.

Raoul Walsh was like Mr. Griffith in some ways. He was talented, hard-working, dignified, polite with women. But in other ways they were completely different.

Mr. Griffith, for example, would never dream of using profanity. Raoul swore all the time. It was the way he started the day. He'd get up in the morning, go to the window, look out, and say, "Christ, what a hell of a fine day."

Mr. Griffith got his best performances from women, and though he could recognize that indefinable something that made women stars, he often failed to recognize star quality in men. In two cases he missed what was as obvious as the nose on his face. He was completely baffled by Douglas Fairbanks' exuberance, the very quality that made Doug a superstar. Later, in 1919, Mr. Griffith wouldn't hire Rudolph Valentino because he thought his face wouldn't appeal to women.

Raoul was just the opposite from Mr. Griffith. He worked best with men. One of his discoveries was a young man in the Fox Company property department who is now John Wayne. Another was a truck driver now known as Rock Hudson. But though I pleaded with him to give a young girl friend of mine a chance—and he did cast her in a couple of walk-on parts—he saw no potential in Carole Lombard.

Rather than romance, Raoul liked to direct action and adventure. His best pictures had plenty of both. Typical of his style were those which made *The New York Times* list of the ten best pictures of the year: *The Thief of Bagdad* in 1924, and *What Price Glory* in 1927. Douglas Fairbanks starred in the first, jumping around over everything. Edmund Lowe and Victor McLaglen starred in the second, fighting in and winning World War I.

Raoul also made films with Humphrey Bogart and Clark Gable. In 1949, in his early sixties, he directed *White Heat*, in which there's a scene no other director of the time would dare to do. In this scene James Cagney, one of the toughest guys of all, sits on his mother's lap. Raoul would try anything.

He'd also tell the wildest tales. He never bored you with the truth. Though we'd been divorced for forty-five angry years, I couldn't help chuckling when I read an article on him in the *Los Angeles Examiner* in early 1972. He told the reporter how he'd grown up on a ranch in Montana and tested broncos for the United States Cavalry. I'd never heard that one before. Oh, that Raoul!

Actually he was a nice Catholic boy, brought up in a New York City brownstone. His father, Thomas Walsh, "Pops" to his children, manufactured military uniforms. Mrs. Walsh died when the children were young, and Pops raised them with the help of a housekeeper. When I came into the Walsh family Alice, the only girl, was married to Willie Hoppe, the world-famous billiards champion, and Raoul and George were both in pictures.

Raoul had come into films as a stagestruck young actor, but his brother George had backed in. Maybe pushed is a better word. Raoul was in California when he got a wire from Pops. George had been fooling around with a married woman, and Pops asked Raoul to get him a job in California to get him out of town.

Raoul was furious about it. "That son of a bitch," he said. "He's always getting into trouble."

But Raoul would do anything for his father and he wired back to send George out. Raoul asked Mr. Griffith to give George a job as an extra, and his was one of the thousands of faces in the crowd in *Intolerance*. While working on *Intolerance* he met Seena Owen, who played the role of the Beloved Princess in the Babylonian sequence. Seena was a beautiful Swedish girl whose mother was a dressmaker. She'd copy expensive dresses for me for ten dollars—that was all I could afford. Seena almost didn't get into pictures. Mr. Griffith interviewed her, and was put off by her cool composure. He told her she was too unemotional to be an actress. "Then I'm an actress, because I'm trembling inside," she said. He hired her immediately. He couldn't pronounce her real name, Signe Auen, and changed it. She had three names in a period of a few months, for she married George Walsh soon after.

Pops was one of the finest men I ever knew. A Victorian romanticist, he kept his wife's bedroom the way she left it until he himself died, forty years later. Her lovely silk dresses hung in the closet, her tiny size 1½ shoes stayed on the rack, and her cut-glass perfume bottles and silver toilet articles remained on her dresser until Pops gave them to me shortly before he died. The maid cleaned and aired the room every week, but the rest of the time Pops permitted no one to enter it but himself.

The family lived in a fashionable house in New York, across the street from the Barrymores. Raoul had gone to the same Catholic boys' school Lionel and John Barrymore had attended, Seton Hall in New Jersey. His name was originally Albert Edward Walsh. While he was working as an actor on the stage in and around New York, he began a long friendship with Paul Armstrong. Paul was the author of a successful play, *The Deep Purple*, which Raoul later made into a movie. Paul thought the name Albert Edward Walsh could be improved upon. They tossed a lot of names back and forth, and finally decided that Raoul sounded the most romantic. For many years he was Raoul A. Walsh, though he later dropped the A.

When I left the Griffith company to begin my married life Raoul was living in his father's big brownstone in New York and I simply moved in with him. We were comfortable and happy. I always loved Pops, and he enjoyed having his family with him. There was plenty of room, and a good thing, too. Alice was there with her husband, Willie. Willie practiced billiards all day. He'd brought in a billiard table and put it in the dining room.

During the day I'd visit with both my new family and my old one, see the new friends I'd made in pictures and my old friends all the way back to childhood. I was having a wonderful time. I was never going to work again. I was going to be a wife and, I hoped, a mother. I wanted a lot of children, and Raoul was cooperating nicely.

Raoul and I were very much in love, but even if he hadn't been, he'd have been glad to come home to me as a relief from Theda Bara. He was directing her in *The Serpent*, another one of her sultry vamp pictures that made so much money for Fox. (She made forty pictures during her thirty-six-month contract with him.) Between falling over cameras and mooing at Raoul she was driving him nuts.

Another thing that bothered him was her insistence on staying in New York. I loved New York, too, and I could understand that, but it was making a wreck of my husband. Fox's studio was a makeshift place in an old building in Fort Lee, New Jersey. The only way to get there was to take the 125th Street ferry across the Hudson River. In the winter the river was full of ice and the ferry took hours going across. The actors were paid all the time they spent on the river. It was costly and frustrating. Raoul wanted to make movies, not look at ice.

He'd come home at night tired and cross after a day spent riding ferries and directing Theda Bara. He longed for California and the long sunny days where one could shoot from sunup to sundown every day for ten months of the year. But Theda Bara didn't want to leave New York and Mr. Fox accepted it. She was making a lot of money for him and he'd do anything to keep her happy.

"It's a hell of a lot different from working with Griffith," Raoul told me one night. "He thought about something besides money."

"You can't compare the two men," I told him. "Mr. Griffith is an artist and Mr. Fox is a businessman."

"Businessman!" Raoul said. "Do you call pants pressing and nickelodeons business?"

That's the way most of the directors and actors referred to Mr. Fox, as a pants presser. It's true he had once owned a cloth-shrinking and -examining business, but he had been a moderately successful businessman before buying his first theater. The picture people took the money he paid them, even though they didn't have much respect for him or any of the high moguls. Actually, I always liked Mr. Fox. He was really a very nice man, kind and considerate. But he was still primarily a businessman, and Raoul was an artist, like Mr. Griffith. We couldn't help wanting Mr. Fox to be like Mr. Griffith. Once you had worked for Griffith, you compared everybody with him.

Though frustrated with the whole setup, Raoul did as

good a job as any director could have done with Theda and *The Serpent*. When it was finished, he got his reward. Fox had realized the practicality of a California studio and acquired one. He immediately set about staffing it with several directors and crews. Raoul was one of the first selected. His first picture would be a four-reeler called *Blue Blood and Red*. The leading man was, of all people, George Walsh, Raoul's brother. Raoul and I went merrily back to California.

That was just the beginning of our travels. All during our married life we were on the go. We'd live in New York for a few months, then go back to California, then on to location.

Then, as now, picture people were berry pickers. Sometimes we'd have an apartment in New York and a house in California, and neither one of us would be in either of them. Raoul would be on location and I'd be in Bretton Woods, New Hampshire, during the hay fever season with my asthma. Picture people traveled back and forth across the country so much the railroads used pictures of actresses in their advertisements.

Wherever we went we had massages and high colonics. They were all the rage with picture people then. The massage was relaxing, and the high colonic was supposed to get rid of the impurities in our systems. We had them in New York, Santa Monica and San Francisco. Whenever we went to a new town, the first thing we'd ask the hotel clerk was where can we get a good massage? Where can we get a good high colonic?

One time I was visiting Norma Talmadge at the Algonquin Hotel in New York shortly before her marriage to producer Joseph Schenck. She had a massage every afternoon in the hotel. Norma and I were admiring the clothes she had bought for her trousseau when the door burst open and a slim brown-haired girl came in wearing a blue terrycloth robe.

"Dahling!" she shouted at Norma in her husky, deep Southern voice. "I'm a wreck. I've got to go on tonight. The leading lady's sick—probably cockeyed. Can I use your masseuse?" Norma introduced me. The girl was Tallulah Bankhead.

Tallulah lived at the Algonquin too, and knew what time Norma's masseuse came. She had timed her entrance so well that the masseuse walked in right behind her.

"Help yourself," Norma said, and Tallulah threw off her robe and fell nude on the nearest bed. I was sitting on the foot of the bed and I can still remember her bare feet. They were as black as coal. At that time, 1916, all New York burned soft coal; you couldn't walk across your bedroom without getting black feet, and Tallulah had walked the length of a hotel corridor. The masseuse didn't seem to notice. She poured oil on her hands, and as I sat there watching, she calmly smeared the dirt from Tallulah's feet all the way up her legs.

A few hours later Tallulah, relaxed by the masseuse and with clean feet, went on in place of the star and started her climb to international acclaim.

In addition to the high colonics and massages, I slapped Elizabeth Arden's pore cream all over my face every night. Being beautiful was one of the reasons we were stars, and we all worked hard to stay that way. When we were in California all the girls went to the Denishawn School to learn from these famous dancers how to be graceful. I had private lessons with Martha Graham, who was later to become the high priestess of modern dance. In one movie I had a couple of weeks between scenes and did so many barres that I lost ten pounds. I opened a door at 107 pounds and appeared on the other side at 97. They had to pour malted milk shakes into me for several days, then reshoot the scene.

The first time we returned to California we lived in a thirty-five-dollar-a-month bungalow. Our nearest neighbors were Wallace Beery and his wife, Gloria Swanson. Beery was a well-known actor then, but Gloria was still having pies thrown in her face in Mack Sennett comedies.

Although Raoul was now making more money, we were still like the Griffith people: hard-working and without glamor. The lifestyle of the directors and actresses making enormous salaries was still unknown to us.

Our only luxury was a full-time cook. I spent hours with her, fussing over her uniform, showing her how to serve the vegetables with one hand behind her back. But I never asked her if she could cook; all I was interested in was the show.

The first night she served dinner, she brought the meat in on a platter and set it down before Raoul. He looked down at it. There were two burned-up lamb chops, so tiny they looked lost on the big dish.

"What the hell is this?" Raoul asked me.

"That's your dinner, dear," I said. "They're lamb chops—don't you like them?"

"Lamb chops," Raoul said. "They look like dog turds to me. Don't you know what I like? You ought to—you sat across the table from me for a whole year."

"I guess I never noticed," I said. "Food just doesn't interest me."

It did interest Raoul, and he fired the cook. The one he found, Theresa, was splendid. Many people tried to hire her away from us over the years, but she stayed with us—even moving across the country with us—until she died.

Now my days were filled with things I liked to do—ride and swim and walk the lonely beaches with Pat and Mike, the two Airedales Raoul had given me. He knew I loved animals and he was always giving them to me. One Easter he gave me some rabbits. I let them run around the bungalow, so we were always stepping on the little black pellets they left everywhere.

Milton Sills and I in The Honor System. *I'm reading to him since he's blind from ill treatment received in prison.*

Charles Clary played the villainous politician, Milton Sills the framed convict, in The Honor System.

Jack Connors
played my child
in The Woman
and the Law.

This is Raoul Walsh with his back to the camera in The
Innocent Sinner. *He got in the scene with me just for luck.*

I played opposite Vincent Serrano in The Deep Purple.

Filming Evangeline. At left are Raoul and his cameraman, J. D. Jennings. Note the status symbol—leggings.

I was made up here to play Evangeline as an old lady.

This shot from Evangeline *is my favorite picture of myself.*

In Serenade *I was
a fiery senorita.*

*The well-known illustrator
Henry Clive played a bit
part in* The Oath.

In this scene from
Kindred of the Dust
*I gazed so soulfully
into the lights that
I damaged my eyes.*

MF 2-81

Ralph Graves and I in Kindred of the Dust.

However, even in our first happy year together, there were intimations of trouble to come. One was Raoul's mania for gambling.

Shortly after we were married Raoul took me to my first horse race at Belmont Park in New York. I had never seen a horse race before in my life. The park wasn't crowded—it never was in those days—and Raoul took me to a table under the big trees. As I sat down a man came over. Raoul introduced him to me. He was a Chicago bookmaker, one of the biggest in the business. When he left, Raoul explained everything to me.

"This is the program," he said, handing me a sheet of paper, "and these are the jockeys and the horses. There are six races and I'm betting on three. I'm going to bet one hundred dollars on the first race."

"What do you mean, Raoul?" I said. "One hundred dollars! That's one-third of your salary. Suppose you lose?"

"Then I'm through," he said. "You're not allowed to lose more than one hundred dollars."

That wasn't much more than our combined weekly income a year before, but now it was "only" one hundred dollars, so I felt better. Then Raoul explained the rest of his betting.

"I'm going to parlay my bet," he said. "I'm only betting on horses owned by Harry Payne Whitney. If I win in the first race, I'll put my winnings on Whitney's horse in the third. If I win that, I'll put my winnings on Whitney's horse in the sixth."

He gave me his binoculars to watch the races with and told the waiter to bring me some coffee. Then he left. I didn't see him again until all the races were over.

I looked at the program and saw that the odds on the first of Raoul's horses were ten to one; the other two were eight to one. I thought Raoul was making a big mistake, but I was comforted to know he couldn't lose more than one hundred dollars.

During the races I stood up next to my chair, for I was too timid to watch from the fence, and kept my eye on Raoul's choices through the binoculars. If I'd known what was really going on I'd have been a lot more excited.

In those days before parimutuel betting, there were no windows to go to. You placed your bets with the book-maker. Raoul placed his bet with his regular bookmaker, the man from Chicago. After his first two horses won, his winnings were so big that the Chicago bookmaker couldn't handle the third bet by himself. He had to lay it off around the country. A bookmaker in New York took some, another in California, until it was covered. There was no question but that they'd make good if Raoul won. Both bookies and gamblers either kept their word or they were dead.

That day they kept their word. All of Raoul's horses came in. He wound up with $90,000, plus the hundred he had started with.

We were making $300 a week and we had $90,000! It was an exhilarating feeling. And so easy! A few days later I went to Belmont Park by myself, found Raoul's book-maker and prepared to win another fortune. I lost $1,100. That cured me. I never bet again.

But losing money never cured Raoul. And there would be days when his losses would be far more than we could afford.

Another incident in that first year cast a shadow of what would be an even greater threat to our happiness. Although Raoul often preferred the company of men, he liked women, too. He possessed a magnetic attraction for them. Women were always falling all over him. And I was so crazy about him that I was terribly jealous. It was a bad combination.

One evening Abe Carlos, one of Fox's vice presidents, and his wife went to the movies with Raoul and me. After-wards Raoul took me home and then went out again. He said he was going back to the studio. I wandered around the house waiting for him to come back. Every time I heard a car on the road I'd race to the window. It was never him.

Thinking maybe Abe and his wife might know where he was, I called their house. Mrs. Carlos answered, and when I told her how worried I was, she just laughed. She was a big, fat woman who knew her husband was cheating on her, but she didn't care. I'd never known women would stand for that. She made me even more suspicious and jealous.

After hours of weeping and running to the window, I went to the kitchen for a drink. Theresa had left a bottle of carbolic acid on the sink. I looked at the bottle. If I drank that I'd never have to worry about where Raoul was again. Impulsively I grabbed the bottle and swallowed what was in it.

I barely got it down before it came up. I ran to the bathroom and held my head in the toilet as all my insides came up.

That's the way Raoul found me. He called the doctor and they took me to the hospital. I had thrown up the whole lining of my stomach. I was a very sick girl, and Raoul was solicitous and loving. But I lived to wonder where he was on many more nights.

My life as a lady of leisure didn't last long. Shortly after we were married Raoul was approached by Henry Christeen Warnack, a Los Angeles newspaperman and drama critic. He wanted Raoul to make a picture of his book, *The Honor System*, which was widely read and discussed at the time. This was a story of prison reform which contrasted the brutal treatment of prisoners under the old system with the new, more humane system that allowed men to get out of the prison for a stipulated time. They were on their honor to return. Raoul was crazy about the idea. He thought it would make a blockbuster of a picture. He told the story to Mr. Fox and got the go-ahead.

It was easy to get the cooperation of the man who had inspired Warnack to write his book. He was George W. P. Hunt, governor of Arizona. Governor Hunt was vitally interested in prison reform. There was every reason why he should have been. The prisons in what had been the territory of Arizona were hell holes where centipedes, snakes and rats were star boarders and lived far more comfortably than the prisoners. Governor Hunt introduced the honor system, and Henry Warnack had written a dramatic story about it.

This would be a picture built around the men. It was just the kind of story Raoul wanted to film. It was all he talked about. "I want to do it with authenticity," he said. "I want to show the real thing—the real prison, the real prisoners."

He went to Arizona to see Governor Hunt and sold him on the idea of shooting most of the action in the state prison. The Governor went all the way, putting all the facilities of the penal system at Raoul's disposal.

Getting me to work in the picture was a lot harder than getting either Mr. Fox to produce it or Governor Hunt to cooperate. As far as I was concerned, I had retired. "It's an important part," Raoul said, "but it's not a lengthy one. You can do it so easily; you're so natural for the part. And if you don't do it, then I'll have to find some female with more looks than brains and have to work with her down there in Arizona for months."

Raoul may not have liked to direct women, but he knew what to say to me. I didn't want to be separated from him for the time it would take to shoot the picture on location. And I got the message about looks—the role called for a pretty young actress.

I knew what working on location was like. You were

thrown together, all day and all evening. Such proximity with emotional people like pretty actresses could be dangerous. I took the part. Because it was not a starring role, but rather an opportunity to be with Raoul, I took it for only a thousand a week. *Only!* My last paycheck had been sixty-five dollars.

I even got excited about the role. Not because I'd be in a picture, not even for the money, but because I was always interested in meeting other people and seeing other places. This was what I really liked about making movies, going places and seeing how different people lived. Until I went into the movies the only places I had ever been were Baltimore, which I don't even remember, Washington Heights and a New York slum. Today people travel all over the world, but in the early part of the century travel was much more difficult. For a young woman of my background it would have been impossible. But the movies got me across the country many times, to Florida when I was still a teen-aged girl, and to locations in southern California and Mexico. Now as Raoul and I set out for Arizona, I had a chance to see what a desert looked like outside a geography schoolbook.

« 16 »

What began as just an excursion for me became one of the great movies of the period when the cinema came into its own. It was the third longest film ever made up to that time. I'm the only person, let alone the lead, who appeared in all three: *The Birth of a Nation, Intolerance* and *The Honor System.*

Like its two great predecessors, *The Honor System* was built on a great humanitarian theme. It was not only entertainment; it contained a message of world-wide importance and delivered it with a punch. Reviewers of the day raved about it, saying it made film history. It also made money. *The Honor System* did not produce the enormous returns of *The Birth of a Nation,* but its earnings far surpassed those of *Intolerance.* If there had been any award for best picture of the year in 1917, the year it was released, *The Honor System* would certainly have won it.

With the resurgence of interest in the early films, it's truly a tragedy that students of the cinema will never be able to see and study this history-making film. It was lost forever in a fire in 1937 that consumed all the early Fox films. Only the reviews and some of the stills I have saved for more than half a century remain of Raoul's masterpiece.

The Honor System was shot at both the old and new penitentiaries in Arizona. We began at the new prison. The air was stifling hot and the sun beat down on the white desert, unrelieved by any shade from anywhere. It was September, and my God it was hot. At Phoenix, where we got off the train, there were very few women. In those days men sent their wives to California in the summer. The heat was utterly unbearable.

The only reason people lived in Arizona was for their health. Everybody we saw was tubercular, even the taxicab drivers. They were always stopping to get ice cream sodas with raw eggs in them, the standard TB treatment at the time. It was only after air conditioning became practical that this area began to grow.

The new prison was in the heart of the desert. It's now the small city of Florence, but back in 1916 there were no housing facilities, no hotels. Raoul had hired almost a thousand men, including actors, extras, cowboys and Indians, and two hundred horses. He had to provide housing and meals for all of them. He erected a tent city outside the prison walls and lived there with the other men. Raoul and I were together but still separated; I lived with the warden and his wife.

At the old prison in Yuma, more than one hundred miles away, conditions were deplorable. The prisoners were tied to stakes and beaten for the slightest reason. I even heard that the guards would turn their backs to allow men to escape, then, as the prisoners swam the Colorado River in hopes of freedom, the guards would entertain themselves by shooting at the prisoners' heads bobbing up and down in the water.

In *The Honor System* Raoul showed how the men lived in dark airless cells with snakes, rats and scorpions crawling through the sand under the doors. It was a sordid scene. To relieve the tension and shock the audience felt, Raoul remembered one of Mr. Griffith's tricks.

"Always relieve a tense situation with comedy," Mr. Griffith had told his assistants, and Raoul had learned his lesson well. He had the prisoners send notes to each other by attaching them to the backs of cockroaches. The audience roared.

Milton Sills, the legitimate stage actor, played the part of a young miner who kills the accomplice of a dance-hall girl in self-defense. Sills was a fine actor, somewhat on the order of John Barrymore, and was enormously popular. As the hero in the picture, he is sentenced to life imprisonment. His experiences as a convict lead to the humanitarian treatment of prisoners and the installation of the honor system, under which prisoners could go out of the prison to work, keep part of their salary, and return to the prison at night.

Some of the highlights of the picture were a battle between Mexican bandits and American cowboys on the Arizona border, a life-or-death fight between Milton Sills and a former prizefighter named Johnny Reese on top of a swaying freight train moving at high speed, and, of course, a prison break.

For the battle scenes Raoul used Mr. Griffith's method of having assistants in costume in charge of a group of extras. As the cavalry charged, Raoul signaled his assistants to join the action. They shouted orders to the extras, then got into the action themselves.

Raoul had been a director for only two years when he started *The Honor System*, an assistant director for only two years before that. Mr. Griffith had worked as a director for six years, turning out 400 films before he attempted anything of that size. But what Mr. Griffith had learned, he taught to his assistants. They all worked the same way he did: innumerable rehearsals before ever going in front of the camera, and writing the day's shooting script on whatever paper was handy.

I don't know if any of Mr. Griffith's scraps of paper still exist, but I do have in my possession one of Raoul Walsh's shooting scripts. I didn't even know I had it until one evening just a few years ago when a pleasant man knocked on my door and, in an English accent, introduced himself as Kevin Brownlow. My blank look forced him to explain modestly that he was a film historian. We started talking—he stayed until two in the morning!—and I pulled out some of my trunks of assorted junk to show him.

One item was an envelope, bearing a three-cent stamp, addressed to Raoul Walsh, Fox Film Company, New York City. It was obviously delivered—in those days you got your three cents' worth. It was from the governor of Arizona, but there was nothing in it, just some scribbles on the outside. I started to throw it in the wastepaper basket, but Kevin grabbed it and squinted at it.

"Fade in," he read. "Girl reads, flash of Joe . . . My God, what's this?"

"Oh, that's just one of Raoul's shooting scripts," I said, and explained how he and Mr. Griffith before him would write down the day's shooting on anything that was handy.

"Mrs. Walsh," Kevin said, "people like me have been looking all over the world for documents such as this. It's the only way we can learn how the early movies were made. This is priceless!"

Unfortunately Raoul's handwriting was lousy, and we couldn't make it all out. But I can see how those scribbled notes—Girl sits down, Mother in and kisses daughter—would make an impression on anyone seriously interested in moviemaking. I remember when script girls suddenly appeared, passing out neatly typed copies of thoroughly worked-out, detailed plans for the day's shooting. But in those early days directors shot entire movies, good movies, with just such scribbled notes.

Along with his own working methods, Mr. Griffith passed on to his assistants the challenge to think of new methods and approaches and the courage to try them. It took a lot of both for a young director like Raoul to make a film of the scope of *The Honor System,* but Raoul was never nervous about it, never worried. He had tremendous confidence in himself.

While shooting *The Honor System* Raoul began gathering his own people around him. My brother Gordon was his assistant; his brother George had a small role; James A. Marcus, a big, fat and coarse man who stayed with Raoul for years worked as a bit player and assistant director. This was the nucleus of a group that worked with Raoul for years. As time went on he added other people who worked with him on many pictures and with different companies. We were Walsh people, just as in the earlier days we had been Griffith people, and it all began with *The Honor System.*

At the time, I confess, I didn't realize the magnitude of the picture, or even the beginning of the Walsh company. During the shooting I found an interest much more absorbing to me than moviemaking.

Most of my scenes were shot in the studio, back in Hollywood. But my exterior scenes were shot on location close to the prison, some right in the prison yard. While the rest of the company went out in the Arizona desert sun, I would stay back at the prison. I had nothing to do and I started visiting the convicts, particularly the sixteen men on death row. Each day as these men returned to their cells from their meals they could see the hangman's noose waiting for them at the end of the corridor.

I always took presents with me—cigarettes, bottles of pop, and magazines, At first some of the men turned their backs on me; others took my small gifts reluctantly. Gradually they all accepted me as their friend, not just another curiosity seeker. After a while, when the big iron door clanged behind me, the men would come to the doors of their cells, press their faces against the bars and watch me walk down the corridor. I'd stop at each cell and talk to each man for a few moments while he finished his drink. The guards always took the empty bottles away. I asked why.

"You don't know these men," one of the guards told me. "They could bust this bottle and use it to kill themselves or each other."

When the guards were gone, the men spoke to me more easily. They told me about their families, their children and their sweethearts. And they always asked me what was going on in the world outside the prison walls. They never mentioned why they were there; and they never looked at the gallows.

I learned a lot about people there. For one thing, the crimes of the Americans were generally cruel and premeditated. The Mexicans, on the other hand, had committed crimes of passion and impulse. Jose, a young Mexican with sad eyes, always brought out a red velvet photograph album to show me pictures of his wife and daughters. All the girls were in their Holy Communion dresses, their hands clasping small white prayer books. I saw this man every day, and every day he brought out the album. I couldn't imagine him killing his own cousin during a family quarrel.

I was especially friendly with one young American prisoner named Race Galpin, a tall young man with brown hair, bronzed skin and white teeth. He looked like a young Apollo, but his eyes were strange. They would change from soft gray to cold green to opaque within minutes.

Galpin had advertised home sites in the Arizona desert for elderly retired couples in Eastern newspapers. When they came to see the property he'd meet them at the train in a horse and buggy and drive them out in the desert. Then he'd murder them and take their money. His grandmother blamed his "style," as she called it, on his mother. She was a writer, and while pregnant had thought out the characters for a novel.

"I suppose the bad man of her story was woven in your brain," Race's grandmother wrote him. "What you need is to be in a sanitarium for mental treatment."

But Race was never helped, and he ended his life in prison.

When I got back to California I sent packages to the prisoners every month with cigarettes, magazines and jams and jellies. Every so often I'd get a letter from the warden telling me to stop sending packages to one of the men. That meant he had died on the gallows. The names were always Mexican. The Americans were never hanged.

After three months we left the desert and returned to Hollywood to shoot the interiors. One day as I was putting on my makeup, I looked at myself in the mirror. My nose looked much too long. Oh, how I wished I had a cute nose like Mae Marsh's. I looked through my makeup box and got out some eye shadow. Then I blackened the end of my nose and went out on the set.

Later that night, when we sat in the projection room looking at the day's rushes, Raoul said, "What the hell happened to her nose?" The projector stopped and everybody looked at my picture on the screen. Raoul fussed at the cameraman, but I didn't say anything. It cost Raoul so much money to reshoot that scene, with my long nose left the way it was, that I never admitted what I had done.

When the shooting was over Raoul worked until after

midnight night after night cutting the film. It had been scheduled to be a six-reel picture, but he had shot so much film on location that he wanted to expand it to ten reels. It was not uncommon in those days to start out with a short picture and, if you had good footage, to end up with a long one. Besides, Raoul felt the subject of prison reform was so important that it deserved to be explored in depth. The only way he could do it was by using everything he had shot.

But ten reels made a long movie. Only Mr. Griffith's spectacular *The Birth of a Nation* was that long. It was, however, still running, and making lots of money for Griffith and his backers. *Intolerance* had not yet been released, and Raoul thought the time was right for a spectacular of his own. He told Mr. Fox it would make lots of money for him. One thing William Fox understood was money. He accepted Raoul's assurance and gave the okay to let *The Honor System* run ten reels.

Several months went by before *The Honor System* opened at the Lyric Theatre in New York on Lincoln's birthday, 1917. Raoul and I made the trip across the country to be present. I was scared to death. I sat holding Raoul's hand tightly during the first half.

At intermission the lights went up and we went into the lobby. I thought the movie was powerful and moving, but what did the other people in the audience think? Suddenly they began coming up to us, clapping Raoul on the back, shaking his hand, and saying wonderful things to both of us.

I'll never forget what Victor Watson of the *New York American* said: "It's bigger than anything that's ever been on the screen." The next day in his review Mr. Watson was even more ecstatic. "*The Birth of a Nation* is eclipsed at last! . . . [*The Honor System*] made new history in the film business."

His wasn't the only good review. Frederick James Smith of the *New York Evening Mail* wrote, "This indeed is the first real attempt of the movies to enlist in a great humanitarian movement. Consequently, *The Honor System* can be said to have the biggest theme of any screen production thus far."

I was happy for Raoul, and I was pleased with what the reviewers said about me, too. Victor Watson wrote, "It put Milton Sills, who plays the hero, and Miriam Cooper, who plays the heroine, in the class of all the leading picture stars."

The Honor System played to audiences around the country for years. In Phoenix 500 people filled the theater and 150 more stood in the rear. When the prisoners escaped from the old prison, the audience stood up and cheered.

Two years later it was still considered so important that it was one of the special events scheduled for the Prince of Wales, the one who later abdicated the throne for "the woman I love." Mr. Fox arranged for the showing to be held at the Academy of Music on 14th Street. Many years before, the Prince's grandfather, Edward VII, had attended the opera there, sitting in a throne-like chair built especially for the 300-pound monarch. Mr. Fox found it somewhere. The prince looked like a little boy sitting in Papa Bear's chair.

He also looked as though the whole thing had been a waste of time. The meaning and the message of *The Honor System* seemed to go right over his head; he looked bored stiff. I realized why at the ball held later that night at the old Waldorf Astoria. New York's loveliest debutantes were there, and the Prince whirled them, and me, around the dance floor. What he was interested in was girls.

After *The Honor System* Raoul was on his way; it enabled him to take a giant leap into the big time and the big money. He received a bonus of several thousand dollars from Mr. Fox, who made millions on it. I received a bonus also: a fur coat. We both deserved them, too, but not entirely because of *The Honor System*. During the period between shooting and opening some significant backstage maneuvering had taken place.

« 17 »

When Raoul began *The Honor System* he was only one of several directors on the Fox West Coast lot. As in the days of the Griffith company, directors were expected to grind out their quota of short features. The big money was in quantity, not quality.

Therefore, when Raoul finished shooting *The Honor System,* he looked forward to cutting and editing it with the care and artistry it deserved. Instead he found himself assigned to a series of pictures. One, I recall, was *The Conqueror,* with William Farnum. It was a successful picture but a terrible comedown from our dreams of what *The Honor System* could be. The only way he could devote the necesary time and effort to cutting and editing *The Honor System* was to do it at night, after a long day shooting something like *The Conqueror.*

I rarely saw him; he'd leave the house early in the morning and not return until long after midnight. Once again life was very lonely for me. Raoul could see that I was fidgety. One night, after he'd come in very late, undressed and gotten into bed, he said, "Racsey"—we had the silliest names for each other—"it looks like it's going to go on like this for a hell of a lot longer. How'd you like to go to New York for a while?"

"Oh, Raoul, honey, I don't want to leave you," I said.

"You're not leaving me," he said. "Hell, you never see me. You might as well not see me in New York as here. You could see your mother and Pops and all your friends, and do some shopping."

I protested prettily, but he was right. And I was always ready to go to New York.

"While you're there," he said, "you can drop in and see Fox. I'm goddam tired of all this crap I've got to do. I want to do big pictures like *The Honor System.* But I never see him. I bet you could talk to him and make him understand. You did a pretty good job with Griffith."

So that was the reason I could go to New York and see all my friends and go shopping. He wanted me to build him up with Mr. Fox. Well, it was all right with me. I was glad to do all I could for Raoul. His life was my life, too. And Mr. Fox really ought to know how he was wasting Raoul's talent on those routine pictures.

I called Mr. Fox the first day I was in New York. "Miriam!" he said. "It's so good to hear your voice. When can you come around to see me?" We set up an appointment.

In the meantime a long letter arrived from Raoul telling me what to say to Mr. Fox. It sounded like a prizefighter's manager giving instructions before sending him into the ring. "Give him the impression I have some ten-reel ideas tucked away in my head," he wrote. "Tell him about some reputable concern that made me a good offer to produce ten-reelers. Give him to believe that there is a vast difference between five- and ten-reel subjects . . . one requires just ordinary work, the other is a deep study. Inasmuch as it plays to a critical audience, he gets a *better price* for it, and why should *I not* get a better salary?"

So now I was supposed to negotiate a raise for him, too. I was perfectly willing to tell Mr. Fox how talented Raoul was, but I wasn't so sure that I could bargain with him. I hadn't had much experience along that line, whereas Mr. Fox had had nothing else but. He was shrewd and suspicious.

It takes one to know one, I figured. I asked Pops, a uniform manufacturer with two sons in pictures, for his advice on how to deal with a cloth-shrinker who owned a whole company. Pops and I sat down in his study and, to the accompaniment of Willie Hoppe's billiard balls going click-click in the dining room, plotted my strategy.

"I don't think you ought to ask Fox for a salary increase for Al," Pops said. Raoul was still Al to Pops. "That wouldn't be businesslike. But let's see. You're going to talk to him about making longer pictures. I don't see why you can't mention that longer pictures ought to have some kind of bonus."

I rehearsed everything I was going to say carefully, just as though I were going to play the part of the wife of a director making a big pitch to his boss.

I dressed carefully, too, wearing my new navy blue suit that I had bought at Mme. Frances. I thought my best approach to Mr. Fox was to be humble and polite. He listened attentively to everything I had to say. He was very nice to me and made it all quite pleasant.

"Vell," he said finally. "So Raoul vants he should make big pictures, hm? With a bonus yet. I don't see vy not—he's a good boy, that Raoul. Of course he should have a bonus—if his big pictures make big money."

To me that was as good as saying yes. Of course Raoul's pictures would make money. I went straight to a telegraph office and wired Raoul the results of the interview, with a promise to give him all the details later. He was very pleased with me and said I'd done a good job.

Once I had taken care of everything for Raoul, I concentrated on shopping and, more important, going to the doctor. I had been having trouble with my kidneys, and that was another reason for the trip. Although we spent a lot of time in California, Raoul and I were real New Yorkers. Just as we went to New York to shop, so we went to New York to go to the doctor.

The doctor took longer than I had expected. He insisted that I have a lot of tests. As long as I was spending so much time with him, I got up the nerve to ask him about something that concerned me more than my kidneys.

"Doctor," I said, "my husband and I want children, but I don't seem to be able to have any."

That brought on more tests. They seemed to be all right. He shook his head, puzzled. "How long have you been married?" he asked.

"Eight months," I said proudly.

"Eight months!" he shouted. "Oh, for God's sake. Come back in eight years."

Raoul was impatient with me, too. Finally he wired me telling me point-blank to come home to him. My letter almost burned up the post office.

"I want you to understand this has been no pleasure trip for me and least of all taking a cross-country trip of five days alone. Most women take such trips with their husbands . . . and if you think I enjoy being in New York without my husband who should be with me seeing that I see a show or two or taking me to an occasional dinner or pleasant evening of amusement you are entirely mistaken."

I guess that told him off. He was very contrite. "If I spoke unkindly I am sorry. There has been rain and fog every day since you left. Consequently all my plans were upset . . . miss you, love, Poppy."

We were two emotional people needing constant assurance of each other's love and devotion. And there was jealousy. Raoul wrote he was going on location with Jewel

Carmen, a beautiful young actress he had engaged for *The Conqueror*. I wired him immediately that I was surprised he was taking such a trip without me. "I shall stand for no gossip. You should know better."

Poor Raoul. He had to get his sister Alice, who was visiting him, to go on location with him to pacify me. Our letters had started out addressed to Boobie-boy and Mimsy, Mommy and Poppy. By the end of my stay in New York I was writing My dear Raoul and he was answering My dear Miriam. The separations were hard on us from the very beginning, and they were going to get a lot worse.

« 18 »

The moving picture industry was a crazy business then—
I guess it still is. When *The Honor System* came out Raoul
and I were riding high. He'd made a wonderful picture, a
box-office picture, and now everybody in the industry
knew the name Raoul Walsh. Mr. Fox certainly did. He
had rented space in the new Biograph Studios up in the
Bronx and brought Raoul back to New York to film his
pictures there. Raoul read plays, books, scripts far into
the night, searching for a subject to carry another big picture, another *Honor System.*

And then Mr. Fox chickened out. *The Birth of a
Nation* was still playing to packed houses all over the
country. *The Honor System* was a big success. Other Fox-
made spectacles by other directors, *The Daughter of the
Gods* and *The Queen of Sheba*, were making money too.
But when *Intolerance* failed at the box office, and with
the United States on the brink of war, Mr. Fox decided not
to risk large sums of money on big pictures. His promise
to me, and Raoul's dreams, went down the drain. Back to
churning out the short features Mr. Fox thought would be
safe at the box office. Raoul filmed whatever the front
office left on his desk at the studio, frequently using his
brother George as leading man.

I had nothing to do with them, directly at least. Of course I heard all about them. Pictures was practically all we ever talked about at dinner. I was as close to the business as I wanted to be. I'd pitched in and helped out on *The Honor System* for Raoul, but now I was fixing up our new apartment in the east seventies, being a housewife, trying to get pregnant, and loving my new life.

But night after night, as Raoul moaned about the pictures he was doing, a new element began to enter the conversation. Winnie Sheehan, Fox's vice president, had discovered one of the fringe benefits of the business—casting girls. He'd sign them, then send them around to Raoul.

"Winnie's girls give me a pain in the ass," Raoul said. "They don't know what the hell they're doing in front of a camera. It takes all my time just to get them to sit down, or smile, or blow their nose, for Christ's sake. I wish I had somebody with Griffith training, somebody I could depend on. Somebody like you."

Raoul and I worked well together. We'd both had our training with Mr. Griffith, so we knew what to expect from each other. He didn't direct me; I just did the scene the way I felt it should be done, and he was almost always happy with the result. If he didn't like it, he'd just say, "Okay, let's try that again and get a little more feeling in it."

So he wasn't fooling me. I knew what he was getting at. I knew even better than he did. Raoul hated directing women and he wasn't very good at it. Mr. Griffith loved to coax a performance out of a girl, patiently, carefully, using all his tricks. Raoul begrudged every minute of it. He liked to stage rough, tough, he-man scenes.

For example, in one movie he made, the good guys cornered the bad guys in a bar. It was to be a real brawl. They used papier-mâché chairs and tables, of course, and everybody was swinging them around, breaking them over each other's heads. Raoul was having the time of his life. When he was directing dramatic or love scenes, he'd copy Griffith and be very dignified. But when he directed fight scenes, he'd jump up and down and wave his hat in the air.

When the action was over, Raoul yelled "Cut" and walked onto the set.

"Not enough action that time, fellows," he said. "Do it again like you really mean it."

The set was put back together again with more papier-mâché chairs and tables.

"Camera! Action!" Raoul hollered and everybody began banging each other on the head again. Raoul got so excited that he threw a couple of chairs into the melee himself. Then somebody picked up a real chair, a sturdy wooden chair, and broke it over another man's head. The blood spurted out. The man who was hit reeled, then pulled himself together, and *he* picked up a real chair. By the time the scene was over, not one piece of furniture was intact, the blood was real, and Raoul was almost out of his mind with joy. It scared me to death, but Raoul loved it and it was a great scene.

That was what he wanted to do, not tell girls how to look sad. And he didn't like the power struggles that took place between the director and sweet-looking female stars who'd as soon cut his throat as look at him. What it all boiled down to was that if he had me working for him it would eliminate a lot of time and bother. He knew what Griffith had demanded of me, and knew that I could deliver.

"With a girl like you playing the lead," he said, "I could concentrate on turning out really good pictures and get established quickly."

As usual, I couldn't resist him. "Well, Raoul," I said, "if you really want me, I'll work for you."

We agreed that I could retire permanently as soon as

he was established. Then we had to work it out with Mr. Fox.

Mr. Fox was delighted to have a Griffith player as one of his leads. "But," he warned me, "we can't afford to feature both you and Raoul. It's either one—either the director or the actress has to have top billing. Then all the money we spend on advertising, the big salary, the publicity, is all on one person. You'll have to decide which one."

If an actress wanted starring roles and offers of huge salaries, it made a lot of difference how the name appeared on a marquee. Actors and actresses were always trying to get top billing in letters ten feet high. I wasn't interested in these things. I had what I wanted, a husband and security. It was Raoul's career that mattered. I never hesitated in my answer to Mr. Fox.

"This is Raoul's career," I told Mr. Fox. "I'm not going to stay in pictures; I'm only doing it to help out. Raoul is the star."

Mr. Fox said he understood. He was a very nice man, not like those fresh guys who would maul you. He agreed to pay me $1,200 a week when I worked, and gave Raoul a raise. I never had a contract; Raoul did. I don't remember Raoul's exact salary, but with his raise and bonus after *The Honor System* the two of us were making thousands of dollars a week.

For someone who thought she had retired I had a lot of exposure in these years during and after World War I. No matter where you were you could see a picture with me in it. *The Birth of a Nation* and *Intolerance* were still playing in the hinterlands. *The Honor System* was booked in all the major cities, and during 1917 alone I made three pictures for Raoul and Fox.

It was easy work for me. Pat, our chauffeur, would drive us to the studio early in the morning. If I wasn't needed for the first shots of the day Raoul would let me sleep late. Then my brother Gordon, who was Raoul's assistant, would call me. "Be on the set in half an hour," he'd say, and Pat would drive down and get me. That was one of the privileges of being married to the director.

Working together so closely, we could make a game of it. One time in a movie called *The Innocent Sinner* Raoul, who hadn't acted since *The Birth of a Nation,* got into a scene with me just for luck. We were sitting at a table in a barroom with Raoul's back to the camera and me facing it. He was only in that one scene. Many years later Alfred Hitchcock got a lot of publicity for doing the same thing.

Although I had privileges, I worked hard on the set. Raoul worked even harder. This was serious business for my husband and me. After the day's shooting we'd both be exhausted. To relax, we had a standing appointment with a masseur from the New York Athletic Club where Raoul was a member. He'd come to our apartment and give Raoul a rubdown and massage me with olive oil. It was supposed to build me up; I was always too thin.

After dinner we'd go back to the studio to see the day's rushes. The day would be over for me, but Raoul would sit up for hours planning the next day's shooting. By the time he came to bed I was sound asleep.

After a while though, my old kidney ailment flared up again and I had to take it easy for a time. It was in 1917, and about the same time the papers were filled with news of a sensational murder trial. A young South American woman named Blanca De Saulles had shot her ex-husband, Jack De Saulles, a millionaire playboy, in an argument over custody of their child. Their pictures, and those of his mistress, were splashed all over the front pages.

An embarrassing coincidence was that Blanca and I looked alike. I'd go into a store or a restaurant and hear people whispering behind my back, "There's Blanca De Saulles!"

Winnie Sheehan thought it would be a great story for Fox to produce. "Let's do it while it's hot," he said.

Since I wasn't available, Raoul chose a society girl to play the part of Blanca De Saulles. She was pretty, but no actress. After a couple of weeks Winnie came to see me.

"Miriam," he said, "this girl is lousy. Do you think you could get down there and do the picture?"

"I'm too sick," I protested.

"But you look like her," he kept saying.

I finally gave in. Raoul's plan was to shoot the interiors in New York and the exteriors in Miami Beach. When it came time to leave for Florida, a nurse went with me. We stayed at a small hotel on the beach. Miami Beach then was just a long strip of sand with a few beach cottages and a couple of big houses which had been converted to hotels.

The picture was called *The Woman and the Law*, and the name De Saulles was thinly disguised as La Salle. Mr. Fox wanted to have me listed in the cast as "Mrs. Jack La Salle, played by . . ." followed by a blank. Then everybody would think the real Blanca De Saulles was actually playing the part. I wouldn't stand for that.

Peggy Hopkins played the mistress, and it was perfect casting: she was one of the most famous courtesans in the country. She later married a man named Joyce and is remembered as Peggy Hopkins Joyce, but she was still a high-class tramp. She wasn't very smart, either, and it was easy to keep the real meaning of the role from her. She never knew she was playing the part of the mistress.

When the film was premiered on Broadway, Raoul, his brother George and I sat in the back of the theater together. Peggy Hopkins was there, too, sitting in the front. A few minutes into the film a subtitle came on the screen describing Peggy's house as a place where "taxi-driver and millionaire alike are welcome." Only then did she know she was playing her real life role. She let out a yelp, jumped out of her seat and came charging up the aisle through the darkened theater looking for Raoul.

"Where's that son of a bitch?" she shouted. "I'll kill him!"

When Raoul saw her coming he climbed over George and me, ran into the ticket booth and hid under the cashier's skirts until Peggy left.

The Woman and the Law got what amounted to an X rating for the time. The picture was advertised with the notation, "No Children Admitted." Critics questioned Fox's taste in using the case as a basis for a picture.

Mae Tinee, drama critic for the *Chicago Tribune*, said, "If you care to spend your time peeping through the curtain at harrowing domestic infelicity, at a ne'er-do-well's unfaithfulness, at a child's helplessness and at the sordidest kind of tragedy, *The Woman and the Law* is what you are looking for. It drips with yellow."

I couldn't argue with her too much, however, because she went on to say, "Miriam Cooper as the mother is a lovely and appealing figure . . . She does some exceedingly good work, this slender, dark-eyed Miriam Cooper."

She was certainly right about my being slender. During the shooting I was still sick and worked the whole time weighing less than a hundred pounds.

After *The Woman and the Law* I had plenty of time to recuperate. I couldn't have worked if I'd wanted to. It wasn't because Raoul was now so well established that he didn't need me—it was to keep him out of the draft. For when the United States entered World War I in 1917 Raoul, who was then thirty, was immediately classified 1-A. Raoul and the Fox people went into a panic. Raoul sure as hell didn't want to go to war, and Fox didn't want to lose a director. I didn't want to lose a husband, either.

Raoul, Mr. Fox and his cohorts got together to figure out a way to beat the draft. He could hardly claim dependents when his wife was earning $1,200 a week. The solution was obvious. I stopped earning it.

I'd been giving Mama $200 a week. Raoul took that responsibility over so that he'd have two dependents. That kept him out. My two brothers, Gordon and Nelson, were married, with children to support, so they weren't called up, either. That left George. He had a wife and baby too, but his wife, Seena Owen, wanted him to do his bit, or maybe she just wanted to get rid of him. Over George's protests and pleadings she signed an affidavit saying she was getting permanent employment. He was made 1-A again, but before he was called up the war ended. And so did their marriage.

Raoul escaped the war in the trenches but he didn't escape it on the screen. Most of the industry went off on an anti-sabotage kick, during which German-Americans were depicted as traitors knifing America in the back. Mr. Fox didn't want to be left out. He assigned Raoul to a story about German-Americans sabotaging aircraft factories.

Raoul didn't want to do the picture. He tried to talk Winnie Sheehan and the other Fox yes-men out of it, but nobody would listen. When it became obvious that he had to do it, at least he did it right. The man he hired to play the villain was the real thing—a German spy who had been captured by the English. In return for giving information about the Kaiser, our government granted the German spy political asylum in the United States. Raoul hired him for authenticity.

Raoul thought I could play one role without jeopardizing his draft status, so I played the innocent all-American sweetheart who is taken in by the spy's glib line and falls in love with him. In the end, of course, I realize he's a bad guy.

The climax of the picture came when the German spies were cornered by a band of hooded men. It was just like the Ku Klux Klan rescuing the Southern family from the Negroes in *The Birth of a Nation*. We had really made progress—from racism to fascism.

Raoul and I were disgusted with the whole movie. Not because we approved of sabotage, but because we knew very well that not every German–American was a saboteur. It was terribly unfair, even dangerous, to many thousands of innocent people. While cutting it, Raoul wrote me:

"It is without a doubt the rottenest picture I ever made. It's my fault to let that gang of yegs bull me into putting a picture on of that sort. I only wish to God this war was over—we would show them something. I will not work for them one day after peace is declared."

The public agreed with him on both the quality of the picture and the falseness of the message. Called *The Prussian Cur*, it was panned by the critics. By the time it was released, only two months before the war ended, all war pictures were box-office disasters. Fox, along with most other companies, lost money on its war films.

I had found a project of far greater interest than movies about saboteurs. After two years of marriage I still wasn't pregnant. I never got a positive medical reason for our inability to have children; perhaps it was related to my kidney problem, or perhaps it was related to Raoul. He never had any children by any of his other wives. Anyway, I grew impatient. Raoul and I could afford to share our good fortune with children. If we couldn't have a child, we could adopt one. I went to an orphanage, the New York Foundling Hospital.

I knew what it was like to be in an orphanage. I had

been sent to one when Mama was ill many years before. I had been so miserable there, and so relieved when Mama got well and I could go home, that I thought I could bring that same happiness to some other child. This was something good Raoul and I could do with our money.

The child we selected was a beautiful blond five-year-old boy. We called him Jackie. When the Sisters tried to tell me his history, I stopped them. I didn't want to know anything about his parents. I didn't care who they were. I firmly believed that a good environment was all anybody needed. I invented parents for our new son. I told him, and everybody else, that his parents had been lost in a shipwreck off the coast of Canada, near Halifax.

Everybody believed me but Jackie. For years whenever I left the house he'd go through my personal papers looking for something about his own mother and father. Theresa, the cook, told me he was always asking her about them, too.

A month or so after we got Jackie, while Raoul was still cutting *The Prussian Cur,* the hay fever season hit New York and I was miserable. I'd had asthma before, but this time it was so bad I could hardly breathe. My doctor suggested I get out of New York and into the clean mountain air. Not only would I be able to breathe, but I could take my new little boy from the city orphanage into the beautiful countryside.

When I went to Bretton Woods, New Hampshire, it was with a full entourage, just like a movie star. There was Jackie, and Theresa the cook, and Bessie Waters, a friend from childhood.

Theresa took charge of Jackie while Bessie and I spent our days riding, swimming and learning to play golf. I fell in love with the game. On clear days Bessie and I spent hours practicing our putting and driving.

Every night after dinner I wrote to Raoul. He had

invented our own special language and we used it all the time. "I'm lonserie and saderie," I wrote him. "I miss you and the niceries," he wrote back. "Niceries" had a double meaning. He had more pet names for me than I can count: Racsey, Mimsey, Little Fellow, My Girl—and I loved them all. I called him Papa, Daddy and Booboo.

His letters were warm and affectionate and full of news of what he was doing. He was staying at the Lambs Club, eating dinner at Dinty Moore's with his cronies, and cutting film until late at night. When he could, he'd take the overnight train and join us.

One time I suggested he cut the film at Bretton Woods, so we could be together. But I also suggested that he and Benny, his cutter, could work somewhere else in town. "I don't think they'd like that kind of operation here at the hotel," I told him. It was a very high-class place.

I didn't even want him to bring his brother George up. I knew George would tell everybody he was an actor. I didn't want that kind of notoriety. People at Bretton Woods didn't know I was in the movies, and I never wanted them to know.

I always shunned publicity. I hated it when people drew attention to me. One time Texas Guinan saw me coming into her supper club. "Here comes Miriam Cooper," she said in her big brassy voice. "Let's give the little girl a big hand."

I was so embarrassed I sat down in the back as fast as I could. One of the men in our party said, "I've never met an actress like you. Most actresses would have loved that and walked right up to a ringside table."

Anyway, Raoul understood my feelings and didn't bring George.

I was always asking Raoul to do things for me and he never refused. One time I asked him to send Pat, the chauffeur, and the car over to take the priests for a ride on their day off. "I know you won't refuse because I ask it," I wrote him. He didn't.

Raoul worried about me all the time. He was always telling me to bundle up, keep warm and wear my heavy jacket. I took shameful advantage of his concern. One time I wrote him I had a sore throat and a cold. "Why don't you charge a narrow ermine scarf at Revillon Frères for me?" I suggested. "If you think I should have it, dear."

A plain woolen scarf from Macy's for $2.98 wouldn't keep me warm; I had to have a $500 ermine from Revillon Frères. But I paid for it with words he wanted to hear, and sincere words, too.

"I received the scarf today and it is a beauty," I wrote him. "It was so thoughtful and sweet of you to think of it.

"Daddy dear, I cannot tell you how much I appreciate all the sweet thoughtful things you do for me. Truly there could be no better lover-husband in this world than mine.

"Not because you have bought me a new scarf. But because you are always so good and sweet . . . you are successful because you are good, and as long as you are good you will always be successful."

When the hay fever season ended, Jackie and I hurried back to New York and Raoul.

« 19 »

Now that the war was over, films like *The Prussian Cur* were gathering dust on the shelves, where they belonged. The new trend would obviously be toward pictures as far removed from violence and fighting as possible. Raoul was now a well-known, highly respected, high-salaried director. I didn't think he needed me as his leading lady anymore. However, we did want to keep his career going up with a good picture. But what would it be?

Like Mr. Griffith, Raoul leaned toward famous novels and plays for his pictures. *The Birth of a Nation, Broken Blossoms, Way Down East,* all Griffith masterpieces, had been successful plays. One of Raoul's first films had been Ibsen's *Ghosts,* his best *The Honor System,* taken from a current best seller. He again wanted to film something well-known, a popular classic.

He'd bought a twenty-volume set called *The Authors' Digest,* which was a *Reader's Digest* type condensation of great popular literature. Authors such as Dickens and Kipling and Longfellow were in it.

One night at dinner we were discussing pictures, as always. "I've been looking through those books you bought," I said. "There's a story by Longfellow in it. I don't think it's very good, but it reminded me of something. What about that poem he wrote about the two young lovers who are separated and search for each other through the years? Finally they're reunited in old age. Do you remember that? The heroine's name was Evangeline— that's the name of the poem—*Evangeline*. Everybody loved it."

"That's not a bad idea," Raoul said. "We could use a modern-day love story as a frame for it. Evangeline— wasn't she a French-Canadian? You'd be perfect . . . dark hair, white skin."

"Why don't you try to get somebody else this time?" I said. "Jackie needs a mother now, and I love to be with him."

"Sure," he said. "I understand."

I didn't realize it then, of course, but Raoul hadn't really dropped the idea. We began recalling what we could about Evangeline, and even discussing who'd play the leads, now that it was definitely understood that I was out of it. Mr. Fox liked the idea. Raoul and I read the poem and talked about it. Fox writers began a scenario.

It was decided to shoot it not in the beautiful Acadian country of Canada and on the lush Cajun bayous of Louisiana, where the story actually happened, but in California. That long Western state has so many climates, so many terrains, that it had already been many other places in many other pictures, and will be many more. Of course that meant Raoul and I would be separated again, as I would stay on in New York.

One night Raoul came home furious. "I'm quitting," he said. "What do you think they sent me today—a bleached-blonde whore to play the part of a sweet dark-haired girl. I'm through. I'm going to China and drive a taxi."

I knew what sweet dark-haired girl Raoul had in

mind for Evangeline. But I could never refuse Raoul. Playing Evangeline would also mean that we would be together, not a whole continent apart. Before dinner was over I was Evangeline, California-bound.

Although I had had some part in the choice of the story, and it was supposed to be just what post-war audiences would pay to see, I never liked *Evangeline* myself. The story was so blah and Evangeline was such a saint. I preferred roles with more emotional charge in them. I wouldn't have hung around under an oak tree all my life waiting for my sweetheart to turn up. I'm impatient, and sometimes I'm a little hot-tempered. One day that temper turned up on film.

We were shooting a scene in which I was standing with a large bouquet of flowers in my arms, looking angelic. Raoul had his head close to the camera, looking through the finder.

"You'd never know she's such a devil, would you?" he said in a low voice to the photographer. He didn't think I could hear him. But I did.

I gave him a furious look and threw the flowers at him, right into the camera. That night Mr. Fox came to see the rushes, along with Winnie Sheehan and some of their yes-men. They did this every once in a while to check up on the director and see how things were going. When the film came to the scene of me with the flowers, I saw myself glare at Raoul, then throw the flowers. They came flying at the camera all over again. I had thought the camera had stopped grinding when I threw them. Everybody laughed but me.

Evangeline was a beautiful picture, but very sad. To keep me in the mood, I'd have an organ brought on the set and the organist play mournful music. Everybody complained about it. One time, as the stagehands wheeled the tiny organ onto the set, somebody said, "Oh, God, here it comes again." I don't blame them for complaining. It wouldn't have been so bad if the musician had played different tunes, but I had the poor man play the same sad song over and over and over.

In the picture I age from a young girl to an elderly woman. One day I picked up the paper to see two pictures of me, one as the young Evangeline and the other as the aged woman at the end of the picture. I looked to see what was written about me. My eyes popped. The newspaper story wasn't *about* me, it was *by* me. I was identified as the author, although I had never seen the article before. It was a story on how to grow old gracefully. A girl in her twenties writing "How To Grow Old Gracefully." Christ! Somebody should ask me to do it today. At eighty-two I could write an article about growing old in three words— Don't Do It.

Evangeline was premiered in New York in 1919, during the hay fever season, so Jackie and I were back in Bretton Woods. Raoul went to the first showing and wrote to me:

"The picture was received with great applause. . . . The house was crowded with the usual *Fox elite* all chewing gum and picking their noses during intermission. . . . Everybody was full of praises for you and said you were the most beautiful girl on the screen."

The reviews were all good. The *Variety* reviewer mentioned the beauty of the film and then talked about me. "Of all the leading ladies developed by D. W. Griffith, she alone remains herself. . . . She is simple, direct, convincing, appealing as few more versatile actresses are, and in playing Evangeline she seems not to be acting, but to be actually that suffering maiden."

Evangeline opened at a most propitious time. There was a strike on in the legitimate theaters. The lines outside our theater were longer than we'd dared to hope for.

To take advantage of the situation Fox rushed a six-reeler to Broadway that Raoul and I had made immediately after *Evangeline*. Called *Should a Husband Forgive?*, it didn't have the depth and beauty of *Evangeline*, but critics considered it a nice summer offering. Practically all I remember about it is that at the climax of the picture, I put on jockey's clothes and ride my sweetheart's racehorse and save his fortune. And that it was no double riding the horse, either. There I was, saving the day, just as I had won the Civil War for Kalem seven years earlier.

After these love pictures, Raoul was itching to get his teeth into what he really liked, manly action pictures. He was a sports nut—boxing, baseball, racing—you name it, he loved it. When Jake Ruppert, the owner of Ruppert's Brewery and the New York Yankees, brought the great Babe Ruth to New York, he and everybody else in town talked about it. A picture on the Babe would give Raoul the opportunity to do his kind of work and rub shoulders with his hero at the same time. Other companies and directors also wanted to exploit the colorful and popular baseball star, but Raoul and Winnie Sheehan turned on their Irish charm and, with an assist from the Fox bankroll, talked the Babe into making his first picture with Fox.

Headin' Home was a comedy about a country boy who nobody thought could play ball. Then the country boy, Babe Ruth, of course, hits a ball through the church window five blocks away. He becomes a baseball star and the picture ends with him hitting a home run in New York.

Raoul hired Arthur "Bugs" Baer, the famous newspaper wit, to write the titles for the picture. The titles poked fun at Babe, and the audience loved it. *Headin' Home* didn't open at a theater, but at Madison Square Garden, on September 20, 1920. Jack Dempsey made a personal appearance. The event was a smash hit.

Raoul worshipped heroes of sports, and he and Babe

Ruth became good friends. Raoul followed him around like a little puppy dog. Raoul was so masculine and liked rugged men so much that it was quite a surprise to walk past his bathroom door one day and see him curling his hair with my curling iron.

With his pictures getting praise from the press, Raoul began talking of going out on our own. "I can get all kinds of backing," he said. "Then I can produce pictures with you." All thoughts of my retirement seemed to have faded from Raoul's mind. "Even Mr. Fox says *Evangeline* is the best picture of your career," he told me. "I think we can produce pictures ourselves. George wants to come in with us. The three of us will make an organization. I have big things in mind for you, Racsey, things that will make *Evangeline* look like thirty cents. I'm going to concentrate all my energies on making you a great star."

The last thing I wanted to be was a great star. I wanted to be a wife and mother like other girls.

But Raoul was ambitious. He wanted to be an independent producer. In a way he already was. His brother George often played the leading man, his wife Miriam played the leading lady, my brother Gordon was his assistant, and we'd squeeze the rest of the family in as extras.

"This isn't Fox Film Corporation," somebody said; "this is Walsh Productions."

So going along with his dream would be good not only for Raoul, but for the whole family. It would also be good for our marriage. When we worked together we were happy. It wasn't only being on the set together. We'd discuss the picture at dinner, see the rushes together and, being free at the same time, play together. On weekends we'd go swimming at Catalina Island with Jackie, play golf and go to the race track. Those were the happy periods of my life. The unhappy times were when Raoul worked on pictures without me. I'd get lonely and jealous.

I could whip up a case of jealousy even when I knew Raoul was working with his writers or cutting the film with his editors.

Once more I gave up my dream of being only a wife and mother. It was crazy, but as my husband's leading lady, seeing him day and night, I was actually a better wife and mother. I'd gone into pictures to get money. Now that I had it, I stayed in pictures for the sake of our marriage.

« 20 »

Raoul and I, and our entourage, always seemed to be in the wrong place. We'd been working in New York, then Fox sent us back to California, and now when Raoul decided to become an independent we had to go back to New York to see the big money men. We had rented a big house in California. We decided that Theresa would stay there with Jackie and the dogs. Pat, the chauffeur, would follow us with the car in order to drive us around—as though you couldn't get a cab in New York.

On the day we left we were in the bedroom packing when Raoul happened to look out the window. A little fat man was coming up the walk to our front door.

"Oh, my God," Raoul said, "here comes Louie Mayer."

I knew very well what Raoul thought of Louis B. Mayer. "He's always over-anxious to make himself agreeable," he had written me before. "I'm not keen on tying up with him."

At that time Mayer was running around toadying up to established directors and stars, trying to get us to sign up with him. Mayer had put together his own company and had made a couple of passes at us, but there was one problem: we couldn't stand him.

Now when Raoul saw him coming up the walk he passed the buck to me. "You go down and get rid of him," he said. "I don't want to have anything to do with him."

Like a dutiful wife I went downstairs and met Mayer at the front door. He told me he wanted to see Raoul and sign us up. I told him we were leaving for New York and Raoul was too busy to see anyone.

Mayer persisted. He kept telling me he had Anita Stewart and Mildred Harris under contract, which we knew. Mildred was a sweet but dumb girl whose only claim to fame was having been married to Charlie Chaplin. That left Anita, and he nearly worked her to death. He needed a female star desperately. Somehow he had signed up the irrespressible Mickey Neilan as one director, and he wanted more directors with talent, like Raoul. He kept saying how much he could do for Raoul and me. He didn't say how much we could do for him.

I kept backing away from him. He was short and fat, with squinty eyes and a big nose and the worst case of halitosis I'd ever been this close to. The odor really made me sick. There was green stuff on his teeth, like moss. The more I retreated, the more he came on. He backed me all the way from the front door to the backyard.

I finally got rid of Louis Mayer, but he got back at the Walsh family a few years later when George Walsh was rehearsing the part of Ben-Hur for the Goldwyn Company in Italy. *Ben-Hur* was to be as spectacular as *The Birth of a Nation*. When Mayer merged with Metro and Goldwyn, he and his right-hand man, Irving Thalberg, replaced George with Ramon Novarro. They didn't even have the decency to tell him to his face; he read about it in the newspaper. It was a terrible blow to George's ego, and his career. He never really recovered from it.

When Raoul and I arrived in New York we went directly to the Plaza. I wanted to get our old apartment on

East 77th Street but Raoul said no. He insisted that we stay at the Plaza.

"But, Raoul," I protested, "we can't afford it." With the big house in Los Angeles, the servants, relatives to support, and Pat with the car, we were running out of money. I'd already taken money out of my savings account where it was getting two and a half percent interest. "We're spending all this money and we're not making any. At least we could live in an apartment."

"You can't do that," Raoul said. "You've got to put up a big front. You've got to look as though you've really got it or these guys will say, 'Well, he's not doing so well; I guess he's on the skids.'" So much about this business was false.

When Raoul made his rounds of the money men he found it wasn't as easy to get money for independent pictures as he had thought back in California. Although it was now early 1920, the industry had not completely recovered from the effects of the flu epidemic of 1918, when many theaters were shut down for months to prevent the spread of the disease. Another problem was the financial pinch resulting from the backlog of war pictures. The money men were still being cautious. Also as the businessmen took over the industry they wanted full say in the production, whether or not they knew what they were talking about.

Finally Raoul found a company that still believed the director was the most important man in the production of a picture. It was the Mayflower Corporation, which chose good directors and put them in charge of their own productions. Mayflower believed that if it had a good director and gave him a free hand, he'd produce good films. This was just what Raoul wanted, to be on his own. He was excited about his new deal and picked his old friend Paul Armstrong's successful play, *The Deep Purple,* as his first picture.

Raoul gathered his old company around him. There were my brother Gordon and Jim Marcus, his two assistants, and me. George was working on a picture in California, but he planned to join the Walsh Company as soon as it was finished.

The Deep Purple was a story about a band of crooks and a sweet young country girl who almost gets accused of murder. It was just what Raoul liked—a fast-paced melodrama with lots of action.

The story takes place in New York, so we could stay put. We sent for Theresa and Jackie to join us. We left the Plaza for a large apartment on West 64th Street. Once we were settled Raoul started casting the picture.

I was the star, playing the sweet country girl. Vincent Serrano, a well-known stage actor, was the male lead, and Helen Ware, also from the stage, played a character role. Helen had a difficult time working before the camera, and Raoul had to retake many scenes before he was satisfied with her performance.

"It's so different from working on the stage," she told me. "I don't see how you do it."

I understood her problem; I'd seen so many stage people come into the Griffith company thinking they knew it all only to find they didn't know anything about movie acting. But though I understood it, I didn't know what to advise her to do about it. After all, I'd never been on the stage. Making pictures was now easy for me, particularly with Raoul. It wasn't that he directed me well, but rather that he left me alone. With Helen, despite her reputation as a stage actress, he had to knock himself out to get a halfway decent performance.

I was now really living the part of the director's wife. I wasn't pushing myself as the star—I still considered him the star, just as we had agreed with Fox—but I took advantage of my position in a way more important to me. I found jobs for just about everybody I knew.

This was common practice in those days. When you were making money all your relatives showed up looking for jobs. The best example of this practice I know involved Constance and Norma Talmadge. They hadn't seen their father for fifteen years, not since he had left the flat one night to go across the street to the corner saloon, carrying a large can to have it filled with beer. Rushing the growler, it was called in those days. He just walked out and never came back. Now that the girls were making gobs of money as Hollywood stars, their old man showed up looking for a job. Norma asked her husband, Joe Schenck, to give him a job as the gatekeeper.

"We can't do that," Joe said, "with you making all that money. How would it look in the newspapers? STAR'S FATHER STUDIO GATEKEEPER."

Joe found a more respectable job for him, and the old man came to the studio every day, twirling his cane, with a fresh boutonniere and spats on. "The old bastard walks around as though he owns the place," Norma told me. "He makes Constance and me want to puke."

At least I could get my family honest jobs. Gordon by now had had five years' experience in films and was thoroughly capable as Raoul's assistant. Lenore had worked as an extra for Griffith, and though she'd given up her dreams of a career in films and gotten married, she could handle the bit parts Raoul gave her. Theresa, our cook, was in our movies, too. In one scene she was walking along holding a child by the hand. Guess who the child was—little Jackie, of course. He got ten dollars a day for his part.

Even Mama worked as an extra in *The Deep Purple*. Raoul asked her himself. "What day does your bridge club meet, Mom?" he inquired.

"Tuesdays," Mama told him.

"Well," Raoul said, "tell all your girl friends to wear evening clothes next Tuesday. They're not going to play bridge; they're going to be in a movie."

Mama's friends were delighted. They met at the studio dressed to the teeth. Raoul used them as part of the crowd in a nightclub scene. They loved it—and made six dollars each.

Getting my friend Bessie Waters a job took a little more effort. Some time before, when Raoul was directing a Theda Bara picture, I got him to cast Bessie as Theda Bara's maid. Bessie filmed one scene in which she leaves the room with Theda. The next scene, in which they come out on the other side of the door, was to be filmed the following day. But the next day Bessie didn't show up.

"Where in the hell is the maid?" Raoul said angrily. Gordon called her to find out why she wasn't there.

"I didn't think you worked on rainy days," Bessie told him. This was a big scene, with a lot of extras. It cost Raoul thousands of dollars waiting for Bessie.

I knew then that Raoul didn't like her, but I asked him to give her another chance, and he used her as an extra in *The Deep Purple.*

While we were shooting *The Deep Purple,* John Mc-Cormick, Raoul's publicity man, noticed Bessie and went for her. McCormick later married Colleen Moore and became her producer, but for a while he and Bessie had a sizzling thing going. Together they cooked up a scheme.

McCormick suggested we put on a contest—the National Salesgirls Beauty Contest. That's all he told Raoul and me, and Raoul told him to go ahead. McCormick got newspapers all over the country to cooperate on it. All any salesgirl had to do was to clip the coupon from the newspaper and send it in with an eight-by-ten photo of herself. The winner would get acting lessons from me, and roles in Raoul's pictures. She would receive $100 a week for six weeks work with Raoul, and then the same deal for six weeks with the Ziegfeld Follies.

It seemed as though every salesgirl in the country wanted to be a movie star. The entries came in by the bagful. McCormick sent reams of material to the newspapers to publicize the contest. One handout, supposedly written by me, said, "I will rehearse her personally and teach her that the secret of success lies in being able to express a thought, a particular thing, or an intention through the medium of pantomime." Another directed to the salesgirl contestants quoted Raoul as saying, "Individuals who make good in the selling game possess the first essential of the motion picture player—personality."

The newspaper stories promised the world. The winner was practically assured she'd be a star.

When the winner was chosen, I was to introduce her to a large audience in a downtown theater in Los Angeles. When the time came, I walked on the stage and McCormick handed me an envelope with the winner's name inside, just like the Oscar winners on television today.

When I looked at the name I nearly fainted. It was Bessie Waters.

I called out her name and she came up, pretending ecstatic surprise. But I was furious. I thought it was a dirty trick. Here these shopgirls, who worked so hard for practically nothing, were spending their money for expensive pictures when they had absolutely no chance of winning. I was so mad at John McCormick I made Raoul fire him.

The contest may have been a fake, but Raoul kept his part of the bargain. After all, she was the "winner." He gave Bessie parts in several movies. Of course, there was nothing in the bargain that said she would enjoy the roles. In one movie Bessie played a nun in a convent. The convent catches on fire, and the nuns pray in the chapel while the firemen put out the fire. Water from the fire hoses drips on the nuns as they pray. Actually the water came from stagehands on ladders around the set.

"Here, pour the water over here," Raoul told them.

And the stagehands dumped their buckets where he pointed—all over Bessie. They almost drowned her.

Bessie didn't get the message. The next time Raoul had her made up to look just awful.

"Raoul," I said, "what are you doing? You know nobody will ever hire her again if she looks that ugly."

"Oh, no," Raoul said. "This is really an outstanding part. I think she'll do fine and get a lot of job offers."

God, he was a liar, but such a charming one. And she never did get any other offers.

Because I was so upset about the poor shopgirls, and because he let me have my own way so much anyway, Raoul let me have practically everything I wanted for our next production.

First came the story. It was the last thing Raoul himself would have chosen. I had read William J. Locke's *The Idols* and gone completely crazy over it. It was a woman's story, a soap opera if there ever was one. Raoul had it adapted for me and changed the name to *The Oath*.

The Oath was a perfect vehicle for an actress—large range of emotion, beautiful gowns, and a tearjerker. It was the story of a rich Jewish girl who marries a ne'er-do-well Christian playboy. Knowing her father would disinherit her, they keep their marriage a secret. But when her father is murdered and her husband is accused of doing him in, the girl breaks her oath of silence and tells the court he is her husband and that she was with him. The playboy, however does not really love her, and in the end the girl decides to end her life rather than live without the man she loves.

To play opposite me Raoul engaged Conway Tearle, the most popular leading man of the day. He was wonderful—smooth and the best actor I ever worked with. He responded to your feelings in a scene. What you felt, he felt. He made you give a good performance. I loved working with him and he seemed to enjoy it, too. During the love scenes Raoul would say, "Show me how much you love this man." I guess I showed more feeling than Raoul wanted. Just as Conway and I were really into it, Raoul would shout, "Okay, that's enough."

When Raoul signed him he agreed to pay Conway $2,500 a week. When he told me that I just whistled. That was twice as much as I was making, and I was the star.

I didn't care, because I was never envious of actors making more than I was. But Tearle also worked with actresses like Norma Talmadge. "Don't tell any of the girls how much he's getting," Raoul warned me. "If they find out he's getting more than they are, they'll raise hell."

Conway was right for the role in more ways than one. Playing a gentile with more than a trace of anti-Semitism, he was playing himself. As more and more Jews came into the industry Raoul and I were never offensive to them, but not Conway. He went around making cracks about Jews. He alienated so many people that although he was really a wonderful actor, he phased himself out of pictures.

Supporting roles in *The Oath* were well cast, too, though not in the same way. Anna Q. Nilsson, the leading lady of my Kalem days, played a small part. After ten years, our roles were reversed. Henry Clive, the famous illustrator, had drawn me for the February 1921 cover of *Theatre Magazine*. He asked Raoul if he could play a small part in the picture "because I'd just like to try it." Raoul said sure, and gave him a bit part.

Raoul used very stylized lighting, making stark contrasts between black and white which were highly dramatic and striking. I got carried away with lighting, too. I arranged for a light on the floor in front of me. It rounded out my thin face, made me look sexier.

And the clothes I wore—I nearly bankrupted us on costumes alone. Up until *The Oath* I had always been very careful to get clothes that fit the character. I had gone to more trouble to dress myself for roles in which I looked tawdry than for roles in which I looked good.

When we began a picture we'd simply tell the Western Uniform Company in Los Angeles what we wanted and they'd send it over. Usually the dresses they sent for me to wear as a girl of average good taste were fine. But clothes for the part I played so many times, the simple working-class girl gone wrong, were often *too* good. They'd have too much style. So I'd go to second-hand stores and get dresses which had not only been worn, but were of poor taste to begin with. Like the role I played in *Intolerance,* for example. I never liked that girl in the first place, and I dressed her as though I didn't like her. That awful hat—just what a small-town girl gone wrong would wear to look respectable.

I'd always dressed for the role rather than for myself, but in *The Oath* I could do both—and I went crazy. Whatever a wealthy girl would wear I ordered, no matter how much it cost. The whole damn movie was composed of dramatic scenes for Miriam, but the final scene was the most melodramatic of all. In it I chose death rather than go on with the husband who did not love me. For this scene I had a dress designed and made that was a knock-out in every way—style, fabric and cost. It was a red chiffon evening gown, and it had real class.

I loved that dress, and I loved the final scene. We shot it on location on an island off the coast of Maine. As I struggle over whether or not to kill myself, I'm on a cliff high above the ocean as the wind whips my red chiffon gown around my body. After a lot of melodramatic emoting with my hand to my head, I jump.

I loved the story and I loved my part. But I was the only one who did. This was the only picture Raoul ever made that didn't make any money. It didn't even get good reviews. What was worse, even after all that arm-waving on top of the cliff, *I* didn't get good reviews.

I was crushed, and when Raoul asked me to be in his next picture I meekly agreed to do whatever he asked in whatever he chose.

The story he chose was *Serenade,* one of our most ambitious productions. It was a Spanish story taken from Felin y Codina's *Maria del Carmen.* A new addition to Raoul's company wrote the screen adaptation. He was J. T. O'Donohue, a young Catholic boy recommended to Raoul by the Jesuit priests. A tall, quiet young man with a moustache, he had just graduated from Loyola University. He was Raoul's scenario writer for years.

Serenade was also the first time William Cameron Menzies, the art director, worked with Raoul. Raoul liked the young set designer. He had great imagination and wasn't at all Hollywoody. Bill was just becoming important in his field, and with a set designer of his caliber around, it was utterly ridiculous to read a newspaper clipping saying that I had designed the sets. The article even went so far as to say that back in my days with Reliance Majestic I was "constantly consulted by Mr. Griffith regarding his sets." Oh, the things you could read about yourself!

Serenade was a good picture, and a most profitable one for the Walsh-Cooper combine. It was a Raoul A. Walsh production, directed by Raoul Walsh, and starred George Walsh and Miriam Cooper (Walsh!). But there was a serious drawback to keeping all the money in the family. It was George. He was impossible to work with. I always dreaded a scene with George; he was such a lousy actor. He was like a stick.

Raoul knew my feelings and agreed with me. In our next production he gave me another leading man, the handsome young star Ralph Graves. The picture was *Kindred of the Dust,* based on a best-selling novel by Peter

B. Kyne, one of the most popular authors of the day. *Kindred of the Dust* was a real old-fashioned melodramatic story, full of tough, straightforward heroes, mean, vicious villains and long-suffering heroines. My costumes in this picture tell the story, all grubby homespun and calico. After reels and reels of hardship and fighting you are convinced that nobody can ever be happy. Then, gee whiz, the heroine—me, of course—has a baby and everything turns out all right. It turned out all right at the box office, too.

It's ironic that *Kindred of the Dust*, which was not my kind of movie, exacted a permanent sacrifice from me. In those days the studios used arc lights. They gave off a blue-white light of great intensity. And they were set up all around, in banks of five, in front and on the sides, even above you.

All that white-hot brilliance could cause severe injury to your eyes. We all knew the danger, but the cameramen and assistant directors were always warning us anyway. "Don't look at the lights, don't look at the lights!" they'd shout.

Being married to Raoul, I was even more conscious of the danger to my eyes. Raoul was almost fanatical about our eyes, his and mine. He has blue, blue eyes—like the actor Paul Newman—with long black lashes. He was always reminding me to protect my eyes. When we were on the train he'd say, "Don't put that towel on your face. You may get some disease."

When we were in California Pat would frequently drive us in our open car down the coast to Tijuana, where Raoul engaged in his favorite pastime, gambling. When cars approached us from the other direction, scattering dust and gravel from the unpaved roads, Raoul would put his hands over his eyes and shout, "Protect your eyes, protect your eyes!"

After all that, you'd think I'd have remembered to be

careful. But in one of the final scenes of *Kindred of the Dust* I had to hold the newborn baby and stare soulfully up to the heavens. I stared all right, right into a bank of lights. Once again I was not playing the part—I *was* the part. I just simply forgot about the lights. I looked too long at them—and burned my eyes.

I lay in a darkened room for two weeks, resting them. My doctor said I had granulated lids, but instead of being on the outside which is very common, mine were on the inside. Even today my eyes are frequently sore and I have to wear dark glasses, just like a movie star, in most every kind of light, even in private homes.

Strangely enough, after all his precautions, Raoul too had an eye accident. He was in an open car when the front wheels hit a jack rabbit. The rabbit's body hit the windshield and shattered it. A piece of glass flew into Raoul's eye. He has worn a black eye patch ever since.

Kindred of the Dust was the last film Raoul did on his own, and the last film in which we worked together. The big studios were taking over the industry. The day of the independent, all-powerful director was about over. In another year even Mr. Griffith would go to work for somebody else—Zukor of Famous Players–Lasky.

Times were changing and we had to change with them.

« 21 »

Now we were the beautiful people. During our six years of marriage we had gone from little nobodies in a grubby business to important people in the fourth largest industry in the country. Our friends were the people whose names were household words in every home across the country. We had everything—youth, good looks and money.

But no matter how successful we were, the very people who spent their own money to see us in the movie theaters looked down on us. They didn't want us for neighbors or friends. When Raoul and I lived in the fashionable area near the exclusive Wilshire Country Club, we couldn't get in the club. Neither could other picture people. We belonged to the Rancho Golf Club run by the Ambassador Hotel, which didn't mind taking our money.

Business people thought of us as gypsies. We couldn't even get insurance for our jewelry. One time I noticed Norma Talmadge wasn't wearing the ten-carat diamond her husband, Joe Schenck, had given her. I asked her why.

"Joe said he can't get it insured," Norma said. "Insurance companies won't insure picture people."

"Why not?" I asked.

"I don't know; I guess they think we're a bad risk,"

she said. "And there are all those bums hanging around the studios looking for jobs. Anyway, I can't wear all the beautiful things Joe gave me. I have to keep them put away."

"What do you do—have a safety deposit box?" I asked.

"Oh, no," she said airily. "I just put them all in a brown paper bag and then I put vegetables on top of them. You know, parsley, lettuce, things like that."

But if we didn't have status in our profession, we could have it in our dogs. Everybody had a dog, and every dog had a pedigree a mile long. You wouldn't be caught dead with a mongrel no matter how cute he was. Raoul and I didn't have just one pedigreed dog; we had *five* of them, huge Airedales with more papers than we had.

But we did feel inferior and self-conscious about our big salaries, and we tried to improve ourselves. We went all-out to buy culture. Georges Jomier, a cultured Frenchman, gave French lessons for a dollar an hour to picture people. Joe Schenck and I took them together. Joe, with his guttural accent, was a riot trying to talk through his nose like a Frenchman.

I took lessons in everything: golf, bridge, ballet, water skiing. I even had Jackie taking them. When he wasn't in school he was learning to ride and to play golf, too. When I went to Lake Placid for ice-skating lessons I took him with me.

We worked hard for our money and we enjoyed spending it. Raoul bought an $8,000 Locomobile for himself, and a Packard limousine for me. The Locomobile stayed in California, but the Packard made the trip across the country with us. I kept that car for years and years. I never learned to drive; I couldn't learn to save my soul. I was always stripping the gears. So Raoul insisted that I have a chauffeur. Having somebody ready to go whenever I wanted at a drop of a hat was almost as much fun as hitching rides had been five years before.

Having come from poor backgrounds, picture people loved huge ornate houses. Raoul and I wanted a permanent home, but we couldn't agree on where it would be, and for years we lived in hotels and apartments. I wanted to live in the city with its bright lights; I was terrified of the darkness in the country. The coyotes howling at night didn't help, either. But I knew Raoul wanted a home, a real home, with dogs and children and home-made bread.

We were living in the Beverly Hills Hotel when Raoul heard about a hunting lodge out in the hills. He dragged me out there to see it. I knew it was the kind of place he wanted—a dozen acres of wild country outside the city— and I said at least I'd look at it. It was a Tudor-type structure, yellow stucco trimmed in brown wood. It was a good buy, only $45,000, but it was so gloomy looking it gave me the willies. I told Raoul I just couldn't live in it.

Well, that gloomy-looking place became one of the most famous houses in the world. Douglas Fairbanks bought it, transformed it into a castle, and brought his bride, Mary Pickford, to Pickfair.

We kept looking and finally compromised on renting a house. Of course we did it Hollywood style—it was a pretentious mansion on West Adam Street, where the society people lived. We were surprised the owners rented it to us.

Everything we did, we did with extravagance. We bought expensive toys and clothes for Jackie. In suits with matching shirts and coats with fur collars, he was so handsome, I was always proud of him. When I wanted a white chiffon dress from Madame Frances I didn't get just one, I got two; then I had one to wear while the other was being cleaned. And all they cost was a mere $250 apiece.

Dresses were an extravagance, but furs were the love of my life. The first one I ever had was a white fox fur piece Raoul gave me. I wore it everywhere, even to the beach walking the dog. Pops, Raoul's father, used his wholesale tailoring connections to help me get a full-length ermine wrap. When I wore that coat, pulled tight around me with the big collar up around my face, I thought I was hidden from the world.

I used to love to hear Harry Richman, a popular singer of the day, sing some particular song—now I can't even remember the name of it. Whatever nightclub he was appearing in, I'd sweep into the club, wrapped from head to toe in my ermine, sit down at a table right on the dance floor, and wait for Harry to sing my song. When he finished I'd wrap my ermine around me again and leave. I honestly thought nobody noticed me.

Raoul was a clothes-horse, too. He was slender and handsome and wore his clothes well, and he knew it. Like Mr. Griffith, he was always impeccably attired on the set. But where Mr. Griffith wore pepper-and-salt business suits and those ridiculous high-button shoes, Raoul liked imported tweeds with a belted jacket and leather leggings. We used to do a lot of work on location in the desert and the woods, where the leggings were sometimes practical, but they also represented a kind of status uniform.

Unlike Mr. Griffith, who wore that awful, big-brimmed hat—sometimes a farmer's straw hat—to make his hawk nose look smaller, Raoul, like other directors of the day, often wore a tweed cap. He usually had it on backwards, with the visor pointed to the back so it wouldn't get in the way when he peered through the camera. Even when he was nowhere near the camera, however, that cap was on backwards. It was the mark of The Director.

Whatever he wore, it didn't come from Los Angeles. Like me, Raoul had to go to New York to have his suits tailored and his shoes hand made. Later his father, through his connections in the clothing industry, recommended a tailor in San Francisco, and Raoul went up there to have his suits made. That meant he could get a suit made to his liking in only two or three trips of two or three days.

Raoul's big extravagance was racehorses. He spent a fortune on them. One time he bought a beautiful little black filly and named her after me. I loved to sit in our box at Belmont Park and hear the crowd cheer Miriam Cooper around the track.

At a party one night I was introduced to an oil man who also liked racehorses. "I shouldn't even be talking to you, Mrs. Walsh," he said.

"Oh, really," I said. "Why?"

He told me that he had owned a horse for three years and the horse had never won a race. One day his trainer came to him and said he had a sucker from California who'd pay $15,000 for the horse.

"Well, I sold it," he went on, "and the sucker raced the horse at Agua Caliente. The damn nag came in first and won $50,000—the highest purse ever paid. It was a long shot, too, and the owner collected a lot more than that when his bets paid off. Then the horse broke his leg and the sucker collected the insurance.

"That sucker, Mrs. Walsh," the man told me sadly, "was your husband."

Raoul bought more horses and started breeding them. But his luck changed, and when he lost, he lost as big as he won. One time I was sitting in the box while Raoul went down to see his trainer. A man in the next box pointed at Raoul and told his friends: "See that man down there? He's the unluckiest gambler in the place. I bet he's lost millions."

Horses, houses, clothes . . . whatever picture people did, we did to excess. Even the time when Mama was sick and Raoul sent her flowers, he didn't send just one bouquet —he sent so many flowers you couldn't get in the lobby of Mama's hotel.

When Norma Talmadge bought a refrigerator for her mansion in Beverly Hills, she bought a hotel-sized freezer. The sides of beef hanging in it looked like dead bodies. The first time I saw it I said, "My God, Norma, it's an abattoir!"

"Call it anything you like," Norma said. "It's an icebox to me."

Newspaper columnists accused us of all kinds of loose living, drinking, drug addiction and adultery. Soon they had actual case histories to prove their insinuations.

One of the first stories to shock the country was the Fatty Arbuckle scandal. Fatty, who'd been one of Mack Sennett's Keystone Kops, was one of the most popular comedians in movies in 1921. I didn't like him myself. Even for a comedian he was particularly vulgar. But his comedies made money.

I've read that Fatty was an innocent victim of a tragic escapade involving a girl who was practically a whore. Well, that's not the way I heard it.

When Raoul and I were living at the Beverly Hills Hotel I got to know a guest in the hotel named Virginia Rappe. She was not at all like picture people. She didn't wear makeup, and wore her hair parted in the middle and drawn back into a knot at the nape of her neck. With her pale skin and dark eyes she was plain but beautiful. She dressed expensively but simply. I thought she was a summer tourist.

I first spoke to her in the hotel garden. She sat down beside me on a bench to drink in the beauty of the mountains and the lush green shrubbery. "It's so beautiful here," she said. "I've been here just a short time and I'm in love with the place already."

I thought she was a lovely sweet girl, probably going back to school in a few weeks. Then it turned out she was movie struck and was just getting started. Before long she and one of Mack Sennett's directors named Henry "Pathé" Lehrman were going together. He had to go on location, and to keep her from being lonely, he asked a young couple who were going to San Francisco for the Labor Day weekend to take her along with them.

I happened to be in San Francisco myself that weekend. It was in 1921, when Raoul was off on location and I was alone. Gerald "Cookie" Fitzgerald, a wealthy Texan who had business interests in California, and his wife Lillian asked me to drive up with them. Cookie was going to inspect some of the warehouses he owned up and down the coast. Lillian and I planned to shop.

We weren't involved in the Arbuckle mess, but Lowell Sherman, an actor who was a good friend of Raoul's and mine, was in the hotel suite when it happened. He told us the real story. He said they were having a party, and Fatty invited Virginia and her friends to come. Fatty had had his eye on Virginia for some time.

Fatty was already drunk. Virginia had to go to the bathroom, which of course was in the bedroom of the suite. Fatty saw her go, followed her into the bedroom, and locked the door. Not long after Lowell said he heard screams coming from the bedroom.

"He's killing me, he's killing me," Virginia was crying.

Lowell and the others pounded on the door, but Arbuckle wouldn't open it. Somebody called the hotel manager. He came up and shouted to Fatty that if he didn't open the door he was going to break it down. Fatty opened the door and came out. "She's all right," he said. "She's just drunk."

Virginia was lying half on, half off the bed, her dress halfway up her body, writhing in agony. Fatty had raped her, falling on her with his huge body. She died four days later of a rupture of an internal organ and peritonitis.

In his official statement to the police Lowell told an

entirely different story. He exonerated Fatty and implied that Virginia was drunk. But that wasn't what he told us privately. I think Lowell was bought off. In fact, I'm sure of it.

Fatty was acquitted, but it took three trials to do it. I and most of the people I knew at the time thought he was guilty. Anyway, it was the end of Fatty Arbuckle. Audiences threw eggs and tomatoes at the screen when his pictures were playing. Club women picketed the theaters showing his pictures, and civic groups demanded that his pictures be banned. Some cowboys in Wyoming shot up the screen of a theater showing a Fatty Arbuckle comedy, took the film outside the theater and burned it.

Leaders of the movie industry decided they had better do something before the industry was permanently damaged. They hired Will H. Hays, former postmaster general in Warren G. Harding's cabinet, as president of Motion Picture Producers and Distributors of America. He was the sole judge of Hollywood's morality. President Harding, who had fathered an illegitimate child himself, was certainly a good one to find a judge for Hollywood's morals.

One of the first things Hays did was to ask Adolph Zukor, whose company, Famous Players, released the Arbuckle films, not to distribute them. Although it cost Famous Players millions of dollars, Zukor agreed.

Shortly after, Raoul and I were guests at a party along with Joe Schenck and Norma Talmadge when Arbuckle turned up. Joe, who had Arbuckle under personal contract, said to Raoul, "That bastard. He'll never appear in another film, and I've got to pay him $5,000 a week for the rest of his life."

The dust had hardly settled on that case when William Desmond Taylor, the director, was murdered. In the investigation that followed, the police determined that both Mabel Normand and Mary Miles Minter knew him well. They found a nightgown belonging to Miss Minter and torrid love letters from her in Taylor's house. Mabel Normand was the last person to see him alive. Both were eventually exonerated, but not until after a lot of dirty linen was exposed.

Famous Players was involved in this scandal, too. Zukor had spent a lot of money on Mary Miles Minter. He hoped that she could take the place of Mary Pickford, who had left him for more money at First National. It was money down the drain, for after Taylor's murder Mary Miles Minter was through.

I was sorry for both her and Mabel Normand. Mabel had been kind to me that day when I, a scared teenager, went before a movie camera for the first time. She wasn't my type, as she was tough and dirty-talking, but all those girls who did comedy were tough. And at the time of the Taylor scandal she already had troubles enough. She was tubercular and alcoholic. She was always in and out of sanitariums. One time while we were living at the Ambassador Hotel I had the grippe and couldn't go to the Tuesday night dance. Mae Marsh and Norma Talmadge came up to visit me. Raoul went out for a while but he left some whisky on the bureau in case anybody wanted a drink.

We were sitting there, talking, when Mabel came in. She sat quietly for a while, then went into the bathroom. She was in there a long time. When she came out she whirled around the room, dancing and singing. Then, with her back to the mirror on the bathroom door, she flicked up her skirt and whooped, "My ass is open to the world."

We all looked at each other. "What's the matter with her?" I whispered to Norma. "She couldn't get a drink in there. How could she get so high just going to the bathroom?"

"I think she gave herself a shot while she was in there," Norma whispered back.

Apparently in addition to everything else, she was on drugs. She was so far gone by the time of the Taylor murder that I doubt if she could have made it back anyway, but after that she didn't have a chance.

Not long after this scandal, Wallace Reid, the popular leading man, died from drug addiction. Wally's death was doubly shocking, for he specialized in playing clean-cut American youths. He was blond and good-looking and an unusually fine actor.

One night, while we were working on *Evangeline*, he visited me on the set. He was no longer the happy smiling young man of *The Birth of a Nation* days; now he was vague and jittery. While we talked I drank cup after cup of coffee from the big agate pot simmering over a sterno near me.

"Why do you swill all that coffee?" he asked.

"How else can I stay awake?" I said. "We've been working since nine this morning and it's nearly midnight now."

"Those slave drivers," he said. "They'll get their money's worth if they have to kill you doing it."

"I don't know about killing me," I said, "but they are killing this set first thing in the morning and we still have several scenes to do. I've got to keep going."

"Why don't you get my doctor to give you something to keep you going?" he asked. "It'll be better than drinking all that stuff."

Just then I was called to the set. "Don't forget to remind me to give you my doctor's phone number," hc called after me. But I did forget and so did he, thank God.

Months later I ran into him at the Rancho Golf Club. He and his wife were sitting at a table in the tap room. Wally was looking down at the table. When he looked up at me I was too shocked by his appearance to speak. His deep blue eyes were dull and long creases lined his sunken cheeks. His jacket hung on him.

When he died all Hollywood was sad. It all seemed so

senseless. And then Olive Thomas, the beautiful Follies girl who married Jack Pickford, committed suicide on her honeymoon. We had all hoped that his marriage to Olive might make a new man out of Jack. He was a worthless drunk living off his sister, though he had a lot of charm and we all liked him. But after her death he was worse than ever.

All this was almost too much to believe. After the scandals, the Hays office had producers insert a morals clause in every contract. From then on if a player was merely accused of some immorality it was enough to end his career. Nobody even waited for proof.

The power of Will Hays and his successors continued on into the fifties, when the U.S. Immigration Department barred Ingrid Bergman from the United States after she gave birth to a child fathered by Roberto Rossellini, the Italian director, before she was married to him. How strange that all seems in this day of explicit sex on the screen, which is made for the same class of people who threw rotten eggs fifty years ago.

The people who took dope or drank too much were usually the top names of the day. They were the hot properties with tremendous box-office appeal. The high moguls wanted to make all the money they could from these stars while the public loved them. After all, these stars were just so many hula hoops to them, a fad to be pushed as hard as possible.

The producers worked their stars until they were ready to drop. People like Wally Reid and, later, Judy Garland started taking drugs to keep awake to finish a picture. And then there would be another picture, and another pill, until it was too late. Their popularity would wane, and the demand for their pictures would end. But by then they were hooked on the pills.

« 22 »

Raoul and I were never driven to dope, and we managed to remain fairly stable, but our life as picture people put many strains on our marriage. One was the shift in our positions. When we were first married I was the star, the one Raoul asked to help him get a job with Griffith and then bigger pictures with Fox.

Then Raoul became the star. He was Raoul A. Walsh, of R. A. Walsh Productions. At parties it was Raoul everybody wanted to talk to. Every day at our house was like Christmas. Every mail brought something: flowers, elaborate and expensive ash trays of rose quartz and jade, and many other imaginative presents. One Chinese actor sent me a beautiful hand-embroidered pink silk kimono from China which I still have.

"Oh, isn't it wonderful the way people love us," I said to Raoul. "And just think, we don't even know them."

"Wonderful, hell," Raoul said. "These guys think if they give *you* a present, I'll give *them* a job."

They not only sent me presents, they followed us around. Whenever I left Los Angeles for New York everybody would come to the train station to see me off. You'd have thought I was going to Europe forever.

Raoul Walsh, the director, and I were married for years.
You can see why he was irresistible to women.

Mae Marsh and I
the filming of The
of a Nation. Don't
look prim and pro

This picture of M
was taken in the l
days shortly after
she was married.

Here I am with Pat, Mike and my
beloved white fox scarf, all presents
from Raoul. I wore the fur day
and night, winter and summer.

Raoul and I had many happy ti
together. This was one of them.

The reasons why I wanted to re[tire]
from films: Bobby, Raoul and J[ackie]

The occasion: I was off to New York for a shopping trip.
You'd have thought I was leaving forever. Left to right,
Lena Bencini, one of my rich Texas friends; my brother
Gordon and his wife and daughter; Jackie; Mama; me; Bobby;
Raoul; May McEvoy and her mother, and Carole Lombard.

Aren't we the beautiful people? Unfortunately, the car was owned by the studio and the house was rented.

I got so mad at this lady, a countess no less, that I tore up the picture she gave Raoul. Here she is with her husband, the Earl of Lanesborough; Raoul on the left, Charlie Chaplin and J. Warren Kerrigan, a popular leading man, on the right.

All my girl friends wanted to meet Doug Fairbanks. He'd always find a minute and pose with them. Raoul and I are at either end. This was taken on the set of The Thief of Bagdad.

Doing what I like best—playing golf.

Pierre and I in 1968.

Jackie and I. Jackie was the first boy we adopted.

But all this attention for me was because I was Mrs. Raoul Walsh, wife of a famous director. I had thought that was what I wanted, but I guess it wasn't. I had never liked making movies, but I did like everything else about the movie industry—the money, the glamor, the travel to offbeat places.

In Hollywood, a honky-tonk town I always hated, I was either Mrs. Walsh or just another pretty young woman who played leading roles in movies. But in my hometown 3,000 miles away I was Miriam Cooper, Hollywood star, and called the most beautiful brunette in New York. Everybody loved me and told me how wonderful I was. All my life I wanted people to love me; in New York they did, and whenever I was there I never wanted to leave.

I was invited everywhere in New York. The bright lights of this big city shone just for me. I went there at every opportunity—to see Mama, to shop, to go to the doctor. While Raoul was cutting and editing *Kindred of the Dust,* I left for New York once more. When he finished he joined me there. I could see he was worried about something. One night we were having dinner alone and he told me what it was: he didn't think he loved me anymore.

The thought that Raoul didn't love me didn't send me to the kitchen for carbolic acid this time. Rather, it brought to the surface something I'd obviously been pushing down into my subconscious—I wasn't so sure about my feelings for him, either. When we were working together we were happy together, but when we weren't or when we were apart, we had problems. And this time we had been apart several weeks.

We discussed it, but we really didn't get to the heart of the matter. Anyway, Raoul and I had been married six years and were good Catholics. Divorce was out of the question. We agreed we'd give ourselves a little time, and see what happened.

Another part of our problem was that I didn't want to live in California. I missed Jackie, but he was busy, too, with school and his own friends. So when Raoul went back, I stayed in New York. At the station, as I said good-by to him, Raoul suddenly said, "I have a feeling I won't see you for a very long time." I told him that was silly, that I'd follow him in a couple of weeks, and as soon as he was ready to work on another picture, I'd be ready too.

But his feeling was right. For as the days, then weeks, went on, no call came for me to work on another picture with him. There was no picture to make. R. A. Walsh Productions wasn't doing a damn thing. I was annoyed with Raoul, though I shouldn't have been. I've always lived in a world of people and everyday things. Things like the national economy and politics never meant much to me. I've never voted in my life—I never met anybody who ran for president, and how could I vote for someone I didn't know? I can't believe what they say in the newspapers; I learned not to believe what my press agents said about me, so why should I believe what some candidate's press agent says about him?

Anyway, I didn't know that there was a big depression in 1921 and that it raised hell with the picture business. Many theaters closed, and the rest were half empty. With no money coming in, a lot of studios were dark. Directors were working as extras in what few pictures were being made.

And they were mostly made by the big companies run by businessmen who could get both financial backing and national distribution. Raoul was no businessman. He was a capable hard-working director with a gambling streak who wanted to be a big wheel in the industry, and that was all. As an independent producer he'd been lucky in good times, but in bad times he, like most others, was squeezed out of business by the high moguls with their big companies and theater chains. R. A. Walsh Productions had no capital to make new pictures—we'd spent it—and no chain of theaters to show them in if we made them. Our distributor, First National, was in trouble, too.

And so our company just died. We had enough money put away to keep up a front, Raoul and Jackie and Theresa in a rented house in Los Angeles and me in the Plaza. Raoul kept busy, but it was the worst kind of work—looking for work.

I didn't know the real situation in Hollywood, and I was happy in New York. By an ironic twist of fate, it was Raoul's brother George who introduced me to the people who kept me away from Raoul. George, a bachelor once more, was dating Leanne Carrera, Anna Held's daughter. Anna Held was the famous comedienne who had been married to Florenz Ziegfeld. Now she was dying of a bone-softening disease in the Sherry-Netherland Hotel across the street from the Plaza where I was staying. George brought Leanne over to see me. She introduced me to a theatrical crowd. In the group was Archie Selwyn, the theatrical producer who, with his brother Edgar and Sam Goldfish, had formed Goldwyn Pictures Corporation.

I liked Archie. He was short and ugly, with a pock-marked face and a big nose, but he was a lot of fun. While I was at the Plaza, Archie would call me from the lobby and say: "This is the police. Get those men out from under the bed. We're coming up to raid the joint."

Archie had a big house up near the Westchester Country Club. On weekends we'd all go up to visit him. One time I said to him, "Archie, you like golf so much and you live so close to the club, why don't you join it?"

I didn't realize the club didn't take Jews and I hadn't remembered that Archie was one anyway. He let out a big laugh. "How in the hell do you expect me to walk in, Miriam? Backwards?"

On these weekends Archie always invited several other men who were in the selling part of the picture business, and there were lots of young chorus girls around for them.

"What are you men doing with all these cute Irish girls?" I asked Archie. "I think you brought them out here just to sleep with them."

"What else are little Irish girls good for?" Archie said.

He was always good for a laugh, and I enjoyed him, but I never dreamed anyone would think we were more than friends. Not long after Raoul went back to California I heard from a friend on the coast that Raoul had a girl out there. I wrote him an accusing letter and told him I was not coming back.

He wrote me that if he believed everything he had heard about me and Archie Selwyn he could accuse me of things, too, and it would mean the end of our marriage. I couldn't understand how he could think there was anything going on between Archie and me—Archie was a married man—but I decided if people could suspect that Archie and I were having an affair, I could give Raoul the benefit of the doubt.

We made up through the courtesy of Western Union, but our marriage was still shaky. Then Archie offered me the lead in a production of one of his stock companies in Springfield, Massachusetts. I had once said that I wished I'd had experience on the stage. I thought it would make me a better actress.

I didn't think Raoul would mind my taking the job because Archie wouldn't be there. And even if I were in California I wouldn't be seeing Raoul; Sam Goldwyn had asked him to look over a script. It was a lucky break to have something to work on, although he'd be doing it for Goldwyn Productions, not R. A. Walsh. Raoul wrote that the story, called *Lost and Found on a South Sea Island*, was terrible, but Goldwyn's scenario department knew it and they were letting him improve it. He thought he'd eventually get a good picture out of it. He'd be scouting locations, casting, and generally busy as hell. There wouldn't be much time for me.

So I took advantage of Archie's offer and became a stage actress for the first and only time in my life. I don't remember the name of the play, but my performance wasn't very memorable either. The qualities that made me a good screen actress—my expressive eyes, my quiet style—were worthless on the stage. The stage did not provide big close-ups. I had to exaggerate my emotions, wave my arms, speak lines for the first time in my life at the top of my voice, and my face was the size of a golf ball to the people in the rear of the theater. Those two weeks were enough. I decided I was no stage actress and it was perfectly all right with me.

Raoul was still working on the script for Goldwyn, but he wouldn't go on salary until he started shooting. All our money was going out; nothing was coming in. Even though I was spending money like water myself, I was worried about our idleness. We were still young, and we had a reputation, but I knew it wouldn't last forever.

In the years before, whenever directors would come up with a role which called for my type—sweet and innocent, but dignified—they'd call me, just in case. "You'll love this part," they'd say. "It's perfect for you."

I'd always said either that I was working for Raoul or that I didn't want to work at all, which was true. I wanted to stay home, be a wife and mother, and maybe play a little golf. So they stopped asking me.

Raoul's business manager at the time must have known our financial picture better than we did. He heard about a picture a small company, the D. M. Film Corporation—which I never heard of before or since—was preparing to shoot. They were going to do it in Detroit. God knows why—maybe they had a financial angel there. There was a part in it for me. It would only take a few weeks, and would pay $650 a week.

I didn't want to work in the first place, and $650 was a lot less than I was used to getting, but I still thought about it seriously. Raoul was working, although without pay, Jackie was in school all day, and we could use the money. Even the title was apt—*Is Money Everything?*

Raoul wrote me to go ahead and do it. "But be sure and get your salary every week. There are a lot of gyp companies around today."

I headed for Detroit. About the same time, oddly enough, George Walsh signed to play opposite Mary Pickford in *Rosita,* the disaster Mary made with the German director she had imported, Ernst Lubitsch. With the three of us working for three separate companies, it marked the final dissolution of the family company.

If the thought had lingered in the back of my mind that I was no longer in love with Raoul, Detroit drove it out. I missed him and Jackie terribly. The loneliness was unbearable. I wrote long letters to him, pouring my heart out.

"I am so tired," I wrote him early in June. "We have been on location thirty miles away every day since we started the picture. We leave at eight-thirty in the morning and do not get home until seven-thirty or eight o'clock at night. I feel too badly about your not writing to me to talk about it. Not even one letter have I received. I am quite sure you do not expect me to believe you care for me and I am fully convinced you have ceased to love me. I do not blame you. These are things which are not controlled by us."

My letter must have touched him. "My heart is breaking for you," he said. "If you tell me you are not coming back I will not live without you. Let me but have you in my arms and one day of love shall widen into eternity. Who knows the earth may crack tonight—or the Sun go down forever in his grave—Who knows tomorrow God will begin to finish the judgment of the world—and when it is all over find you sleeping in my arms."

Two days later I told him, "I guess after six years there is little doubt of whether people really belong to each other body and soul and I feel that as I always have, so I always shall be yours heart, soul and body. I love you so much, Daddy, wait for me . . ."

But the wait stretched out. The picture I was making was far behind schedule. The people I was working with were all very nice, but they were heavy drinkers. Norman Kerry, the leading man, drank up his salary almost as fast as he got it. Luckily he was married to a nice, rich woman.

I tried to hold on to my money. Someone offered me a bargain on two $1,000 Liberty Bonds and I bought them. Deducting the expenses of a maid, hotel and food, I was clearing $475 a week. I figured I'd have saved $3,000 by the end of the picture.

Raoul had his own plan for saving money. He had decided, and Goldwyn had agreed, to do *Lost and Found on a South Sea Island* in Tahiti, the romantic island in the South Pacific. The company would be gone about three months. It would be the first film Raoul would do without me since leaving Fox two years before. He hadn't seriously considered me for the leading lady's role; it wasn't my type and, besides, Sam Goldwyn wanted Pauline Starke, another of Mr. Griffith's protégées, to play the part.

Raoul looked forward to seeing this exotic part of the world, and, more important, he was eager to be working and getting paid. Further, all expenses on location would be paid by the company. We'd given up the big house we were renting and were living in hotels. The rest of Raoul's coterie could go with him, on company money. Jim Marcus and Gordon would go as his assistants and Jim O'Donohue would work on the scenario. Pat, the chauffeur, would go as an all-around handy man. Theresa, the cook, was the only person Raoul couldn't find a place for, but she agreed to take half salary while we were away.

Raoul wanted Jackie and me to go with him. The company would pay my expenses, he wrote, which would leave only Jackie's expenses for us to pay. We would all take the boat that sailed on July 4 and have a leisurely holiday. Raoul called me to talk it over.

"There's not much hope of finishing the picture before the boat leaves," I said. "We're very far behind now. We've been working until late at night every night and Sundays. The director says I am in every set in the picture and he can't do anything without me."

I didn't want to go anyway. For one thing I was an awful sailor. I was always seasick. "Why must you go so far away?" I asked. "Can't you get the same effects in Florida?"

"I've checked into it," he said, "but hell, I can't find anybody there who looks like a South Sea island native."

I finally gave in and told him I would follow on the August boat, but I still wasn't happy about the situation. I brooded over it, and then wrote him a bitchy letter.

I realize dear that you must go as no one knows better than I how badly we need the money. But above all you must make your pictures quickly. You are much too slow between pictures. Too slow getting started. Just think you have been out there five weeks and have not started and no salary yet. You simply must make the money while you can as it will not last forever and under the conditions you are not making much you know, with two pictures a year. Why don't you make it a point to try and make four pictures a year especially this year and at the end of the year you will have a nice little bankroll if you save it.

I didn't know how bad the situation was in Hollywood and I shouldn't have fussed at him. Fortunately I ended the letter on a different note. "I shall never stay away from my Daddy so long again. Good night sweet love."

Raoul and I needed to be together, away from pictures and picture people, but Tahiti! The idea scared me half to death. This was 1922, remember. People didn't just take off for such remote places then. Our cameraman in Detroit had been in Tahiti just the year before and told me white people contracted dreadful fevers and were laid up for weeks. I wrote Raoul to be sure to get injections before he left. I also told him I thought it was foolish to take Jackie: ". . . He may be very sick, not just seasick, but contract a fever."

But I knew that for the sake of our marriage I had to go. I wrote: "I will travel to the end of the earth to be with you."

And that's where I thought I was going, to the end of the earth. We finally finished *Is Money Everything?* It was such a horror I'm glad I don't remember any more about it. I hurried to San Francisco to get the August boat. Raoul had gone on, after persuading me to bring Jackie. I took him to Confession the day before we left and Holy Communion the morning of departure. I left all of my affairs in good order because I was sure I was going to die.

It took two weeks for the boat to get to Tahiti. Other passengers, going to New Zealand and Australia, would be on the boat twice as long. The food was terrible. There was no icebox to keep food from spoiling, so our meals consisted of fish—freshly caught every day—and potatoes. I love seafood, but not every day.

Aimee Semple MacPherson, the famous evangelist—the female Billy Graham of her time—was on board with her young son. He was about Jackie's age, but the two boys never played together. When I asked Jackie about it he said, "His mother won't let him play with me because my mother is an actress."

I thought that was a pretty un-Christian attitude and a cruel thing to say to a little boy.

On Sunday Mrs. MacPherson held services in the salon below deck. Everybody on the ship went, except me. While she was down there preaching, I sat up on deck, knitting, sitting where everybody could see me through the open door. The captain asked me if I wouldn't like to hear Mrs. MacPherson preach. "No, I would not," I said.

As the ship approached Tahiti, we could see its mountains jutting high into the sky. The island was surrounded by a still and beautiful blue lagoon and coral reefs. Waterfalls cut the mountainsides, falling to clear, deep pools where the natives did their bathing and washing. Bananas, mangoes, breadfruit and avocados were everwhere, along with pineapples and papayas and fish. Lush tropical flowers bloomed in fiery colors. It was the most magnificent place I had ever seen. Heaven can't be any better.

Raoul met us at the pier. I was so happy to see him that all our problems were forgotten. We had a comfortable bungalow and we enjoyed our life among those beautiful people.

The girls were so lovely with their long black hair hanging to their waists and bright flowers tucked behind one ear. Their beautiful round breasts were bare above their colorful *pareaus.* Here and there you could see a girl in a Mother Hubbard dress, evidence that the white missionaries were having their effect on the islanders. The missionaries changed their way of life and taught them that sex was a sin. To the Tahitians sex was as natural as eating and drinking. Their life was beautiful; the people never fought, all creatures on the island lived in harmony. There were no hungry Tahitians, no neglected old people, no abandoned children. Tahitians, the saying goes, take care of each other, and nature takes care of them all.

The big event on the island was the return of the pearl divers after six weeks at sea. The natives gathered around large bonfires on the beach. The few foreigners—people like us—sat on the *lanai* of the French Club sipping liqueurs. We all watched as the boats picked their way through the passage in the reefs. When they got to shore a dozen or more golden-brown young men and one lone Tahitian girl, who went on the voyage to take care of the men, jumped out. The crowd on the beach hugged them and everybody laughed and shouted and milled around. It was a beautiful sight.

Through the movies I learned to question things I had accepted as truths as a child. That is something making pictures on location did for me. I was able to see things for myself. In Arizona I saw how we treated the Mexican prisoners as compared to the white prisoners. In Albuquerque I saw the way we treated the Indians. And on Tahiti I saw the way the white missionaries were ruining the innocent natives. I came to the conclusion that the white man wasn't so hot.

The picture Raoul directed, *Lost and Found on a South Sea Island*, now shortened to *Lost and Found*, was the story of a dastardly white trader who almost ruins the life of a young girl and the man she loves. The climax has a Griffith-like chase with the girl's father rushing to rescue his daughter from the warring natives. And for that we had traveled thousands of miles to Tahiti. But, for us, it had been worth it.

« 23 »

There's nothing like a stay in Tahiti with salary and expenses paid and the view of topless native girls to rejuvenate a marriage. Raoul and I came home very much in love, and with $20,000 in the bank and more coming in as he cut the film.

We rented a house and settled down comfortably with Jackie, Theresa, Pat and the dogs. It had finally dawned on me that they all couldn't afford for me to retire yet again. But it didn't matter, for I was happy and I wanted to work. The industry was opening up and the phone began ringing again. I had so many offers I could afford to be choosy. Over the next several months I made five pictures, but the one I liked most was the first. It was for B. P. Schulberg Productions, My salary was $1,000 a week.

I liked Mr. Schulberg. He was a gentleman. Unlike the pants pressers and nickelodeon operators, he had a background as a newspaper reporter. He'd come into the movies as Adoph Zukor's first press agent and had quickly picked up a knowledge of business details, then had become a top executive with Paramount. Now he wanted to be an independent producer. With the big companies in the saddle in Hollywood the odds were against him, and indeed he did go bankrupt in 1925, but he gave it a good try.

The picture he wanted me for was called *The Girl Who Came Back*. It was a fitting title for me, as I'd been out of circulation for a while (the Detroit thing didn't count in Hollywood). The plot was one I'd done so many times I could do it again with my eyes shut. I'm a sweet innocent girl of course, but wouldn't you know, I unwittingly fall in with a bunch of gangsters and become a Fallen Woman. Of course somehow I wind up as the same sweet and innocent girl in the last reel.

The director was Tom Forman, who'd been a handsome leading man before taking up directing. It was a happy crew. I think one of the stories about me and the picture is interesting. It was included in a *Los Angeles Sunday Times* wrap-up piece about several stars who were supposed to be making a comeback—Mae Marsh, Blanche Sweet, Bessie Love, Theda Bara and me.

Once, long ago, when Griffith wanted a dark-eyed girl to express hurt pride, broken heart, in *The Birth of a Nation,* he picked Miriam Cooper out of a crowd of extras. She had come to California for her health, was delicate, thin, white, aristocratic looking.

Griffith broke her spirit, for he was cruelly harsh in his direction. He got the look that he wanted, and Miriam Cooper was made.

She started her starring career with Fox, but got some godawful stories. Besides which, Raoul Walsh, her husband-director, let her do about what she pleased in the pictures, which meant that she faced the camera every minute and chewed up the scenery. She failed.

She came near retiring from pictures altogether and devoting her life to her little adopted son. But the divine spark was there, after all, and she comes back most triumphantly and appropriately in *The Girl Who Came Back.*

In all that nonsense was a germ of truth. I did feel the divine spark and it *was* a minor triumph. The statement that Raoul let me do as I pleased was all wrong, of course, as was the reference to Griffith's cruelty. It's true that I knew more about playing my type of role than Raoul did, but the writer of the piece obviously hadn't been around when Raoul would make me do a scene over and over again.

"Let's do that scene one more time, Miss Cooper," he'd say. (Like Mr. Griffith, Raoul always tried to be formal, even with his wife.) And we'd do it again and again, with the camera grinding. With Mr. Griffith we'd rehearse a scene many times, though rarely on the actual set. But when the money came in we'd rehearse on the set, then burn up film in retakes until we got it right.

Actual direction on the set wasn't the important thing anyway. With nearly every director I ever worked with we'd talk about the character of the person I was playing before we ever thought of rehearsing. It might be at a party, or at lunch on the lot, or in a special meeting.

"What do you think about this part?" the director would ask. "What's she like?"

I'd think a minute, then say what I thought, he'd say what he thought, and we'd talk it over. By the time rehearsals began I knew exactly what kind of girl I was, who I was, and then I'd *be* her. Shooting the scene was easy after that, but a good director would still make sure that everything went right.

The leading man in *The Girl Who Came Back* was Gaston Glass, a quiet Frenchman who spoke with an intriguing accent. I loved to listen to him; it was a shame feminine movie audiences couldn't hear him.

I was in New York when *The Girl Who Came Back* opened at Grauman's Million Dollar Theater in Los Angeles. Raoul wired that the picture was "a wonderful personal triumph" for me, and that all the papers gave me a good review. "Makes me very happy," he said. "Schallert of the *Times* called me up especially to tell me how much he liked your work. Congratulations, dear."

Before the picture came out word got around that I gave a good performance. Mr. Schulberg asked me to do two more for him, and I also did two others for other companies, none worth mentioning. The third Schulberg movie, *The Broken Wing*, sticks in my memory for many reasons. For one, my old friend from Griffith days, Walter Long, was the villain, only this time I didn't kill him as I did in *Intolerance*. This time it was the Secret Service who foiled a foul plot Walter concocted. Despite all his villainy on the screen, Walter was actually a genial, gentle man and I enjoyed working with him.

For another, this was the first time I refused to do what the director asked me to do. The title, *The Broken Wing*, refers to an airplane that has crashed into the house I live in. The director, Tom Forman, told me to get into the airplane. I refused. I was afraid it might start off with me in it.

"Just sit in it," Tom said. "We'll take your picture and you can get out."

"No," I said, "I'm too scared to even sit in an airplane." It was almost fifty years before I did ride in one.

What I remember most vividly about *The Broken Wing* was Tom Forman himself. He'd become a lush. He was always drunk, even when he was supposed to be working. Some days he didn't know what was going on, and he didn't care. He let the picture get completely out of hand. I knew there wasn't much hope for the film, but I hoped at least I could salvage something through my performance, for my own self-respect if for nothing else.

My big scene came on the last day of shooting. I saw Tom the night before. "Please don't drink anymore," I pleaded with him. "Please let's do this last scene right."

But he paid no attention to me. The next day he was still drunk. He just staggered around, not knowing what was going on and not caring. I tried very hard, but nothing went right. We made one take and I waited for him to do it again. Instead he just waved at the cameraman to pack up and shuffled off to get a drink. I called after him but he didn't even turn around. Maybe he was afraid he'd fall down if he did. That was the end of *The Broken Wing*.

It was also the end of Miriam Cooper.

When the picture opened in Hollywood I went with some friends. When it was finally over, I was in tears. I'd never been so embarrassed. It was not only the worst movie I'd ever been in, it was the worst movie I'd ever seen.

After *The Broken Wing* I never wanted to make another picture. After all the times I thought I'd retired for good and then came back to films, I finally wound up my career in a stinker made by a drunk. What a hell of an ending.

« 24 »

As my movie career was ending like a thrown-away whisky bottle, Raoul's was beginning again with a new spark.

During good years and bad he had kept up his interest in sports and in his own physical fitness. He liked to work out at the athletic club. Another sports nut in Hollywood, the number-one physical fitness addict of them all, was Douglas Fairbanks. Doug was also the number-one actor in Hollywood. From that bouncing stage actor Mr. Griffith had tried to slough off on Mack Sennett, Doug had risen to a height in popularity and wealth that far surpassed Mr. Griffith, or anyone else. After years of making buckets-ful of money in four-reel formula movies, he'd taken a chance on big spectacles, and it had paid off. His *Robin Hood* was acclaimed the best picture of 1922. As actor, co-owner of United Artists and, with his wife Mary Pickford, social leader of the picture colony, Doug was at the top of the heap.

He and Raoul used to work out together. They were a great pair. Doug always called Raoul "Irish." One day he asked Raoul over to his own private athletic club—track, gym, steamroom and pool—at the United Artists studio. They ran around the track together.

Without breaking stride, Doug suddenly said, "Irish, I'm going to make a picture and I want you to direct it."

That one sentence got Raoul started on a glittering production involving hundreds of people and thousands of dollars.

The picture was *The Thief of Bagdad,* a marvelous fantasy. Raoul was very excited about it. He'd been making melodramas for so long he loved the idea of doing a fantasy.

When he brought the script home I couldn't believe the size of it. It was enormous. Everything was worked out to the last detail. "I guess you won't be writing what you're going to do tomorrow on the back of some scrap of paper," I said.

"Hell, no," Raoul said. "These guys put charts up on the wall telling you what to do each day."

The old days of working in a casual manner were just about over. It was happening everywhere. The men who supplied the money wanted directors to stick to production schedules and produce. Doug's company worked on schedule, but the schedule was flexible. Doug would frequently decide to take off on another project for a few days, but there was plenty for everybody else to do.

Working for Fairbanks, who had friends and relatives of his own, Raoul wasn't able to give jobs to all the old gang. I was automatically out of it even if I had wanted to be in it. Doug didn't want established recognizable people in the picture. The female lead was an unknown girl named Julanne Johnston.

Raoul did take some of the old company with him. Jim Marcus and my brother Gordon went along. There was no place for Jim O'Donohue, as Doug's scenario writer was somebody Raoul could neither hire nor fire—Elton Thomas. Hint: Doug's real name was Douglas Elton Thomas Ulman. Raoul's brother George was in Italy, working on *Ben-Hur,* before Louie Mayer fired him.

William Cameron Menzies, our set designer on *Serenade* and *Kindred of the Dust,* went along as art director. Doug is sometimes given credit for discovering Bill's fine talent, but he had already been discovered by Raoul and was considered the best designer in the business. He's best remembered for his Academy Award-winning sets for *Gone with the Wind.*

Raoul and Doug showed Bill the script and sent him home to design the sets. When he had finished his designs he brought them into the studio. Doug, who kept a close watch on all parts of production, looked the sets over with Raoul. They were just what Doug wanted; they looked like a fairyland. The solid buildings that made up the city of Bagdad seemed to be hanging in the air. The illusion was created by painting the foreground and streets a glossy black that reflected the light. You could see your reflection in the gleaming surface. The Crystal City, which was supposed to be under the sea, looked mystical and unreal.

In this picture Fairbanks played the part of Ahmed, a notorious crook who tries to reform when he falls in love with a beautiful princess. He performs many magical tricks: flying up staircases on a magic carpet, climbing a magic rope right straight up in the air and, most amazing of all, producing a whole army from a handful of dust. This was trick photography at its best.

People were always visiting the set; Doug loved to perform before an audience. Doug and Mary had brought respectability to the movie colony; nobility, society people, politicians, as well as people like me stood around gawking. Several times I took a group of movie-struck girl friends out to the studio and introduced them to Doug. They were so excited they could hardly talk. We all stood around having our pictures taken with him. When the picture taking was over, Raoul would get him back to work.

On days when Doug was doing his stunts on the outside of the mythical castle, he'd send buses into downtown Los Angeles to pick up hundreds of people to come out and watch. Sometimes they were treated to more action than they'd anticipated.

To get the rough-looking characters he needed for some of the scenes, Raoul had gone to the obvious places— third-rate speakeasies in Los Angeles. The bums he picked up looked the part, all right—they *were* the part. They'd get into brawls on the set and Raoul would have to get in them himself to break them up.

At the end of the day Raoul would meet with his assistants and cameramen to set up the next day's shooting. Our house had a big, comfortable study, but Raoul rarely used it; he preferred to work in our large bedroom. He would lie on the chaise longue and his photographers and writers would sit on the French chairs and work at the little marble-topped tables.

While the men worked, I'd sit over in a corner knitting or rolling my stockings into little piles. I always liked my bureau drawers to be neat.

The men would usually have a drink while they were working, but Raoul seldom did. Raoul liked to give the impression that he didn't drink. When we had guests he'd fix drinks for everybody but he never had a drink himself. One night I went into our bedroom for a handkerchief and I saw him in the closet taking a big swig from a bottle. I never let on that I saw him but I often wondered about it. Why sneak a drink? In any case, alcohol was never Raoul's problem.

Usually the men would stay on for dinner; we rarely ate alone. Sometimes a writer or an assistant director or an actor would stay on to discuss changes. These meetings lasted far into the night.

Working on a Fairbanks picture was hard work, but it was also fun. Doug loved practical jokes and was always pulling them on his friends.

After the day's shooting, when they weren't conferring with the others, Raoul and Doug would go to the steamroom and discuss the picture. Charlie Chaplin usually joined them. They'd all take a steam bath, then jump into the pool to cool off.

One day Raoul and Doug called the ice company and had huge chunks of ice put into the pool. When Charlie joined them in the steamroom the three of them sat around for a while. Charlie got restless, stood up, and said, "Well, I think I'll cool off now."

He ran out of the steamroom and jumped into the icy pool. He let out a scream and flailed the water getting back to the side while Raoul and Doug laughed and pounded each other.

Speaking of Charlie, we had known him in less boisterous days. When Raoul and I were first married, we lived in a duplex at the bottom of a hill. His mansion was on top. He was already a comedy star and we were nobodies then. We used to see him driving up the hill past our house in his big chauffeur-driven limousine. The girls in the car were always teen-agers.

Four years later we were living at the Ambassador and Charlie discovered us. He was lonely. His first marriage to Mildred Harris, one of the beautiful extras in *Intolerance*, had been a brief unhappy one. They had parted shortly after their baby died. He was then the most successful and sought-after comedian in the world but he was alone and unhappy. He was also gloomy over his mother. He was trying to get her into the United States but was having difficulty because she had been in mental institutions in England for some time.

It was a tragic, unhappy time for Charlie and he showed it. Every Tuesday night Raoul and I would go to the Coconut Grove for dinner and dancing. Charlie would come in and join us. Everybody in the place would be having a good time, laughing and dancing. But not us. We had to sit there with Charlie, who was depressed and morose. I couldn't stand it. I was young and gay and I wanted to have fun.

I was so desperate one night that when Rupert Hughes, Howard Hughes' uncle and a well-known writer, asked me to dance I jumped up and went to the dance floor with him. Hughes, unlike his tall and skinny nephew, was short and fat.

He was also a chaser: when he danced with me he held me so I could feel everything all up and down his body. I was embarrassed and mad but I couldn't say anything. As I walked back to my table the girls all laughed and said, "How'd you enjoy your dance with Rape Hughes?"

At least Charlie never did anything like that. He was always a perfect gentleman when I knew him. I don't even remember him ever swearing. I liked Charlie. He could be very entertaining when he was happy. But most of the time he was unhappy. He would call us or visit us at the worst possible times.

At four o'clock one morning the phone rang. Raoul answered. "Hello, Charlie," he said. He listened a minute, then said, "Oh, hell, Charlie. . . . Okay, sure, I'll come take a walk with you."

He got out of bed and started dressing. "Charlie's depressed," he said. "I'll go walk on the beach with him awhile."

"My God, Raoul," I said. "It's four o'clock in the morning. You've got to be at the studio ready to work in a few hours."

"Charlie's unhappy and he needs me," Raoul said. I thought Raoul was nuts but he went.

Other times Charlie would come to the house after work. Late one afternoon he came in before Raoul did. He looked even more depressed than usual and I didn't want to put up with him. I deliberately tried to get rid of him. I went into the bedroom and sat down in the middle of the floor and began putting polish on my toenails. I couldn't think of anything much more disgusting than that, but it didn't bother Charlie. He followed me into the bedroom and sat there looking miserable until Raoul came in.

When Charlie's mother finally was permitted into the country he put her up in a lovely cottage at the beach. An elderly couple took care of her. Every Sunday Charlie would take his mother for an automobile ride. Once she was settled some of his depression left him, and we didn't see as much of him until Raoul began working with Doug on *The Thief of Bagdad*.

The Thief was scheduled to be a long picture—fifteen reels—and what with all the special effects, we knew at the beginning that it would take a long time. (It turned out to be eight months.) I don't remember how much Raoul was making but it was plenty, and it would keep coming. I had been putting away nearly all of the $1,000 a week I'd been receiving.

Now at last we could have a house of our own. We bought a ten-room pink stucco house on Plymouth Boulevard in a fashionable section of Los Angeles. I'd have loved any house of my own after all those years, but this was perfect. It was truly my dream house. Now that our bank account was healthy again, I spent all my time—and money—furnishing it.

I bought Oriental rugs and seventeenth-century prints in New York. I spent hundreds of dollars on tablecloths and napkins from McCutcheon's, and thousands on hand-chased silver from Gorham. I drove to San Francisco to get Chinese lamps with silk shades and Oriental antiques from Gumps. Our furniture and an ornate French clock came from a rich young couple who had moved to California, then found they didn't like the place. Before going back to Boston they had sold all their furniture. I spent a lot of money for these things, but they are works of art today.

Our Japanese gardener kept the grounds looking like a fairyland and the house full of freshly cut flowers.

At last we had a permanent home and could live like a real family. We even started negotiations with the New York Foundling Hospital for another child. He was a tough, swaggering kid from Hell's Kitchen. The people at the hospital told us that he might not work out, but Raoul wanted to give him a chance.

Although it was my idea to adopt children, Raoul always went along with it. I don't think he cared whether we had children or not, but he let me do whatever I pleased. Once we had them Raoul liked them and was a good companion to them whenever he had the time.

We called the second child Stewart, my mother's maiden name. Raoul used to mimic him perfectly, walking in sideways, like he was looking for a fight. Jackie soon began complaining that Stewart was picking on him. Jackie was such a sweet, well-mannered boy with us that we sympathized with him, and reluctantly returned Stewart to the orphanage. In the light of what happened later, we may have made a mistake. In Stewart's place we took another good-looking fair-haired boy we named Bobby. Bobby worshipped Jackie and did everything he did. We were pleased about this then, but if we had known what "everything" was, we'd have been furious.

For a while Raoul and I were happier than we had been for years. There were friends and picture people around all the time. Often we'd go over to visit Doug and his wife, Mary Pickford. Pickfair, home of the two most glamorous people in the world, was more famous than the White House or Buckingham Palace. One night Mary and Doug invited us to a party for Lord and Lady Mountbatten.

Everybody who was anybody in Hollywood was there. Most picture people had very humble beginnings and to hobnob with people with titles was all the rage. The Mountbattens probably felt the same way about Doug and Mary and the rest of the movie world.

The women wore gorgeous gowns and all their jewels, and all the men looked elegant and prosperous. At such a party you'd expect the champagne to be flowing, but it was a dry evening. As long as I knew her, Mary never served a drop of anything alcoholic.

Members of the nobility were always visiting Doug and Mary. Like everyone else I was properly impressed with them, but the English lady who made the biggest impression I never even met. I was in New York buying up the town when Raoul wired me that Doug was on a camping trip and he was entertaining their houseguests, the Earl and Countess of Lanesborough. "Charming people," he called them in his telegram.

I didn't think anything of it then, but when I got back to California I heard from friends that the charming Countess had quite a case on Raoul. She'd show up on the set early every morning and coo at him. It got to the point that she was distracting not only Raoul, but everybody on the set. Doug was annoyed over the delay she was causing, but he could hardly be rude to his houseguest. From what I heard Raoul had had enough of the Countess, too.

One day they ran into technical problems on the set and called off the shooting. The Countess practically insisted that Raoul take her to the beach. He had no excuse to get out of it, but he whispered to Doug that he was going to take her out and drown her. Later that day Doug got a call from someone who said he was at the Santa Monica hospital.

"We have a lady here in serious condition," the man

said. "She says she's your houseguest and somebody threw her off the pier."

Then he started chuckling and Doug recognized the voice of one of his practical joker friends.

I heard the story and laughed politely. But if Raoul hadn't drowned her, what *had* he done? I was suspicious and jealous. And when I found a portrait of the Countess with a flowery inscription to Raoul I tore it up and burned the pieces.

In spite of such episodes I was almost as sorry as Raoul when he finally finished work on the picture. It was not only stimulating but financially rewarding. I remember one of the investments Raoul made with the money he made on *The Thief*. He and Frank Hutton, the New York investment banker, bought a mountain together. Raoul put up $24,000, and a year later sold his half to Will Rogers, the cowboy comedian, for $75,000.

We remained good friends with Frank. His wife had died and their daughter lived with an aunt and uncle in Santa Barbara. Frank would come out to see her, and bring her with him when he came to see us. I know it sounds hard to believe, but at that time Barbara Hutton, who became the beautiful, thin, sad-eyed and much-married millionairess, was a plain fat little girl.

In the meantime, *The Thief of Bagdad* opened at the Liberty Theatre in New York to the accompaniment of Oriental drums, Oriental songs, burning incense, perfumed air and magic carpets. During intermission the ushers, in Arabian costumes, brought Turkish coffee to all the ladies in the audience.

Mama, Lenore, Bessie Waters and several other women went with me to the premiere. After the performance we wired Raoul, who was in California, that it was marvelous and we loved it.

The Thief of Bagdad was chosen one of the ten best

pictures of the year. One of the other ten was *Isn't Life Wonderful?*, D. W. Griffith's latest picture. Griffith went to see Raoul's picture, in the same theater in which *The Birth of a Nation* had been so successful almost ten years earlier.

« 25 »

After the success of *The Thief of Bagdad,* Raoul was more in demand than ever. A lot of people thought he was a genius. He had offers from many companies. Finally he signed with the man who had tried to get him almost ten years earlier, Jesse Lasky of Famous Players-Lasky. Raoul worked with many famous stars of the day—Wallace and Noah Beery, Tyrone Power (the father, not the son) and Ricardo Cortez. One of the most famous was the Polish star of German films, Pola Negri. Raoul was assigned to direct her in Somerset Maugham's *East of Suez,* with Edmund Lowe as her co-star.

Pola was one of the most fascinating women I ever met, and one of the most striking. The effect of her jet-black hair, large blue eyes and white skin was startling.

Pola was between love affairs, and she was lonely. Raoul brought her home for dinner practically every night. After dinner we'd play mah-jongg for a few hours. At midnight Raoul would drive down to the delicatessen and get the kind of food that Pola liked—small raw fish floating in sour cream was one of her favorites.

Pola without a man was like California without sunshine, and it wasn't long before she had one. He was Rod LaRocque, the handsome leading man who later married

Vilma Banky. She kept on coming to dinner with us, bringing him along, only now instead of playing mah-jongg after dinner, Pola and I would go up to my bedroom and she would cry on my shoulder. She told me Rod was mean to her. It didn't surprise me. I always thought he was crude. Mama would have said he was common as dirt.

Then suddenly it wasn't Rod LaRocque anymore; it was Rudolph Valentino. When we went to my room after dinner Pola said, "Oh, Meeriam, I haf loff."

"You do? What about Rod LaRocque—you were crazy about him last week."

"Ach, it's like the peasant and the prince," Pola said. She and Rudy were more like the prince and the princess. Both were great stars with millions of slavering fans who gobbled up everything printed about them. The love affair was a press agent's dream, but it was also the real thing. Rudy probably deserved his title as The Great Lover, but he was also a pleasant and polite young man. Once after he had had dinner with us he sent a silver water pitcher as a thank-you present. It's still one of my cherished possessions.

Shortly after that their affair ended with Rudy's sudden death. The picture of Pola weeping at his funeral must have been carried in every newspaper in the world.

Even after Raoul finished *East of Suez* we continued our friendship with Pola. I'll never forget her impromptu performance one night.

Raoul and I used to give formal parties two or three times a year. They'd begin at seven at night, with perhaps sixteen people for dinner, all dressed to the hilt, with the women wearing all the diamonds they had. A small string orchestra would play dinner music. Around midnight some jazz musicians from Watts would arrive and the party would go on in a less sedate fashion until seven in the morning.

When Pola came she always monopolized the conversation. One night she had an exciting tale to tell. Though we were seated at two tables in the dining room, Raoul at one, me at the other, Pola demanded the attention of both tables. She had been robbed; she'd come home and found the house ransacked, all her jewelry gone.

"Oh, my Gott," Pola said, "I talk to myself. 'Oh, Pola, what you do?' I say. I go to the weendow to get help. I open the weendow and put my head out. Then I sheet, and I sheet, and I sheet!"

Raoul and I looked at our plates. We were afraid to look at each other. Nobody said a word. We were all trying not to laugh. If she'd only waited a few hours we'd have roared, and she'd have laughed with us, but it was too early, and too sober.

Pola herself loved to entertain. She bought a huge mansion and became one of Hollywood's leading hostesses. The most distinguished visitors and important people in the industry were invited. At one of her parties William Randolph Hearst was my dinner partner. Shortly before we sat down, I went into Pola's pantry for something. The butler was mixing drinks in the biggest cocktail shaker I had ever seen. While I was standing there Marion Davies, Hearst's beautiful "good and great friend," dashed in, grabbed the shaker from the butler's hands, upended it and chugalugged half of it. Then, still not saying a word to either the startled butler or me, she ran back to the party.

That was one surprise. The next one was when Mr. Hearst spoke to me. I couldn't believe my ears. He had a high-pitched voice that you'd expect from a little puny fellow, not a big imposing-looking man like Mr. Hearst. Then, out of the clear blue sky, he told me, "Marion doesn't drink or smoke."

"Is that so?" I said.

Pola served champagne with dinner. When I reached for my glass to take my first sip, it was empty. I gave the young man on my right a withering look. When the waiter refilled the glasses I kept my eye on mine. Nothing happened. I looked away, then back, just in time to see Marion take my full glass and replace it with her empty one.

It amazed me how this girl could fool so successful a man. He had fallen in love with her when she had appeared in the Ziegfeld Follies chorus. The house he built for her, San Simeon, was a three-story mansion with a marble swimming pool and about ninety rooms, all lavishly furnished with art objects and priceless paintings.

He also built a beach house for her, just five houses from us. We all had reasonably large houses, but when hers was going up it was so big we thought it was the new club. Mr. Hearst would come bicycling past our house and give us a big wave, and Marion would invite us to her parties. We didn't go; Raoul wouldn't let me enter a kept woman's house.

But there were many other places to go. We were now established members of the Hollywood social set and were invited to everybody's parties.

When we weren't going out, Raoul would bring friends home for dinner. He hated to eat in restaurants. He'd even come home for lunch. He'd drive all the way home from the studio for a bowl of graham crackers and milk.

Sometimes Raoul's businessmen friends would show up with girls, extras and bit players they'd practically picked up. I got mad at a friend of ours named A. C. Blumenthal, a wealthy real estate broker, when he came by one New Year's Day to take Raoul to the Rose Bowl game. He had a girl with him named Jane Peters. Blumey was only as big as a peanut, but he owned half the expensive real estate in Los Angeles. His wife spent most of her time in New York and while she was gone he cheated on her. Girls liked him because he spent a lot of money on them.

I thought Blumey had a lot of nerve bringing that cheap-looking girl to the house. She was plump and had dirty knuckles. As I got to know her, though, she was so friendly and funny I couldn't help liking her. She wore a lot of cheap jewelry; I didn't like most of it, but I did admire the long rope of pearls she wore. One day she met me downtown and took me to her jewelry store. I bought eight long ropes of pearls—one wasn't enough for me—all for a dollar each. I loved getting so much for so little—I'd been spending a fortune for pearls.

Jane had been hired by Allan Dwan, one of Doug Fairbanks' favorite directors, when she was an eleven-year-old schoolgirl in Fort Wayne, Indiana. She played a bit part in his picture, *The Perfect Crime*. "That's when I got the acting bug," she said. She quit school a short time later and went to California where she hung around the studios. When she was fifteen she was hired by Mary Pickford's studio. "But when Mary saw I was a blonde with curls," Jane said, "she fired me."

In 1926 I took Jane with me on one of my annual shopping trips to New York. One morning she came bursting into my room while I was having breakfast in bed.

"Look at the new star," she said, whirling around the room. "I'm not Jane Peters anymore. I'm going to change my name and start all over again."

"What's your new name?" I asked.

She giggled. "You know that drugstore at Lexington and 65th? It's been there for ages. It must be a good name."

I knew the one she meant. It was owned by two men and was called the Carroll, Lombardi Pharmacy.

She danced around the room again. "How do you like it?"

I told her I loved it, and that's how a star named Carol Lombard was born. She lost weight, and when we were back in Hollywood Raoul gave her a job as Blond

Rosie, a gangster's moll, in a picture called *Me, Gangster.*

Later Jane—now Carol—added an *e* to her first name. She was a great believer in numerology. She thought that one extra letter would bring her luck.

It must have. As Carole Lombard she played leads in light comedies and became a star. She also became one of the most popular women in Hollywood. She'd do anything for her friends. She loved to play jokes on people. When she was married to the king of the movies, Clark Gable, she sent him a present after seeing the premiere of one of his pictures—a great big ham.

The plump, sloppy teenager became a beautiful, chic movie star. She was at the peak of her stardom in 1942 when she died in a plane crash.

Though Raoul enjoyed the type of entertaining in which girls like the young Jane Peters would show up, his Thursday night stag dinners were his favorite. Thursday was the cook's night off, and when I discovered that Fanny, our Mexican laundress, could make great chili, I asked her to take over. Raoul began inviting his friends, and it wasn't long before Fanny's hot, spicy Mexican suppers were the talk of Hollywood. Writers, directors and actors all came to them. There were Ernest Hemingway, Douglas Fairbanks, a now happy and amusing Charlie Chaplin, and many other prominent men from the screen and stage and the sports world. I didn't attend officially, but many a night I sat at the top of the stairs in the dark listening to the conversation.

I'd like to be able to repeat long stimulating discussions about the meaning of life, or the future of the movie industry, or the stories behind Hemingway's novels and short stories, but that wasn't what they talked about. As a matter of fact I usually started dozing off and went to bed. What they talked about was prizefights, horse racing, the jokes they'd pulled on their friends—and dirty stories.

I'll give you a sample. The only reason I remember it is because I must have heard Charlie Chaplin tell it a dozen times. It was about Billy Sunday, the evangelist.

Billy was walking down the street one day when he saw a drunk lying in the street. "I'll give you five dollars," Billy said to him, "if you'll come to my tent at twelve o'clock today."

The drunk took the money and at twelve o'clock went over to the tent.

Billy was giving his sermon. "Do you see that man?" he said, pointing to the drunk. "His father drank—not much, just a little bit. His mother drank—not much, just a little bit. Now look at him—a big drunk!"

Then the drunk stood up. (Charlie used to mimic him, pulling himself to his feet and swaying.) "Do you see that man?" he said, pointing to Billy Sunday. "His father had diarrhea—not much, just a little bit. His mother had diarrhea—not much, just a little bit. Now look at him—a big shit!"

One of the regulars I emphatically did not like was John Barrymore. He was a drunk. We had a beautiful white player piano and he used to sit at it and make a noise he thought was singing. One morning I came down after a party and found a burned-out cigarette right on top of it. I never could get the mark out. I know John Barrymore did it.

One night, after listening for a while at the top of the stairs, I got sleepy and went to bed. I was sound asleep, lying on my stomach, when I was awakened by a kiss on the back of my neck. The party was over and Raoul was coming to bed, I thought sleepily, and rolled over to put my arms around him.

But I got a blast of whisky breath and I knew it wasn't Raoul. It was John Barrymore. I pushed him away, hard. I was startled and angry.

"What are you doing here?" I demanded, as if I didn't know.

"I'm looking for the bathroom," he said, barely coherent. The smell of whisky was so strong it nearly knocked me out.

"This is not the bathroom," I told him indignantly. "Get out of here."

He staggered out, falling against the furniture on his way. I got up and locked the door so he couldn't get back in. To me The Great Profile was just another lecherous drunk.

« 26 »

The life we led, gay and happy sometimes, was also often lonely. Now that we weren't working together I rarely saw Raoul. He would go off on location, or when shooting in Hollywood, he'd come in late night after night.

I knew that all good directors got caught up in their jobs and stayed on at the studio long after working hours. I understood that, but I understood something else, too—their vulnerability to the star-struck girls who chased them like bitches in heat. Everybody in the business wanted to go up, up, up.

It was an occupational hazard. Girls pursued Raoul with desperation. Extras wanted to play bits, bit players wanted leading roles, leads wanted to be stars, stars wanted to stay stars. I could understand the little nobodies and try to tolerate their antics, but the established stars made me mad.

Why would Ethel Barrymore, with both an established name and talent, want to throw herself at my husband? It happened while he was directing *The Thief of Bagdad*. Ethel Barrymore was one of Doug and Mary's innumerable house guests. She and Raoul would take long rides into the countryside late at night.

I'm still a little ashamed of myself for having done it, but one night I telephoned her.

"You're old enough to be his mother!" I shouted. "Leave him alone!"

After I hung up I wrote Raoul a note saying I was through with him forever, and had the chauffeur drive me to a hotel in downtown Los Angeles. I wasn't there very long when someone knocked on the door. It was Raoul. I let him in and he tried to talk me into returning home. I told him no, I was through.

We argued for hours. Everybody in the hotel must have heard us. Finally I shouted, "I've had enough. I'm going to get a divorce!"

"You can't get a divorce," he said. "I've been in your room for two hours and no judge will give you a divorce if you've been alone with your husband that long."

"It's your word against mine," I shouted at him. "I'll say you weren't here."

"But we've had a witness all this time," he said. Then he went to the door and opened it. Out in the hall was an actor named Carl Harbaugh. He was a good friend of Raoul's, and Raoul had had him standing in the hall all the time we were together in the hotel room.

That really made me mad. I told Raoul I was going to get a divorce anyway. It really shook him up. He promised that he would never even *look* at another woman.

"I'll sign an oath!" he said. "Come on, we'll go down to the lawyer's office and he can prepare it and I'll sign it in front of witnesses!"

We were actually in the car, on the way to the lawyer's office, before I realized how silly it was. We turned around and went back home. But I wasn't completely satisfied.

"If I feel this way when I'm still in my twenties," I sniffled, "what will it be like when I'm fifty?"

Raoul knew better than to mention that I was no longer in my twenties. "When you're fifty I'll be fifty-four," he said. "Who'll look at me then? I'd never think of anyone else when you're fifty."

Oh, Raoul is so sweet, I thought. When I'm old and gray—fifty!—he will still be considerate of my feelings. So we made up again.

But we had a long way to go until we reached our fifties, and Raoul obviously didn't want to waste those years on just one woman. Later that very year, 1924, I came home from New York to learn that my husband was engaged.

The way I found out began when I opened up the pile of bills and found one from a local furrier. I knew I hadn't bought any furs, so I called the furrier and asked him about it. He told me the name of the girl to whom the coat was sent. "Mr. Walsh told me to send the bill to his home."

I guess Raoul had forgotten that I handled all the bills. I had heard of the girl's family; the name was always appearing in the society columns. But I never would have thought Raoul would be interested in their daughter. She was only seventeen.

I called her mother and asked her to have tea with me. She arrived just before Raoul came home from work. When he came in and saw us he blanched under his tan. I asked him to join us and turned back to my guest.

"Why did my husband buy your daughter a fur coat?" I asked her.

"It's an engagement present," she said. "They're going to be married as soon as your divorce is final."

"What divorce?" I said. She looked at Raoul in confusion and then back at me.

"Why, weren't you in New York getting a divorce?" she said.

"I was not," I said. "I was in New York shopping."

The lady stood up. "There must be some misunderstanding," she said. She left without saying a word to Raoul. Raoul, usually so glib, didn't have anything to say. He sat there looking sheepish the whole time.

The coat was returned to the furrier and that was the end of that episode.

But it was no way to live. Night after night I'd lie awake until one o'clock, two o'clock, three o'clock in the morning. I'd call the studio to see if he was there. I'd wake up the chauffeur and send him out to look for Raoul. Then Raoul would come in with a reasonable-sounding explanation and reassure me and we'd make up. But the same sort of thing would happen again.

In 1925 Archie Selwyn brought *Charlot's Revue* to the States. *Charlot's Revue* was a highly successful English show starring Gertrude Lawrence and Bea Lillie. It had a sell-out run in New York, then came to the West Coast.

Gertie and Bea were very popular. Everybody wanted them to come to everything. One Sunday some millionaire invited Raoul and me to spend the day on his yacht. Bea Lillie was one of the other guests.

We all got in the dory to row out to the boat. It was rough that day, and the waves were high. Everybody was soaked. Bea was very frail and pale. I was tanned and athletic-looking. Raoul took off his jacket and put it around Bea. I sat there soaked and shivering.

When we got back that evening Raoul said, "Let's get a rare roast beef for Bea; she looks anemic."

I liked Bea, and she did look as though she needed a good meal, so I asked her to stay on for dinner. After that we had her to dinner several times.

One night when Bea did not come over Raoul said, "Let's go to bed early tonight; I'm half dead."

That was all right with me. I'd had a tough day. I started my nightly routine. I put on my wrinkle patches, smeared my face with Elizabeth Arden's pore cream, and put my hair up in curlers. One time when Mama saw me going through that routine she said, "Miriam, if you go to bed made up like that you won't have a husband." I guess she knew what she was talking about.

We read for a while, then Raoul got up and started getting dressed.

"Hell, I can't sleep," he said. "Let's take a ride."

"After all I've gone through getting ready for bed?" I said. "You go on if you want to."

He did, and, I learned later, wound up at *Charlot's Revue* and took Bea out for supper.

Well, it was fine of Raoul to be nice to Bea and fatten her up; however, I thought she was beginning to take advantage of the situation. But I knew how to end it.

Raoul hated to see a woman drunk. It disgusted him. Bea had always been sober around us, but I'd been to parties without Raoul and seen her drinking like a fish.

So I invited her to come for cocktails on her day off. I set the time a little early, before Raoul was due home. Just before she was due to arrive I made her a drink. What a drink! I put everything in the bar in it. For good measure I threw in some cleaning fluid. Raoul thinks she's so grand, I thought, well, wait'll she finishes this. It's a wonder it didn't kill her.

Bea sat on the edge of the big high-backed needlepoint chair in our living room as she drank her cocktail. In her sober moments no one could be more dignified than Lady Peel, Bea Lillie's title in private life. Her back was very straight, and her feet barely touched the floor. But by the time Raoul came in my concoction was taking effect.

When Raoul asked her if she wanted anything, she said, "No, thank you, Ra–ohl." She began to slump in the chair, her voice began to slur, and one eye began to droop. One of Bea's eyes always drooped when she got drunk.

Raoul looked at her, then at me. "Did you give her anything to drink?" he asked me.

"Just a little cocktail," I told him innocently.

Then Bea passed out cold. I told Raoul I'd put her to bed.

"Put her in the guest room," Raoul said.

"Oh no, dear, I couldn't do that," I said. "She might fall out of bed and get hurt. She can sleep in your bed."

"The hell she can," he said. "I'll never sleep in a bed after any drunken woman."

"Don't worry, dear," I told him. "I'll have it fumigated."

That was the end of that friendship. Raoul was through with Bea Lillie right then.

I got rid of Bea Lillie, but then I brought the next one in myself. My friend Lillian Fitzgerald—the woman I was with in San Francisco on the weekend of the Fatty Arbuckle scandal—and I used to take bridge lessons together. We met two sisters and started a regular game. The sisters were both married; their names were Lorraine Miller and Ruth Hollister. Ruth later divorced her husband and married Walter Pidgeon. One afternoon Raoul came home while we were playing and I introduced him to them.

Those two were a great pair—and I was a great sucker. I took Ruth with me on a shopping trip to New York. Apparently, before Ruth had come to New York with me, she'd had a long talk with her sister Lorraine. Lorraine was married to a rich young man, but they lived in Bakersfield and she was doing her own washing and cleaning. Ruth talked her into leaving her husband. "Concentrate on the one man who can do you some good," she told her.

That one man was my husband.

When I got home from New York Jackie met me as I walked in the door. Before I even had a chance to hug him he said, "Mommy, Lorraine's been sleeping in your bed."

· 225 ·

What a homecoming! "How do you know that?"

"Her hat and handbag were on the piano," he said. "When I took the paper up to your room Daddy didn't let me in the way he does when you're home. He just reached his hand out the door and took it from me."

I was furious. I picked up my unpacked bags and headed for New York. Raoul was once again working with the Fox Film Corporation, and I knew that Mr. Fox's chief attorney, Nathan Burkan, liked me. I went to him and asked him to represent me in a divorce suit against Raoul.

"Miriam, I'd love to do it, but I can't," he said. "Mr. Fox would never stand for it."

But after I agreed not to let Mr. Fox know he was advising me, he told me what to do. "Send for the children," he said. "And maybe it would be a good idea to hire a private detective agency to keep an eye on Raoul."

I got in touch with the agency he recommended, and sure enough, before long I had all the evidence necessary to prove adultery. Raoul and Lorraine weren't even playing it smart. They were blatant about it.

Mr. Fox heard what was going on and asked me to come see him. As I've said, I always liked Mr. Fox, and I went. He got right to the point. "If you do this, Miriam," he said, "Raoul will be through. He'll never get another job in the business."

The scandals of the early twenties had left their mark on the industry. Now if there was any whisper of scandal about someone, that person was through. The Will Hays office had put the morals clause in every contract, and the whole industry was scared to death of it.

At first I didn't give a damn whether Raoul Walsh ever worked again, but Mr. Fox was persuasive. He turned on the sentiment and made me recall the happy days Raoul and I had spent together when we were young and in love. After he softened me up he threw the clincher at me.

"And if he doesn't work, Miriam, who'll support you and those two fine boys?"

I didn't want to finish Raoul's career, for both his sake and mine. I promised Mr. Fox I would not divorce him for adultery, which would mean a messy trial with my private detectives telling the whole sordid story in front of the Hollywood press corps, but would settle for the more acceptable grounds of incompatibility.

My lawyer had never handled a divorce case before. Recommended to me by some friends who were corporate executives, not picture people, he was Oscar Lawler, the best-known corporate attorney in Los Angeles. I think he was intrigued by the case. He said he'd take it, but as a business transaction rather than a divorce. After all, our marriage had been a business partnership as well as a romantic one. I had made a great deal of money on my own over the years and had thrown much of it into the family pot. My financial settlement would not be alimony, but return on investment. Raoul agreed.

When word got out that we were separating, Hollywood was shocked. We had been considered the ideal couple. Everybody knew we were both Catholic; we went to church together. As Catholics, we could never marry again. (Raoul married again, of course, but I never did.)

As the rumors that we were breaking up got out, the press drove us crazy. On the day the case was to be heard, reporters descended on the court like an invading army. But they were too late. Mr. Lawler had arranged for the judge to open court an hour early, and by the time the reporters got there it was all over.

Then they all charged out to the house. The only person I let in was Louella Parsons. I considered our relationship to be that of two close friends, not reporter and movie star. Apparently I was wrong. Our friendly conversation appeared on page one, under headlines so big you'd have thought war was declared.

The night before the divorce Gloria Swanson gave Raoul a party. Norman Kerry, who'd married a Texas oil heiress, and his friend Erich von Stroheim gave a party for me. When I arrived the butler ushered me into the drawing room. The first thing I saw was a big photograph of Raoul on the grand piano—framed in a toilet seat.

There was a lot of liquor floating around and after a while people began jumping in the swimming pool with all their clothes on. It was a hell of a party.

After the divorce I left for New York with the two children, Theresa, the dog and the canary. Always before, as a star and the wife of a prominent director, I'd been seen off by a crowd of people even when I was just going home to visit Mama. Now I was no longer a star, no longer the wife of a director. The crowd seeing me off consisted of just one person, Norman Kerry.

I laughed at the irony of it, but it was all right with me. I was just as through with picture people as they were with me. I was disgusted with the whole lot of them.

« 27 »

When I am through with something I never want to have anything to do with it again. I felt that Hollywood had ruined my marriage and my life, and I vowed not to go back. I never entered a movie studio again. I didn't even go to movies. Right after our divorce one of Raoul's best pictures, *What Price Glory?* was playing in a big theater on Times Square in New York. I frequently passed the theater, but I never went in. I wanted to put movies out of my life forever.

I tried to find the good life. I traveled with the beautiful people of the time, the café society crowd in New York. I enjoyed it for a while, but then I realized how empty the life of the women was. They got up at noon, had lunch at the Ritz, played bridge, shopped or went to a matinee, then dressed again, guzzled cocktails, and went out to dinner and the theater. Day after day.

The parties were particularly asinine. At one, a baby party given by the president of one of the biggest corporations in New York, the host, a man with gray hair and moustache, crawled around the floor in a diaper, sucking on a baby bottle.

At another there was a donkey telling fortunes. The

trainer would ask a question and the donkey nodded or shook his head. In the midst of the performance the donkey let go all over the priceless Oriental rug.

I was amazed; I had thought society people were something great. But they weren't any better than picture people. At least picture people *worked*.

I was used to being busy and I tried hard to be good at everything I did. Theresa and I took care of the boys. I played golf; I played bridge. I was happy in New York with my two boys. But as they grew older, bringing up two lively sons by myself became more difficult. Jack, now barely in his teens, was more than I could handle.

One night I got a call at the Delmonico Hotel, where we lived, and a man's voice said, "This is the police. We have your son in custody."

"Don't be silly," I said. "My son is in boarding school." I hung up. I'd put Jack on the train for Peekskill Military Academy just a week before. He was wearing his military uniform with all those brass buttons and the cape thrown back to show the red lining. He looked like a million dollars. I knew very well where he was.

The phone ran again. The man said he was Sergeant So-and-So of some precinct, and he really did have Jack.

I'd put Jack on the train all right—but he'd gotten off at 125th Street. I had enrolled him as a member of the New York Athletic Club for the athletic program and he and a friend of his had gone there and got a room together. They had had a high old time, having rubdowns and charging meals and theater tickets to his account, until their money ran out. They didn't have enough for a train ticket so they appropriated a car. They were on the way back to school when the police stopped them.

The boys were expelled from school, though I hired an attorney who kept them out of jail. Funny thing was, the man they stole the car from did go to jail. It turned out that he ran a whorehouse in Harlem and the police had been looking for him.

That was just one of the scrapes Jack got in. And to make things worse, Bobby, the younger boy, worshipped him.

"Jack is so clever," he told me. "When we go shopping he buys something, and pays for it. Then while the clerk is wrapping it up, he stuffs lots of other things in his pockets and doesn't pay for them. He's smart."

I could see what kind of influence Jack was having on the younger boy. And stealing wasn't all he was teaching him. Bobby was getting into trouble at school, too.

I wanted to do the right thing with Jack but I didn't know how. I knew he had an unusual and difficult background—first an orphanage, then parents who as busy picture people were never home, and finally the divorce. I had thought I was giving him something good when I took him out of the orphanage, but as a motion picture star I hadn't been able to give him what he needed most: a stable home life with a mother and father around all the time. Now that I was divorced, Theresa and I tried to do the job, but the damage had already been done.

Finally, our priest suggested that I send him out to live with Raoul. "He needs the discipline a man can give him," he said.

Raoul by that time had a ranch and was willing to have Jack. I could see how that life might be better for him. I gave him up, along with the money I was getting for his support, and sent him to California and his father.

In the meantime Raoul and Lorraine had gotten married. Lorraine wouldn't have Jack in the house and he lived with George Walsh in another house at the ranch, near the stables. By this time George had retired from pictures and was managing Raoul's racehorses and stables.

If Lorraine didn't like that souvenir of her husband's first marriage, there was another she liked even less—the agreement under which he sent me $500 a week. Raoul conveniently forgot that that money represented both my own investment and my willingness not to end Raoul's career. Anyway, even before I sent Jack out to him, he had stopped my payments and started proceedings to break the contract. I sued him for back payments and went to California for the case.

In court the judge looked at both of us and said, "You people make more money in a week than I do in a year."

I got the picture right away. The judge didn't like picture people. I knew I had to let him know I was not living the way he thought all picture people lived—big house, big swimming pool, lots of marriages.

He asked Raoul and me to come into his chambers. When we were seated there, I asked the judge if I could speak to Raoul. He nodded.

"What are you trying to do to me?" I asked Raoul. "You have the girl you wanted, you have the job you want. What more do you want from me?"

Then I turned to the judge and said, "Your Honor, I don't have a big house in Beverly Hills. I don't have a swimming pool. I live alone in a seven-room apartment in New York with my children, a nurse and a cook. All I want is enough money to live quietly."

The judge nodded and took us back to the courtroom. After I had been on the witness stand an hour, the judge said, "You've been on the witness stand for some time, Mrs. Walsh. Would you like a glass of water?"

I turned my big brown eyes up to him. "I would like a cup of coffee, Your Honor," I said very quietly.

The judge adjourned court so I could have a cup of coffee.

I won that case, but I wasn't through with Raoul and lawsuits. In 1939 he stopped sending me money again. All in all we had three lawsuits going at the same time. I sued him for $56,000 in back payments; he sued me to void the contract, and he had Jack sue me for a third of all the money I'd received while he was living with me.

That made me mad, and it hurt, too. I left New York to go to California to fight back. I rented a cottage on the beach, next door to Douglas Fairbanks and his new wife, Lady Ashley. When summer came Bobby left his school in Goshen, New York, and joined me.

One day Bobby asked me if he could visit his father. I was rather surprised because he hadn't seen him since he was a small child. But I said yes, called Raoul to tell him Bobby was coming over for the weekend, packed his suitcase and called a taxi for him.

Bobby came back raving about Raoul's ranch and all the things Jack had. Raoul had bought Jack a specially built car, and a specially built gun, and specially built saddles for his horse. For all I know the horse was specially built too.

I'd been giving Bobby five dollars a week for his allowance; I thought that was enough for a sixteen-year-old boy. Now he had seen how the other half lived, and he wanted to join them. I was furious.

"Would you like to live with your father?" I asked him.

"I sure would," he said.

"Good," I told him, and packed up all his clothes and sent him to Raoul. Before my lawsuit with Raoul was over he had Bobby suing me, too. I had acted impulsively and regretted it many times as the years went by.

With everybody suing me, I needed a lot of lawyers. I had five, including the famous Hollywood divorce lawyer, Jerry Geisler. Raoul had four. Once when the judge saw all of them standing before him he said, "This looks like an array of counsel for a murder trial."

We finally settled with the agreement that inasmuch

as I was no longer responsible for the boys, my weekly income would be reduced. I retained the $100,000 worth of insurance on Raoul's life which had been part of the original divorce settlement.

Not long after that Raoul returned from a trip to find that his house had been burglarized. Everything of value was gone—paintings, silver, everything. He called the police to investigate and offered $10,000 as a reward for their return.

A few weeks later the police called to tell him they had the culprit. Raoul hurried over, the police took him to the cell where they were holding the thief—and there was Jack. Raoul had to pay the $10,000 reward for the police to catch his son, and then pay out more to keep him out of prison.

He disowned Jack after that. But Jack had the last laugh on the Walsh family. He ran off with George's girl friend, married her and went to live in Oregon. And that's the last I heard of him. I never heard from Bobby again, either. I don't know if either of the two boys is alive or dead.

As Raoul continued his career, naturally I heard plenty about him. He and Lorraine were divorced after ten years of marriage. In 1947, when he was sixty years old, he announced his engagement to the seventeen-year-old daughter of a Kentucky horse trainer. When Mama heard about it she laughed.

"Raoul had better marry that girl before she's too old for him," she said.

"What do you mean, Mama?" I asked. "She's only seventeen."

"Yes, I know," Mama said, "but she'll be eighteen very soon."

After the long-drawn-out lawsuits, I returned to New York. When World War II started, I became part of the army of volunteers on the home front. As a Red Cross volunteer I handed out doughnuts and coffee to servicemen and wrote letters for wounded soldiers in hospitals.

After the war I looked around for something to do. I had always wanted to go to college, and when I was in my late forties I finally made it. At a dinner party one night I sat next to Nicholas Murray Butler, president of Columbia University, and told him I was interested in writing. He said Columbia offered a fine course. I had never been to high school, of course, but I'm not shy about going after what I want. I asked how I could get in the class.

"What writing have you done?"

"Well," I said, "I've written a book of poems."

"Oh, then it will be easy for you to take the class," he said, and he arranged it. Much later I found out he thought I meant that I had had a book of poems *published*. Actually it was just a notebook with some lousy verses scribbled in it. It's still lying in my bottom bureau drawer.

One of the well-known writers who spoke to the class was Louis Bromfield. He told us about the advantages of writing on his farm. That sounded like a more productive life than café society, so I started looking around for a farm. When I heard of one with a pre-Revolutionary farmhouse near Chestertown, Maryland, I immediately went to see it. After all, I'd heard enough about my Maryland ancestors. I'd be returning home. The house was quaint and lovely, and I bought it—with some help from the bank.

But the writing didn't work out. All summer I had guest after guest after guest. Everybody I knew wanted to spend some time on the eastern shore of Maryland. But in the winter I was alone. I've always loved people and I was lonely and bored—a good atmosphere for writing, but not for me.

I did produce some work, however. I wrote a novel, unpublished, and two plays. The plays were based on two pictures I had made. One was *The Woman and the Law,* the other *The Oath.* I sent them to Twentieth Century-Fox, the same studio that had produced *The Woman and the Law* thirty years earlier. Both were returned to me with the following letter:

Dear Miss Walsh:
I am returning your two scripts. . . . I am afraid that neither of them is material for pictures.

That was funny, but discouraging. About that time I met an executive with Campbell Soup who said the company was interested in developing new varieties of tomatoes. Well, if I couldn't be a great writer maybe I could be a great tomato grower. We planted the whole farm with tomatoes. They looked good to me and I guess the company liked them, too. When harvest time came there were advertising people crawling all over the place taking pictures of me with the workers.

In the winter I went south and played golf. I've shot a hole in one in three different states. In the early fifties I passed through Charlottesville, Virginia, and played golf at Farmington Country Club. I fell in love with the town and with the golf course. I sold the farm and bought a small house on a pine-covered hill in Charlottesville with a view of the Blue Ridge Mountains.

I still wanted to write. I organized a writers' group in Charlottesville and invited the University of Virginia writers-in-residence and the famous authors living in the area to come to speak to us. The group lasted for years. A couple of the women did go on to publish magazine articles and books.

I didn't. I was trying to write a novel about a nun—*A Nun's Story,* I called it. After my hectic life, and lack of success as a wife and mother, I thought the life of religious service was ideal. A professional writer I met looked at it. He seemed a little puzzled.

"I don't get the feeling that you know a lot about being a nun," he said. "What did you do in your earlier life?"

"Well," I said, squirming, "I was in silent pictures."

"Good Lord," he said, and shoved my manuscript back at me. That was the end of *A Nun's Story*.

But there were still golf and bridge and charity work and friends, a full life for a woman in her sixties. None of my friends had ever had anything to do with pictures. I had long since lost touch with all the people I used to see every day. Mae Marsh, my closest friend, and I had fallen out long before, while I was still married to Raoul. She had married Louis Lee Arms, a Chicago newspaperman turned scenario writer. One night Louis got so drunk at our house I asked Mae to take him home. She did, but she didn't speak to me again for years.

The next time I saw her was when I was in Los Angeles for the lawsuits with Raoul and the boys. My chauffeur drove me out to the beach cottage where she was living. It was a terrible dump. She had no money. Friends had warned me not to give her any because Louis would get it from her and drink it up. He wouldn't leave us alone so, on some pretext, I got Mae to go into the bathroom with me. When we were in there I gave her $20. Louis came to the bathroom door and rattled the knob. "What are you doing in there?" he shouted at us.

When we came out I took Mae to the store and bought groceries for her and their three children. Louis couldn't drink up the food and he couldn't pawn it, either. That was the last time I saw Mae. I've heard since that Louis went on the wagon and became a highly respected newspaper publisher on the West Coast.

A few years ago I was playing duplicate bridge at the club. One of the players, a newspaperman, looked at me while we were sorting our cards. "Did you hear your friend died?" he said.

"Which friend?" I asked him.

"Mae Marsh," he said. "She died of a heart attack yesterday in California."

I was stunned. I thought he had meant some casual acquaintance in Charlottesville. I couldn't go on playing. Sweet, lovable Mae.

I kept up with Mr. Griffith for a few years after I left the company. I knew that he had made some good films— *Broken Blossoms, Way Down East,* and *Isn't Life Wonderful?* I also knew that he and Lillian Gish had broken up.

When I left Hollywood I lost track of him completely, along with everybody else in pictures. Somehow, during those years, I had gotten the impression that Mr. Griffith was living in Europe, probably in some great chateau, still wearing his big straw hat. He once told Mae Marsh and me that he had bought an annuity which would give him $500 a month at some later date—it impressed the daylights out of me at the time. With that, and the income I assumed he was getting from his films, I was sure he would be a millionaire the rest of his life.

Then one day while I was still living in New York, I ran into Lillian Gish in Elizabeth Arden's. After reminiscing a little, I asked what I thought was a perfectly natural question—where was Mr. Griffith and what was he doing.

"How should I know," she said, tossing her head. Then she told me he was living in a second-rate hotel on Seventh Avenue.

I couldn't believe it. I had a big apartment on Park Avenue and money to spend in Elizabeth Arden's. Now I learned that I was better off than Mr. Griffith, who had made it all possible.

After seeing Lillian, I heard other stories about him, including how he was drinking, something he had never done when I knew him. It never occurred to me to visit him. I had been out of touch with him for so long.

I know now that his last film, *The Struggle,* was made

in 1931. For the last seventeen years of his life he was neglected by the very people he had made rich and famous. For a man who had made some of the world's greatest pictures, who had worked on every detail of production and directed the thousands of people in them, this inactivity must have been a living hell.

Nobody knew what to do about him, so they took the easy way out. They ignored him. Sometimes they'd cross the street when they saw him coming. The men who had made the money from an industry he had brought from infancy to maturity, the pants pressers and the junk dealers, turned their backs on him. They eased their consciences by giving him an honorary Oscar for his services to motion pictures, then forgot him again. The high moguls could have helped him and they didn't.

He was back in Hollywood, forlorn and forgotten, when he died in 1948. A handful of people paid their last respects at the funeral parlor—Mae Marsh and Cecil B. DeMille were among them. I was not; I was living in New York. When the reporters and the cameras were there for the funeral, everybody came. He was buried in the family plot in LaGrange, Kentucky, in a quiet church cemetery.

A year or so later a writer visiting the cemetery wrote a story about the plain little marker and the neglected grave. That shamed the Screen Directors Guild into doing something. They did it in true Hollywood style. They erected a stone so big it dwarfed everything around it; anything that size should have been in Washington next to the Lincoln Memorial. Raoul Walsh and Albert S. Rogell represented the Screen Directors Guild at the ceremony. Once more only a handful of people were there, but I think Mr. Griffith would have been happy to know that two of them were Lillian Gish and Mary Pickford.

That was the last I heard of him until he came back into my life with a bang, or at least the ringing of bells, in

1969, when I was seventy-eight. The phone rang one day and a man's voice said, "Mrs. Walsh?"

I said yes. The voice said, "Mrs. *Raoul* Walsh? *Miriam Cooper* Walsh?" I said yes again. "Mrs. Walsh, we just found out you were still alive!" the voice blurted out.

Still alive! Jesus, what a thing to say to an old lady. The man apologized and said he was with the film history department of the Library of Congress.

After that I began receiving calls, letters and visits constantly. Even universities got involved. In 1970 the University of Louisville invited me to attend their first D. W. Griffith Student Film Festival. It was the first time I'd ever been in an airplane. It was also my first knowledge that college students were studying motion pictures. One of them, a nice young man, offered to drive me to the cemetery where Griffith was buried.

When I stood at his grave, the tears began streaming down my cheeks. The young man must have sensed all the emotions going through my head and heart. He suddenly leaned over and kissed me.

Perhaps it was the trip, or the excitement of the film festival, but I think it was seeing the grave of the man who had done so much for me. Whatever it was, my heart couldn't take it. I was rushed to the hospital and stayed there several days before I was well enough to go home. It was the beginning of heart trouble which has bothered me ever since. Lying in bed most of the day, I have plenty of time to think about Mr. Griffith and how he was forgotten and neglected.

But Lillian Gish cheered me up a little when she visited me in the spring of 1972. Lillian travels over the United States and Europe, giving lectures, and is in contact with many people. "The young people have redis-covered Mr. Griffith," she said. "He knew the power of the screen and he took the responsibility for what he put up there. Much of what the world is today is a result of what's been up there."

The movies changed the world, and they changed my life along with it. For years, after leaving Hollywood, I thought the movies ruined my life, but now I'm not so sure. During those years I did things as a movie actress I wouldn't have done as a housewife. I traveled to many places and saw how people lived; I saw condemned murderers on death row, and the sweet unspoiled people of the South Seas. I made a lot of money, and it not only took me out of poverty, but enabled me to help others.

I was able to help my family from the time I first started working in pictures. After *The Birth of a Nation* when I began making big money as a girl still in her early twenties, I lavished it on my mother and brothers and sister. I always helped my family when they needed it. I put Nelson through Columbia, and whenever anyone got sick there I was with my checkbook. Mama was ashamed of me when I first went into pictures, but it was the money I earned in pictures that supported her until she died.

I never begrudged a nickel of it. In Mama's later years she lived at the Barbizon Hotel. She was an awful hypochondriac and she liked to have the house physician visit her. He would come by in the morning, take her pulse, hold her hand, tell her she would be fine, then rush downstairs to the cashier and get his fee.

In the meantime Mama would get up, go to lunch and play bridge. At five, when the doctor was due to come again, Mama would rush up to her room and get into bed. He'd come in, go through the same routine, and collect another fee. I didn't care. She could have been going to the theater for the same amount. I was glad to make her happy.

I was glad to be able to take two children from the New York Foundling Hospital and give them a good home and schooling. It didn't work out, but at least I tried. I have found, though, that giving money and helping people makes you feel better than the person you give help to.

If I have any regret at all it's that, though my money helped a lot of people live better lives, it never bought their love. One thing I know now is that you can't buy love.

Today I am alone except for the friends who visit me regularly. My housekeeper, Christine Garland, who has been with me for almost twenty years, comes in for a few hours every afternoon. I don't know what I would do without her.

The only close relative I have left is Lenore, who is widowed. Lenore now lives in Los Angeles; her friends are former picture people.

I used to think picture people were terrible. Now that I've lived with the café society set and the country club set, picture people look pretty good by comparison. So they hopped into bed with each other. So does everybody else.

And picture people are generous. They are always willing to put on benefits for good causes. They'll lend their names, emcee a show or perform in it. All they have is their talent, and they give it away over and over. It's a good habit and I'm glad that I still have it. Not long ago, just before I became sick, I gave a big party—seventy-five tables of bridge—and raised enough money to buy an ambulance for our local rescue squad. When I heard of a group of retarded school children who were going without lunch, I bought their meals for a year.

All of us, back in the early days, thought that money was to help people and bring happiness. We all helped our families and our friends. There are only a handful of us left now, those of us who have seen the motion picture industry grow from nickelodeons in vacant stores to an art form.

When young people come to see me, wanting to know

all about those early days, it makes me feel I'm a part of something important, a part of movie history. Mr. Griffith knew it, even back then.

"What you do here today will be seen around the world," he told us when we were making *The Birth of a Nation*. We laughed, but he was right.

Now, almost sixty years later, it's nice to know that long after I'm gone, young people everywhere will still be seeing me, not as an old lady, but as Margaret Cameron, the Southern girl who marries the Northern soldier and symbolizes the birth of a nation.

1911   *A Blot on the 'Scutcheon:* Biograph; D. W. Griffith, director, with Dorothy Bernard; extra, Miriam Cooper.

1912   Kalem, Florida Stock Company; Keenan Buel, director; Storm Boyd, assistant; with leads, Guy Coombs and Anna Q. Nilsson; character parts, Helen Lindreth and Henry Hallam; heavy, Hal Clements; ingenue, Miriam Cooper.

Victim of Circumstances

Battle of Pottsburg Bridge

Tide of Battle

War's Havoc

The Drummer Girl of Vicksburg

The Colonel's Escape

The Bugler of Battery B

The Soldier Brothers of Susannah

The Siege of Petersburg

The Darling of the CSA

Saved from Court Martial

A Railroad Lochinvar

His Mother's Picture

The Girl in the Caboose

The Pony Express Girl

Battle in the Virginia Hills

The Water Right War

The Battle of Wits

A Race with Time

1913   *A Sawmill Hazard*

A Desperate Chance

The Turning Point

The Battle of Bloody Ford

A Treacherous Shot

The Farm Bully

The Toll Gate Raiders

Infamous Don Miguel

Captured by Strategy

1914 *The Stolen Radium:* Reliance Majestic; Christy Cabanne, director; with Eugene Pallette, Irene Hunt, Sam De Grasse.

For His Master: Reliance Majestic; Christy Cabanne, director.

When Fate Frowned: Reliance Majestic.

Home Sweet Home: Reliance Majestic; D. W. Griffith, director; with Lillian and Dorothy Gish, Bobby Harron, Mae Marsh, Henry B. Walthall, Spottiswoode Aiken.

A Diamond in the Rough: Reliance Majestic; with Edna May Wilson.

The Gunman: Reliance Majestic; Christy Cabanne, director; with Eugene Pallette, Sam De Grasse, Ralph Lewis.

The Dishonored Medal: Reliance Majestic.

The Odalisque: Reliance Majestic; with Blanche Sweet, Henry B. Walthall, Wallace Reid.

The Double Deception: Reliance Majestic.

The Birth of a Nation: Epoch Producing Corp.; D. W. Griffith, director; with Lillian Gish, Henry B. Walthall, Mae Marsh, Wallace Reid, Walter Long, Bobby Harron, Raoul Walsh, etc.

1915 *The Fatal Black Bean:* Reliance Majestic.

His Return: Reliance Majestic; with Elmer Clifton.

The Burned Hand: Fine Arts; Tod Browning, director; with William Hinckley, Cora Drew, W. E. Lowery.

1916   *Intolerance:* Wark; D. W. Griffith, director; with Mae Marsh, Bobby Harron, Walter Long, Lillian Gish, Eugene Pallette, Edward Dillon, Spottiswoode Aiken, Josephine Crowell, Elmer Clifton, Constance Talmadge, etc.

1917   *The Honor System:* Fox Film Corp.; Raoul Walsh, director, with Milton Sills, Gladys Brockwell, George Walsh, Johnny Reese.

   The Silent Lie: Fox Film Corp.; Raoul Walsh, director.

   The Innocent Sinner: Fox Film Corp.; Raoul Walsh, director; with Charles Clary, Jane Novak, Jack Standing.

   Betrayed: Fox Film Corp.; Raoul Walsh, director; with Hobart Bosworth, James A. Marcus, Monte Blue, Wheeler Oakman.

1918   *The Woman and the Law:* Fox Film Corp.; Raoul Walsh, director; with Ramsay Wallace, Master Jack Connors, Peggy Hopkins, George Humbert, Agnes Neilson, etc.

   The Prussian Cur: Fox Film Corp.; Raoul Walsh, director; with Ralph C. Faulkner, Captain Von der Goeltz.

1919   *Evangeline:* Fox Film Corp.; Raoul Walsh, director; with Albert Roscoe, Spottiswoode Aiken, James A. Marcus, Paul Weigel.

   Should a Husband Forgive?: Fox Film Corp.; Raoul Walsh, director; with Mrs. James K. Hackett, Eric Mayme, Vincent Coleman, Lyster Chambers, Percy Standing, James A. Marcus, Johnny Reese.

1920   *The Deep Purple:* Mayflower Prod., released through Realart; Raoul Walsh, director; with Vincent Serrano, Helen Ware, W. J. Ferguson, Stuart Sage, Bird Millman.

1921   *The Oath:* Mayflower Photoplay Corp.; Raoul Walsh, Prod.; Raoul Walsh, director; with Conway Tearle, Robert Fischer, Henry Clive, Ricca Allen, Anna Q. Nilsson. From William J. Locke's *Idols.*

Serenade: Assoc. First National Pictures; R. A. Walsh, Prod.; Raoul Walsh, director; with George Walsh, Rosita Marstini, James A. Marcus, William Eagle Eye, Elizabeth Waters. James T. O'Donohue, scenario; George Peters, photography; William Cameron Menzies, art director.

1922 *Kindred of the Dust:* First National; R. A. Walsh, Prod.; R. A. Walsh, director; with Ralph Graves, Lionel Belmore, Eugenie Besserer, Elizabeth Waters, Maryland Morne, Caroline Rankin, Pat Rooney, John Herdman, Bruce Guerin. James T. O'Donohue, scenario; Charles Van Enger, Lyman Broening, photography; William Cameron Menzies, art director.

1923 *Is Money Everything?:* D. M. Film Corp.; Dist., Lee-Bradford Corp.; Glen Lyons, director-writer; Alven Knechtel, photography; with Norman Kerry, Andrew Hicks, John Sylvester, Martha Mansfield, William Bailey, Lawrence Brooke.

The Girl Who Came Back: B. P. Schulberg; Dist., Preferred Pictures; Tom Forman, director; Evelyn Campbell, adaptation; Harry Perry, photography; with Gaston Glass, Kenneth Harlan, Fred Malatesta, Joseph Dowling, Ethel Shannon, Mary Culver, ZaSu Pitts.

Daughters of the Rich: B. P. Schulberg, Prod.; Dist., Al Lichtman Corp.; Louis Gasnier, director; Olga Printzlau, Josephine Quirk, adaptation; Karl Struss, photography; with Gaston Glass, Ruth Clifford, Ethel Shannon, Josef Swickard, Truly Shattuck.

Her Accidental Husband: Belasco Productions; Dist., C.B.C. Film Sales; Dallas Fitzgerald, director; Lois Zeller, story; with Mitchell Lewis, Richard Tucker, Forrest Stanley, Kate Lester, Maud Wayne.

After the Ball: Renco Film Co.; Dist., Film Booking Offices of America; Dallas M. Fitzgerald, director; James Colwell, scenario; Charles K. Harris, story; Ross Fisher, photography; with Gaston Glass, Thomas Guise, Robert Frazer, Edna Murphy, Eddie Gribbon.

The Broken Wing: B. P. Schulberg Productions; Dist., Preferred Pictures, Al Lichtman Corp.; Tom Forman, director; with Kenneth Harlan, Walter Long, Miss Du Pont, Richard Tucker, Edwin J. Brady, Ferdinand Munier, Evelyn Selbie.

« INDEX »

Academy of Music, 134
Aitken, Harry E., 38–39, 42
   77, 79, 86, 108–09
Aitken, Roy, 38–39, 42, 86
Alden, Mary, 55–56, 65, 69,
   75–76, 88, 91, 104
Alexandria Hotel, 47, 53
Algonquin Hotel, 118–19
Ambassador Hotel, 205
American Mutoscope and
   Biograph Studios, 40
Arbuckle, Roscoe "Fatty,"
   178–80
Arms, Louis Lee, 237
Armstrong, Paul, 116, 162
Arts in Virginia, 66–67
Arvidson, Linda, 36, 58
Auen, Signe. *See* Owen, Seena
Authors' Digest, 153

Baer, Arthur "Bugs," 157
Bambrick, Gertrude, 52–53
Bankhead, Tallulah, 118–19
Banky, Vilma, 213
Bara, Theda, 101, 103, 116–
   18, 165, 197
Barbizon Hotel (N.Y.), 241

Barrymore, Ethel, 220–21
Barrymore, John, 115–16,
   218–19
Barrymore, Lionel, 42, 115–
   16
*Battle of Pottsburgh Bridge,
   The*, 30
Beery, Noah, 212
Beery, Wallace, 120, 212
Belmont Park (N.Y.), 121–22
Ben-Hur, 161, 202
Benoit, Georges, 103
Bergman, Ingrid, 183
Bernard, Dorothy, 11, 58–59
Bernhardt, Sarah, 107
Beverly Hills (Calif.), 4, 45
Beverly Hills Hotel, 178
Biograph Girl, The, 11
Biograph Studios, 6, 11, 24,
   32–34, 57
Birth of a Nation, The, 1, 3, 4,
   21, 34–35, 39, 52, 55, 60–
   79, 80–81, 84–86, 87, 88,
   92, 93, 95, 96, 99, 106–10,
   112, 126, 133, 141, 144,
   145, 149, 153, 182, 211,
   241, 243

Bitzer, G. W. "Billy," 12, 38, 41, 67, 70, 75, 98
Blackton, J. Stuart, 36
Blot on the 'Scutcheon, The, 11
Blue Blood and Red, 118
Blumenthal, A. C., 215–16
Bogart, Humphrey, 114
Bowser, Eileen, 51, 86
Boyd, Storm, 27
Brady, Matthew, 75
Bretton Woods (N.H.), 118, 150–52
Broken Blossoms, 153
Broken Wing, The, 199–200
Bromfield, Louis, 235
Browning, Tod, 99
Brownlow, Kevin, 71, 129
Buel, Keenan, 27–30
Burkan, Nathan, 226
Burned Hand, The, 99
Burns, Bob, 89
Butler, Nicholas Murray, 235

Cabanne, William Christy, 12, 33–35, 43, 45, 46–47, 90, 109
Cabanne, Mrs. W. Christy (Vivian), 43
Cagney, James, 114
Campbell Soup Company, 236
Carlos, Abe, 122–23
Carlos, Mrs. Abe, 122–23
Carmen, 101–03
Carmen, Jewel, 139–40
Carrera, Leanne, 187
Carroll, Lombardi Pharmacy, 216
Chaplin, Charles, 68, 108, 161, 205–07, 217–18

Charlot's Revue, 223–24
Chicago Tribune, 147
Clansman, The (Dixon), 63, 77, 80, 81
Clements, Hal, 27, 28
Clifton, Elmer, 64, 99
Clive, Henry, 168
Clune Auditorium (Los Angeles), 80
Columbia University (N.Y.), 17, 235
Conqueror, The, 136
Coombs, Guy, 27
Cooper, Gordon, 13, 16–18, 25–26, 43, 83–84, 103, 130, 145, 148, 158, 164, 192, 202
Cooper, Julian, 14–17, 21, 23
Cooper, Lenore, 16–18, 20–21, 26, 74, 83–84, 164, 210, 242
Cooper, Margaret Stewart, 13–21, 23–26, 43, 44, 81–82, 83–85, 148, 149–50, 177, 210, 234, 241
Cooper, Nelson, 16–18, 43, 83–84, 148, 241
Cooper Union, 6, 23–26
Coppedge, Walter, 21, 66–67
Cortez, Ricardo, 212
Crowther, Bosley, 94

Daughter of the Gods, 141
Davies, Marion, 214–15
Deep Purple, The, 116, 162–65
De Grasse, Sam, 51
DeMille, Cecil B., 102, 103, 110, 239
Dempsey, Jack, 157
Dempster, Carol, 110–11

Denishawn School, 119
De Saulles, Blanca, 145–46
De Saulles, Jack, 145–46
Detroit (Mich.), 189–91
De Varona, Donna, 28–29
De Varona, Mrs. Joseph. *See*
Cooper, Lenore
Dillon, Edward, 99
Dixon, Thomas, 63, 77, 81
D. M. Film Corporation, 189–90
*Drummer Girl of Vicksburg,
The*, 27–28
Dwan, Allan, 216

Eagle Eye, 43
East of Suez (Maugham), 212
East of Suez (motion picture), 212, 213
Edison, Thomas, 36, 106
Edison Company, 24, 39–40
Edward VII, 134
Edward VIII, 134
Emerson, John, 56, 109
Epping, Johannes Charlemagne, 46, 76, 77
Evangeline (Longfellow), 154
Evangeline (motion picture), 154–58, 182

Fairbanks, Douglas, 99, 108–09, 113, 114, 175, 201–05, 207, 208–10, 217, 233
Famous Players-Lasky, 107, 172, 180, 181, 212
Farmington Country Club, 236
Farnum, William, 136
Farrar, Geraldine, 91, 102, 103

Fatal Black Bean, The, 99
First National, 181, 187
Fisher, Harrison, 23
Fitzgerald, Gerald, 179
Fitzgerald, Lillian, 179, 225
Florence (Ariz.), 127
Forman, Tom, 197, 199–200
Fox, William, 92, 102, 107, 117–18, 133–35, 137–38, 141, 144, 148, 154, 155, 226–227
Fox Film Company, 92, 117–18, 136–38, 141–49, 153–59, 226
French Connection, The, 78

Gable, Clark, 114, 217
Galpin, Race, 130–31
Garland, Christine, 241
Garland, Judy, 183
Gates Hotel (Los Angeles), 44
Geisler, Jerry, 233
Gentlemen Prefer Blondes, 49
Ghosts (Ibsen), 91–92, 153
Gibson, Charles Dana, 23
Girl Like I, A (Loos), 111
Girl Who Came Back, The, 197–98
Gish, Dorothy, 3, 48, 56–57, 108
Gish, Lillian, 3, 30, 38, 42, 48, 50–52, 54, 56, 57–59, 64, 66, 68, 72, 73–74, 79, 98, 108, 110–11, 238, 239, 240–41
Glass, Gaston, 198
Goldfish, Sam. *See* Goldwyn, Sam
Goldwyn, Sam, 4, 107, 109–10, 187, 188, 191

Goldwyn Pictures Corporation, 107–08, 109–10, 187
Goldwyn Productions, 4, 188–89, 191–95
Gone with the Wind, 203
Graham, Martha, 31, 119
Graves, Ralph, 170
Greaser, The, 50
Great Train Robbery, The, 98
Griffith, David Wark, 2–3, 6, 11–13, 19, 31–42, 46, 47, 49–50, 54–55, 56, 57–59, 62–81, 82–83, 84–86, 87, 88, 89–90, 91, 92–99, 101, 102, 104–05, 106–12, 113, 115, 116, 117, 128–29, 142–43, 153, 156, 170, 172, 176, 197–98, 201, 211, 238, 239, 240, 243
Griffith, D. W., Student Film Festival, 240
Griffith, Jacob Wark, 63
Guinan, Texas, 151
Gunman, The, 51

Hallam, Henry, 27
Harbaugh, Carl, 221
Harding, Warren G., 180
Harris, Mildred, 67–68, 161, 205
Harris, Mrs., 67
Harron, Robert, 34, 38, 49–50, 56, 64, 74, 78, 94
Hays, Will H., 180, 183
Headin' Home, 157
Hearst, William Randolf, 214–15
Hearts of the World, 57
Held, Anna, 187
Hemingway, Ernest, 217

His Return, 99
Hitchcock, Alfred, 145
Hollister, Ruth, 225
Hollywood (Calif.), 44
Home Sweet Home, 49–50, 57
Honor System, The (motion picture), 123–35, 136–37, 141–42, 144, 153
Honor System, The (Warnack), 123–24
Hopi Indian Reservation, 103
Hoppe, Alice Walsh, 114, 116
Hoppe, Willie, 114, 116
Horse Wrangler, The, 51
Hudson, Rock, 114
Hughes, Howard, 206
Hughes, Rupert, 206
Hunt, George W. P., 124
Hunt, Irene, 43–44, 46–47
Hutton, Barbara, 210
Hutton, Frank, 210

Ibsen, Henrik, 91
Idols, The (Locke), 167
Independent Motion Picture Company, 24
Innocent Sinner, The, 145
Intolerance, 1, 4, 39, 92–99, 106, 110, 111, 112, 115, 126, 133, 144, 169
Is Money Everything?, 189–93
Isn't Life Wonderful?, 211

Jacksonville (Fla.), 27–31
Johnson, Julanne, 202
Jomier, Georges, 174
Joyce, Alice, 27, 31
Joyce, Peggy Hopkins, 146–47

Kael, Pauline, 112
Kalem, 24–31
Kerry, Norman, 191, 228
Keystone Kops, 11
Kindred of the Dust (Kyne), 171
Kindred of the Dust (motion picture), 170–72, 185
Kleine, George, 24
Korte, Walter, 2–3, 21, 64–65, 79, 99
Kyne, Peter B., 170–71

LaGrange (Ky.), 239–40
Lanesborough, Earl and Countess of, 209–10
La Rocque, Rod, 212–13
Lasky, Jesse, L., 90–91, 92, 103, 107, 110, 212
Lawler, Oscar, 227
Lawrence, Gertrude, 223
Lee, Jennie, 73
Lehrman, Henry "Pathe," 179
Lewis, Ralph, 64
Liberty Theatre (N.Y.), 81, 210
Library of Congress, 24, 240
Lillie, Bea, 223–25
Lindreth, Helen, 27, 28
Little American, The, 30
Locke, William J., 167
Lombard, Carole, 114, 215–17
Long, Samuel, 24, 31, 36, 106
Long, Walter, 71–72, 93, 95–96, 199
Longfellow, William Wadsworth, 153–54
Loos, Anita, 49, 56, 111
Los Angeles (Calif.), 44–46
Los Angeles Examiner, 114

Los Angeles Times, 197
Lost and Found, 188–95
Louisville, University of, 240
Love, Bessie, 112, 197
Loveridge, Marguerite, 58
Lowe, Edmund, 114, 212
Lubitsch, Ernst, 190
Luchow's Restaurant (N.Y.), 13
Lyric Theatre (N.Y.), 133

McCormick, John, 165–66
McLaglen, Victor, 114
McMahon, Monsignor, 17, 23, 81–82
McPherson, Aimee Semple, 193–94
Madison Square Garden (N.Y.), 157
Man's Genesis, 58–59
Marcus, James A., 130, 192, 202
Maria del Carmen (Felin y Codina), 170
Marion, Frank, 24, 31, 36, 106
Marsh, Lovey. *See* Loveridge, Marguerite
Marsh, Mae, 3–4, 6, 37–38, 42, 48, 49, 54, 56, 58–59, 65–67, 71, 73, 74, 75–77, 83, 88, 89, 93, 94, 96–97, 109–10, 132, 181, 197, 237–38, 239
Marsh, Mrs., 49
Mary Christopher, Mother, 19
Maugham, Somerset, 212
Mayer, Louis B., 107, 160–61, 202
Mayflower Corporation, 162
Me, Gangster, 217

Menzies, William Cameron, 170, 203
Metro-Goldwyn-Mayer, 161
Miami Beach (Fla.), 146
Miller, Lorraine, 225–26, 231, 232, 234
Minter, Mary Miles, 180–81
Moore, Colleen, 165
Mother and the Law, The, 94, 95
Motion Picture Producers and Distributors of America, 180
Mountbatten, Lord and Lady, 209
Moving Picture World, 29–30, 51
Museum of Modern Art, 50–51, 86
Mutual Film Corporation, 38–39, 76, 108

Negri, Pola, 212–15
Neilan, Marshall "Mickey," 52–53, 161
New York American, 133–34
New York Athletic Club, 230
New York Evening Mail, 134
New York Foundling Hospital, 149, 208, 241
New York Public Library for the Performing Arts, 50
New York Times, The, 114
New York Yankees, 157
Nichols, George, 91
Nilsson, Anna Q., 27–31, 168
Normand, Mabel, 11, 30, 58–59, 180–82
Novarro, Ramon, 161

Oath, The, 167–70, 236
O'Donohue, J. T., 170, 192

Owen, Seena, 115, 148

Pallette, Eugene, 38, 43–44, 51, 87
Parade's Gone By, The (Brownlow), 71
Paramount Pictures Corporation, 107
Parsons, Louella, 227
Payne, John Howard, 49
Perfect Crime, The, 216
Peters, Jane. *See* Lombard, Carole
Pickford, Jack, 183
Pickford, Mary, 3, 11, 24, 30, 42, 48, 51, 52, 58–59, 108, 175, 181, 183, 190, 201, 203, 208–09, 216, 239
Pidgeon, Walter, 225
Plaza Hotel (N.Y.), 161, 162, 187
Porter, Edward Stratton, 39–40, 106
Power, Tyrone, 212
Prussian Cur, The, 149

Queen of Sheba, 141

Rappe, Virginia, 178–80
Reel Life, 51
Reese, Johnny, 128
Reid, Wallace, 182–83
Reliance Majestic, 46, 51
Rescued from the Eagle's Nest, 40
Richman, Harry, 176
Robin Hood, 201
Rogell, Albert S., 239
Rogers, Will, 210
Rosalita, Sister, 15, 18
Rosita, 190

Rossellini, Roberto, 183
Rubaiyat of Omar Khayyam,
104
Ruppert, Jake, 157
Ruth, George Herman
"Babe", 157–58

Saint Bibiano's Catholic
Church, 88–89
Saint Walburga's Academy,
15, 19, 23
Sampson, Teddy, 9–11, 53–
54
Sands of Dee, The, 59
San Fernando Valley (Calif.),
45
Schenck, Joseph, 118, 164,
173–74, 180
Schulberg, B. P., 196, 199
Schulberg, B. P., Productions,
196–200
Screen Directors Guild, 239
Selwyn, Archie, 4, 187–89,
223
Selwyn, Edgar, 107–08, 187
Sennett, Mack, 10–11, 42, 54,
178
Serenade, 170
Serpent, The, 118
Serrano, Vincent, 163
Seton Hall, 116
Sheehan, Winfield A.
"Winnie", 142, 146, 148,
155, 157
Sherman, Lowell, 179–80
Should a Husband Forgive?,
157
Sills, Milton, 128, 134
Smith, Albert E., 36
Smith, Frederick James, 134
Smith, Jimmy, 78, 79

Smith, Rosie, 76, 78, 79
Squaw's Love, The, 30
Stardom (Walker), 71
Starke, Pauline, 110, 191
Sterling, Ford, 54
Stewart, Anita, 161
Stewart, Colin, 97
Stewart, Mrs. Colin (Annie),
97
Stewart, Margaret. *See*
Cooper, Margaret Stewart
Struggle, The, 238–39
Swanson, Gloria, 120, 228
Sweet, Blanche, 3, 42, 51, 52,
58–59, 91, 108, 197

Tahiti, 191–95, 196
Talmadge, Constance, 3, 39,
42, 48–49, 67, 164
Talmadge, Natalie, 48–49
Talmadge, Norma, 48–49,
83–84, 118–19, 164, 168,
173–74, 178, 180, 181
Talmadge, Peg, 48–49
Taylor, William Desmond,
180–82
Tearle, Conway, 167–68
Thalberg, Irving, 161
Theatre Magazine, 168
Thief of Bagdad, The, 114,
202–05, 207, 209–11, 212,
220
Thomas, Olive, 183
Tide of Battle, The, 29
Tinee, Mae, 147
Twentieth Century-Fox, 236

United Artists, 201

Valentino, Rudolph, 113, 213
Van Dyke, W. S., 99

Variety, 86, 156
Virginia, University of, 2–3, 236
Virginia Commonwealth University, 21
Vitagraph, 24, 83
Von Stroheim, Erich, 99, 228

Walker, Alexander, 71
Walsh, Albert Edward. *See* Walsh, Raoul
Walsh, Bobby, 208, 231, 233
Walsh, George, 114–15, 118, 130, 141, 146–47, 148, 151, 158, 161, 170, 187, 190, 202, 231, 234
Walsh, Jack, 150–52, 158, 160, 163, 164, 174, 186–87, 190, 192–95, 196, 208, 225–26, 230–34
Walsh, R. A., Productions, 184–87
Walsh, Raoul, 2, 38, 43–44, 49, 68, 87–92, 100–05, 111, 113–35, 136–52, 153–59, 160–72, 173–78, 184–95, 196–98, 201–11, 212–15, 217–18, 220–28, 229, 231–34, 239
Walsh, Mrs. Raoul (2nd). *See* Miller, Lorraine
Walsh, Stewart, 208
Walsh, Thomas "Pops", 114–16, 138, 175–76

Walthall, Henry B., 38, 42, 64, 66, 69–71, 91
Wanamaker's Department Store, 13
Ware, Helen, 163
Warnack, Henry Christeen, 123–24
Waters, Bessie, 150, 165–67, 210
Watson, Victor, 133–34
Way Down East, 30, 153
Wayne, John, 114
Welch, Raquel, 3
West, Billie, 50
Western Uniform Company, 168
What Price Glory, 114, 229
White Heat, 114
Whitman, Walt, 97
Wilson, Woodrow, 81
Woman and the Law, The, 146–47, 236
Wood, Rita, 6–9, 24
Woods, Frank C. "Daddy," 46, 76, 82

Young, Clara Kimball, 108
Yuma (Ariz.), 127

Ziegfeld, Florenz, 187
Ziegfeld Follies, 165, 215
Zukor, Adolph, 107, 108, 172, 180–81